WINNER!

BEST TRAVEL GUIDEBOOK AWARD

MIDWEST BOOK ACHIEVEMENT AWARDS

"Very homey. Illustrations are charming.
Hits all the right questions."
—*Citation from the 1992 MBA Awards*

"Great Affordable Bed & Breakfast Getaways
...describes each B&B and includes information
on the unique features nearby."
—*Travel Holiday*

"A marvelous guidebook for travelers that want
the relaxed atmosphere of a bed and breakfast but who don't
want to spend a small fortune for a weekend vacation."
—*Ann Rudie, North Suburban Press*

"Dipping into the contents can give even the most confirmed
homebody the urge to travel."
—*Union Recorder, Milledgevile, GA*

"Clarity of thought and presentation, inherently interesting
material, and a flair for descriptive writing makes (this book)
a must acquisition for any serious, budget-minded traveler."
—*Midwest Book Review*

NEW! INCLUDES
FAVORITE B&B RECIPES!

GREAT AFFORDABLE BED & BREAKFAST GETAWAYS!

Your best national guide
for a B & B mini-vacation
at a reasonable price

LORIS G. BREE

MARLOR PRESS, INC.

Great Affordable B&B Getaways

Published by Marlor Press, Inc. All rights reserved.
No part of this book may be reproduced in any form
without written permission of Marlor Press, Inc.

Copyright 1993 by Loris G. Bree

Distributed to the book trade by
Contemporary Books Inc.
Chicago, Illinois

Printed in U.S.A.

ISBN-943400-67-8

Disclaimer: This guide is not responsible for prices, services, or facilities at listed B&B's, country inns, and chalets. Though the author and the publisher have made best efforts to secure current prices and reports at presstime, the B&B's prices, services, and facilities may change at any time. When contacting a B&B, or other facility, vacationers should check to determine that prices, facilities, services, etc., are prevailing at the time of their visit and that the facilities will meet their own needs. In any event, Marlor Press, Inc. is not responsible for price changes, schedules, services, availability, facilities, agreements, loss or injury of any kind.

Marlor Press, Inc.
4304 Brigadoon Drive   Saint Paul, MN 55126
(612) 484-4600   FAX (612) 490-1182

Contents

Introduction and organization, VI & VII

United States B&B's

Alaska, 2
California, 6
Colorado, 14
Florida, 24
Georgia, 26
Hawaii, 32
Idaho, 34
Illinois, 36
Indiana, 50
Iowa, 52
Kentucky, 56
Louisiana, 58
Maine, 62
Maryland, 74
Massachusetts, 76
Michigan, 90
Minnesota, 100
Missouri, 102
Montana, 110
Nebraska, 112

New Hampshire, 114
New Jersey, 124
New Mexico, 126
New York, 128
North Carolina, 148
Ohio, 164
Oregon, 172
Pennsylvania, 178
Rhode Island, 184
South Carolina, 186
South Dakota, 194
Tennessee, 198
Texas, 200
Utah, 204
Vermont, 210
Virginia, 224
Washington, 234
West Virginia, 246
Wisconsin, 250
Wyoming, 252

Canadian B&B's

Alberta, 260
British Columbia, 266
New Brunswick, 276

Nova Scotia, 280
Ontario, 282
Quebec, 294

B&B Reservation Service Organizations

United States, 300

Canada, 306

Introduction

This book is a **guide to the best places** to have an affordable B&B vacation in the U.S. and Canada. It is not strictly a directory of B&Bs alone. To be represented here, each afford able B&B was invited to send us information, photographs of the inside and outside of the B&B and a completed questionnaire about its property. Three judges independently rated each B&B's entry. Only those with very high ratings were included in the book. Judges also selected the B&B's recipes, which are found throughout this book.

Background

B&Bs are very popular in the United States and in Canada. They have a special appeal. Usually a B&B or country inn is owned by someone who is a personal host and who will greet you and make you feel comfortable. These hosts are proud of their accommodations and the hospitality they offer.

The lodging itself is often special, ranging from contemporary modern structures to restored large old mansions or inns, sometimes of historical significance. Typically, these have been lovingly furnished with antiques, paintings and other distinctive possessions.

Your host often will serve a special breakfast. This is a wonderful way to begin a morning when you are on vacation. You'll find recipes from some of these special breakfasts, or other special meals, throughout this book.

The innkeeper takes personal care in meeting the needs of the guests and can give them advice on how to see the countryside and enjoy their B&B vacation. Often, the host can help arrange itineraries. Most travelers find that a B&B is a special experience and quite different from ordinary hotels and motels.

Organization

Great *Affordable Bed & Breakfast Getaways* is organized alphabetically by state and then by city. Each listing is set up this way:

A thumbnail sketch of the **special attractions** of an area, such as visiting a unique or historic site, scenic location or special attraction.

The **name** of the B&B, followed by a complete **mailing address** and **telephone number**.

Prices for **two** people.

Registration information, such as **when to call**, whether the B&B takes **credit cards**, the name of the **hosts** and the **number of rooms** and **baths** available.

The type of **breakfast** you can typically look forward to.

A **description** of the lodging and its surroundings, such as: "Restored Victorian mansion in a quiet, wooded neighborhood."

Dining suggestions for the area, including the names of outstanding nearby restaurants and their specialties. If the B&B provides a special dinner, with advance ordering needed, we list that also.

The special **things to see and do around the B&B**, such as hiking in the woods, or just sitting under an apple tree.

Many *recipes* or *special meals* featured at some of the B&B's listed in *Great Affordable B&B Getaways*.

In all, there's a wealth of information so that you can find a great getaway at an affordable B&B or country inn.

Alaska

Fairbanks

You'll want to see and learn all you can about fascinating Alaska. A good way to begin is with a cruise on the **Riverboat Discovery**, docked at Discovery Rd., near Airport Way, for a four-hour trip down the Cherna to the Tanana River. This is a terrific way to see some of Alaska's wilderness and wildlife, look at a fishing camp and an Indian village and learn more about Alaska's special history.

Sightseeing trips are available to remote areas of the state. You can arrange your own driving tour in Fairbanks or to nearby areas. Maps are available at the Visitor Information Center, 550 First Ave.

Visit historic **Gold Dredge Number 8**, on Goldstream Rd., off SR 6, the historic five-deck ship built in the 1920s to dredge for gold. You may also pan for gold after you tour the ship. The **University of Alaska Museum**, on the campus West Ridge, has exhibits that include the carcass of a bison killed by a lion 36,000 years ago and preserved in permafrost. If you feel like a walk, take a guided walking tour of the **University of Alaska**. Tours depart from the museum at 10 AM, June through August.

Alaskaland Pioneer Theme Park, at Airport and Peger roads, has many old buildings, a sternwheeler, a presidential railroad car, a narrow gauge railroad, and a pioneer museum. See the **Satellite Tracking Station** of the National Oceanic Atmospheric Administration, on Steese Expwy. Free guided tours are given Monday through Saturday in the summer.

Visit the bird sanctuary or take a hot air balloon ride. Obviously, you won't run out of things to do here.

● Ah, Rose Marie Bed & Breakfast

302 Cowles St., Fairbanks, AK 99701. (907)456-2040.

$40-45/S; $50-65/D; $10/ex. prsn.

Call anytime. Answering machine calls are answered. For summer reservations start calling in February.
•No cr. crds.
•Innkeeper: John E. Davis.
•*3 double, 4 single rms, 3 sb.*
•Full breakfast served with fine china and sterling silver. A typical menu would include a fruit platter, Alaskan sourdough bread, muffins and cakes, juice, egg dishes, cereals, local jams and jellies.
•No pets, no smoking.
•Centrally located in Old Fairbanks, three blocks from the river, downtown and the train depot.

This 1928 home has hardwood oak floors and an enclosed front porch. Your host is a world traveler and elementary school counselor who enjoys providing outstanding hospitality.

For dining, seek out Pasta Bella (Italian), Seoul Gate (Korean), Thai House (Thai), the Pump House or Pike's Landing (on the river) or the twice-daily Alaskaland Salmon Bake.

When you visit you'll be welcomed by the friendly Husky, Snowball, and the cat, Tyla.

Rest, read or chat on the sunny front porch and, at 11 PM, watch the horizontal golden sun rays come down Third Avenue. Stroll out to the small greenhouse featuring Alaskan flowers and vegetables.

Alaska's 7 Gables Bed & Breakfast

4312 Birch Lane, P.O. Box 80488, Fairbanks, AK 99708.
(907)479-0751 / Fax· 479-2229.

Oct - May: $40-50. Jun - Sep: $50-55.

Call 7 AM to 10 PM, AST. •V, MC, D, DC, CB.
- Innkeepers: Paul & Leicha Welton.
- 9 rms, 3 pb, 3 sb. Rooms or private suites, phones in every room.
- A full 3 or 4 course, gourmet breakfast. A typical menu might include fruit streusel crepes, cheesy scrambled eggs, sliced melons, Kona Inn Banana Bread, orange juice, coffee and tea.
- No pets indoors, smoking only in designated areas.
- 5 min to airport, 5 min. to UAF Museum, 300 yards from Chena River.

This spacious Tudor home, once a fraternity house, is located on a landscaped 1 1/2-acre lot near the river. It is surrounded with floral gardens, and, inside, has stained glass, an entry waterfall and cathedral ceilings. Your hosts enjoy music, carpentry, education, skiing, and fishing.

For dining, you'll enjoy the Pump House Restaurant, with its oyster bar and its historic location; the Two Rivers Lodge, with exquisite cuisine, Alaskan decor; Alaska Salmon Bake, featuring grilled salmon, ribs and halibut; or, Pike's Landing, one of the newest and finest in the area.

When you visit, enjoy the two-story floral greenhouse. You can bicycle on nearby bike paths, wooded areas, or open fields; canoe down the Chena River to local restaurants; relax in the whirlpool or enjoy a complimentary snack from the refrigerator. You can go cross-country skiing or view the Northern Lights; go snow shoeing or ice skating in the Alaskan Winter Wonderland.

Crescent Souffle

From Leicha Welton, **Alaska's 7 Gables B&B**
Fairbanks, Alaska

1 can crescent rolls
1/4 cup sweet hot mustard
8 eggs, slightly beaten
2/3 cup milk
2 cups grated cheddar cheese

Spray a 9 x 13 glass baking dish with a vegetable spray like PAM. Line the bottom of the pan with the crescent rolls to form a crust. Spread sweet hot mustard over the dough. Spread grated cheese over the mustard. Mix together eggs and milk and pour gently over cheese. Bake at 350F. for 30 minutes. Serves approximately 10.

California

Burlingame

You'll want to visit San Francisco Bay and the Pacific Ocean. Perhaps you'll want to spend part of your stay enjoying the wonderful cosmopolitan city of San Francisco and part enjoying the country atmosphere of Burlingame.

For those times when you want to stay in the immediate area, visit Moss Beach and the **James V. Fitzgerald Marine Reserve**. In this intertidal region, you can observe marine life and explore. See, but don't collect, rocks, shells or plants — that's illegal.

North on Hwy. 101, is South San Francisco, and **Acres of Orchids**. Here you can see many different varieties of orchids and other flowers. The laboratory is open daily from 8 AM to 5 PM, except on holidays. One-hour tours are given at 10:30 AM and 1:30 PM.

Just south of Burlingame, on Hwy. 101, is San Mateo. Visit **Central Park** to see a lovely Japanese garden. In **Coyote Point Park**, see the museum and biopark where dioramas, electronic demonstrations, manipulative displays and insect colonies show the natural environment and people's impact on it. The park has picnic facilities and wildlife habitats. Year around, you can use the beaches, hiking trails or go ice skating in this area.

● **Burlingame Bed & Breakfast**
1021 Balboa Ave., Burlingame, CA 94010. (415)344-5815.

$40/S; $50/D; $10/ex prsn.

Call anytime.
•No cr crds.
•Innkeepers: Joe & Elnora Fernandez.
•1 rm, 1 pb.
•*Continental breakfast, with croissants, juice and fruit, in season.*
•No pets, no smoking, no alcohol.
•In Burlingame, 1 blk from bus, 5 blks from train, 15 mi. S of San Francisco.

You'll have an exceptionally clean and cheerful upstairs king-size bedroom, with a king-size bed, in this 1920's built home. You'll enjoy your own private dining area where breakfast is served on fine china and silverware. Look out on a creek and its flora and fauna. Your hosts enjoy traveling, literary discussions and foreign languages. Joe speaks English, Spanish and Italian.

For dining, you'll have the choice of nearby restaurants. Of course, you're only minutes away from San Francisco's many famous restaurants. Ask your hosts to help you find something to meet your preferences.

When you visit, the neighborhood has regional parks, a historic train depot and many natural areas. You can feed birds, squirrels or go fishing. If you prefer, you may browse through the extensive library for reading material.

Ione

You'll want to come here when you need to escape the pressures of life. There are many things to see and do to absorb your interest, but you can also find peace and tranquility, if you want it. Antique shops are abundant in the small towns throughout the county.

The **Amador County Museum**, in Jackson, features working models to tell the history of gold mining in the area. Ask about the Kennedy Driving Wheels driving tour of old mines.

Visit the **California Caverns**, at Cave City, near San Andreas, for adventuresome water or rappel tours or a calmer 80-minute guided tour. While you are in the area, you may want to see the ghost town of **Campo Seco** and the **Calaveras County Historical Museum**, with its garden and mining artifacts.

Moaning Cave, at Vallecito, is worth a visit; it also has adventure tours or a 45-minute guided tour. **Indian Grinding Rock State Park**, in Volcano, has a re-created village and museum and picnic areas.

The **Sierra Foothill** wineries are charming and hospitable for tasting and touring.

● **The Heirloom**
214 Shakeley Lane, Ione, CA 95640.
(209)274-4468.

$55-85.

Call after 10 AM.
•No cr crds.
•**Innkeepers: Melisande Hubbs & Patricia Cross.**
•*6 rms, 4 pb, 1 sb.*
•Full breakfast, featuring fresh juice, fruit, baked breads, featuring such entrees as crepes, souffles, Eggs Mornay.
•In center of small town, 45 min from Sacramento, 15 min from Jackson-Sutter Creek.

This Colonial antebellum brick mansion, circa 1863, has columns and balconies, and is furnished in antiques. On 1 1/2 acres it is surrounded by trees, vines and gardens. The spacious romantic English garden is filled with gardenia, magnolia and wisteria.

For dining, you'll enjoy Tazza's, Ballads, Theresa's, the Imperial Hotel, the Pelargonim and Buffalo Chips Emporium Ice Cream Parlor.

When you visit you'll want to stroll in the beautiful garden, relax in the hammock or on the old fashioned glider. Enjoy breakfast in the garden or on the balconies. In cooler weather, enjoy the fireplaces, while perusing the fine collection of art books and reading materials.

Nipton

You'll want to visit this old railroad town when you want to "get away from it all."

Nipton is near the Nevada border. It is in the heart of the **East Mojave National Scenic Area**, and on the **East Mojave Heritage Trail**, a 700 mile off-road trail. This is a great area for riding horses, bicycling or hiking. Rockhounds, balloonists, off-roaders, campers, rock climbers, photographers, boaters, hunters and other desert lovers will have a wonderful time here. See desert wildflowers in the spring; find petroglyphs that are over 10,000 years old; find abandoned mines and desert camps. But, don't try to leave existing routes and be careful to fill your gas tank when you have the opportunity. In October enjoy Old Nippeno Days, a festive week-long celebration. This unique little desert town has maintained the flavor of the 1900s.

For a total change, you'll have just a short drive on I-15 to the glitz and gambling in Las Vegas. Or instead, visit Boulder City, the only town in Nevada without legalized gambling and the gateway to **Lake Mead National Recreation Area, Hoover Dam, Lake Mead, and Lake Mohave.**

This area is certain to provide a unique and enjoyable getaway.

Hotel Nipton
*72 Nipton Road, HC1, Box 357
Nipton, CA 92364. (619)856-2335*

$48/S or D.

Call 9 AM to 6 PM.
• V, MC.
• **Innkeepers: Roxanne and Jerry Freeman.**
• *4 rms, 2 sb.* • *Continental breakfast.*
• No pets.
• Nipton is 60 miles SW of Las Vegas.

This historic old hotel built in 1905, in the railroad town of Nipton, was restored in 1986 as a bed and breakfast inn. The large parlor and bedrooms are furnished with antiques and memorabilia of the area.

For dining, you'll want to travel to nearby towns, have a sandwich at the Lottery Lounge or picnic with food from the trading post. Ask your hosts for dining recommendations.

When you visit you'll enjoy seeing the rooms and looking at the historic pictures of the area. From the front porch there is an unobstructed panoramic view of the Ivanpah Valley, the New York Mountains and Castle Peaks. An outdoor whirlpool is especially inviting at night when star gazing is superb. The entire town of Nipton is owned by your hosts.

Oroville

You'll want to start a tour at the **Lake Oroville Visitor Center**, viewing Lake Oroville and Oroville Dam. Exhibits depict the gold rush era, and present-day water and wildlife projects. The Oroville Dam is the world's tallest earth filled dam and it is basic to water projects throughout California. A Chinese temple, at the corner of Elma and Broderick, was built in 1863 and was furnished by the Emperor of China. It has a courtyard garden, collections of puppets, customs and tapestries. The **Lott home** is typical of a home built by an affluent family during the gold rush, with authentic furnishings and gardens. If you have time, visit the **Feather River Hatchery**, 5 Table Mountain Blvd., where salmon and steelhead are raised for release into the Feather River. Spawning season is in October and early November — an interesting time to visit. There are many antique stores in this area for browsing.

Just north on SR 191 is Paradise where the **Gold Nugget Museum**, has a replica of a gold mine, a miner's cabin, blacksmith shop and general store. Open Wed.-Sun., from noon to 4 PM.

West of Paradise, on SR 32, in Chico, where the **Bidwell Mansion Historical Site** is an example of Victorian architecture, built in the 1860s. The home has a huge collection of vintage clothing. Guided tours are given daily from 10 AM to 4 PM, except Thanksgiving, Christmas and New Year's Day.

● Jean's Riverside Bed & Breakfast
P.O. Box 2334, Oroville, CA 95965. (916)483-1413.

$55-95 Eight rooms are available at the lowest rate year around.

Call 8 AM to 9 PM.
- V, MC, DC, CB.
- Innkeeper: Jean Pratt.
- 15 rms, 15 pb.
- A full breakfast is served in the dining area overlooking the Feather River. In good weather, you may eat on the deck. Expect fruit, a sourdough specialty, home made jam or jelly and fresh ground coffee.
- No pets, no smoking, no children under 12.
- 1 1/2 minutes from Oroville.

The window walls in this cedar building allow you to enjoy the outdoors as a part of the indoor decor. Comfortable and interesting antiques enhance your relaxation. The inn is surrounded by five acres of wooded waterfront. You're likely to sight ducks, geese, jack rabbits, squirrels and birds of all sorts here.

For dining, you will want to find The Depot, in an old Western Pacific Railroad Station, Cornelia Lott's, in a nostalgic Victorian Garden, or Table Mountain Tavern, an old restaurant facing scenic Table Mountain.

When you visit you may enjoy swimming in the Feather River or, if you prefer, fishing and panning for gold. This is a marvelous spot for bird watching because the river and trees provide a natural habitat. You'll find facilities to play horseshoes, badminton, croquet or ping pong.

Colorado

Estes Park, Fort Collins

You'll want to enjoy not only the magnificent scenery of the Rocky Mountains, but hiking, rock climbing, wildlife, horse shows, rodeos and ranger-guided activities, in the summer, and Alpine and Nordic skiing in the winter.

If you are going to Fort Collins, take the scenic, mountainous, SR 14, to the **Cache la Poudre River and Canyon**, through the **Roosevelt National Forest**. This community is the home of Colorado State University. The **Fort Collins Museum**, 200 Matthews St., specializes in the history of northern Colorado. The **Annheuser-Busch Brewery**, 2351 Busch Dr., offers tours of the brewery, a horse barn, beer garden and outdoor show area for a team of Clydesdales. It's just a 30-mile drive to Estes Park and Rocky Mountain National Park for wonderful scenery, hiking, climbing, horseback riding, scenic motor routes, fishing, and picnicking. An aerial tramway just south of the post office in Estes Park will take you to the summit of **Prospect Mountain**. The **MacGregor Ranch and Museum** interprets the life lived by a homesteader of the 1870s and the **Estes Park Historical Museum** has exhibits on the history of the entire area, and includes a Stanley Steamer automobile. The **Ricker-Bartlett Pewter Casting Studio and Gallery** gives guided tours of their casting process daily; **Rock 'N River Trout Farm** and **Trout Haven** have fishing ponds stocked with trout which you may fish without a license; Estes Park Adventures will arrange rafting trips and balloon rides. Estes Park has many unusual shops, antique stores, theaters, art galleries, flea markets, and restaurants. Also in the area are two golf courses (one 18 hole, one 9 hole). The community is at the eastern entrance to **Rocky Mountain National Park**. When you visit the park, you may want to rent a tape and tape player for self-guided auto tours. Talks and campfire programs are presented every night at campgrounds and park headquarters. Take a nature-study walk or field trip. Climb to **Longs Peak**. Drive **Trail Ridge Road** or one of the other scenic routes. Have fun!

● **Wanek's Lodge at Estes**
P.O. Box 898, Estes Park, CO 80517. (303)586-5851.

$49/D; $108/suite.

Call in evening.
• No cr. crds.
• **Innkeepers: Jim & Pat Wanek.**
• *2 rms, 1 sb; 1 3-rm suite/pb.*
• Expanded continental breakfast with homemade baked goods, fresh fruit platter, juice, yogurt, beverage.
• No pets, no smoking, no children under 10 yrs.
• In the town of Estes Park, 5 miles from Rocky Mountain National Park, 75 mi. NW of Denver.

Wanek's is a modern mountain inn, with wood beams and stone fireplace, located on a Ponderosa Pine-covered hillside, above Lake Estes. With its plants and surrounded by beautiful scenery, the inn provide a comfortable and relaxed atmosphere. You'll feel like you were in the home of old friends. Your hosts are former educators and lovers of the mountains, the mountain wildlife and plants. They enjoy books, music, national parks, Colorado Geography, and history.

For dining, there are many fine eating establishments with a variety of ethnic foods. We'd suggest you try Mama Rose's, Poppy's, Villa Tatra, or Johnson Cafe.

When you visit you'll find books, magazines, cards, puzzles, and board games in the library for relaxing fun. You're welcome to enjoy the family room, to sit by the huge moss rock fireplace, or to photograph the wild animals that often come right through the yard. Morris, the cat, will help to make you feel welcome.

●Elizabeth Street Guest House Bed & Breakfast
202 E. Elizabeth, Fort Collins, CO 80524. (303)493-2337.

$44-64.

Call 8-10 AM; 5-8 PM. An answering machine is always available. •V, MC.
•**Innkeepers: John & Sheryl Clark.**
•*3 rms, 1 pb, 1 sb.*
•Full breakfast of fruit or juice, beverage, cereals, breads, Scotch eggs or Dutch Babies.
•No smoking, no pets, no children under 10.
•In Fort Collins.

A 1905 American four-square brick home, restored and furnished with family antiques, plants, old quilts and handmade items. Special features are the leaded windows and oak woodwork. A three-story miniature house graces the entry.

For dining, excellent food is available at the Jefferson Grill, Rainbow Ltd., Rio Grande, Silver Grill or Caninos Italian Restaurant. John and Sheryl have a menu basket and will be happy to talk to you about area restaurants.

When you visit be sure to ask for peanuts to feed Chubby the Squirrel. You'll enjoy relaxing in the garden area or browsing through the games and books available to guests. Feel free to use the guest refrigerator and ask your hosts for directions to area attractions.

Heart Healthy Spinach Souffle

From Melisande A. Hubbs, **The Heirloom**
Ione, California

4 tablespoons margarine
2 tablespoons flour
2 green onions, chopped
2 cubes chicken bouillon
1/2 teaspoon salt
1/2 teaspoon pepper
dash of nutmeg
2 cups lowfat milk
2 - 10 oz packages frozen spinach, cooked and squeezed dry
1 cup Swiss cheese or low-fat substitute, shredded or finely chopped
8 egg whites

In a heavy saucepan, melt the margarine. Saute the green onions just until cooked through. Add the dry bouillon cubes, flour and seasonings and mix well. Add milk to make a sauce. Cook until slightly thickened. Remove from heat, add cheese and stir until melted. If necessary, return to low heat to melt but do not let boil. Off heat, add spinach and mix with cheese sauce.

Beat egg whites just until peaks are formed. Fold into spinach mixture. Pour into ungreased souffle dishes. Melissande uses 3 - 2 cup dishes or 6 - 1 cup dishes. Place in a pan of hot water. Bake at 350F. for 40-50 minutes, until a knife inserted just off center comes out clean. Serves 6.

Pagosa Springs

You'll want to discover the panorama of outdoor activities available here: high country fishing trips, horseback riding, sleigh rides, balloon rides, rafting trips, cross-country skiing, golfing, tennis, mountain biking, day hiking, BBQ haywagon rides, snowmobiling, photography.

The city is named for the thermal springs that burst from the ground, providing mineral baths and heating for some community buildings. It is surrounded by the San Juan National Forest, is about two hours drive from Mesa Verde National Park and is less than 20 miles from Wolf Creek Pass Ski area.

Just west of the city is Durango and the **Durango and Silverton Narrow Gauge Railroad**. The train runs through the mountains, the San Juan National Forest to Silverton. If you want a stressful but breathtaking drive, you may drive US 550 from Durango to Silverton. The road is steep and has frequent overlooks, but there are no guardrails. West of Durango, just south of US 160, is **Mesa Verde National Park**. There are many large canyons across the mesa and in the cliffs are well preserved cliff dwellings, dating from about 500 AD. Trips to the dwelling ruins are conducted by park rangers all year.

● **Davidson's Country Inn B & B**
Box 87, Pagosa Springs, CO 81147. (303)264-5863.

$44-62/D. Discount for stay of four or more days.

Call 8 AM to 8 PM.
•V, MC.
•**Innkeepers: Gilbert & Evelyn Davidson.**
•*8 rms, 3 pb, 1 sb.*
•Full breakfast, served in a family setting.
•No smoking, no pets without permission.
•2 mi. east of Pagosa Springs.

A three-story log country inn located on 32 acres of property surrounded by the beautiful San Juan mountains. Each room is decorated with family heirlooms, antiques, quilts, and handmade furniture. Many rooms are large enough to hold families or small groups. A two-bedroom cabin with kitchen, living room and bath is also available.

For dining, you'll enjoy the Ole Miner's Steak House.

When you visit you'll have 32 acres to hike and explore. The covered porches and gazebo are wonderful places for reading and relaxing. You'll want to join other guests or create your own teams for games of horseshoes or volleyball. There is also an indoor game room and library for times of leisure. Have fun!

San Isabel National Forest — Buena Vista and Salida

You'll want to drive or hike scenic routes in this forest that covers over 1,000,000 acres. There are several recreation areas providing summer activities and many popular ski resorts, for winter sports. Mining ghost towns are scattered throughout the forest.

Buena Vista and Salida are historic mining towns and ranching communities. The spectacular mountain peaks provide a marvelous backdrop for recreation opportunities. Both towns are in the valley of the Arkansas River. White water rafting trips, ghost town jeep tours and tram trips to mountain peaks are popular entertainment. Hot spring pools and baths are piped in from the Poncho Hot Springs.

On U.S. 20, 22 miles west of Salida, the **Monarch Aerial Tram** climbs over 11,000 feet for a view of the Rockies. Just 1 mile west of Salida, on SR 291, visit the **Mount Shavano State Fish Hatchery**, producing trout for the surrounding streams.

North of Buena Vista, on U.S. 24, is Leadville, famed for its golden history. At an altitude of over 10,000 feet, it is thought to be the highest city in the country. This is an interesting place to spend several hours learning about the Colorado gold rush. The **Healy House**, 912 Harrison St., is a museum of gold rush artifacts. Guides are costumed to portray the 1800's Victorian lifestyle of the house's boarders. Also on the property is the **Dexter Cabin**, owned by an early millionaire.

While in Leadville, you might ride the **Leadville, Colorado and Southern Railroad** for a 2 1/2-hour narrated train trip. See the narrated presentation of the city's history, **The Earth Runs Silver**, at 809 Harrison Ave. See the **Tabor Home**, 116 E. Fifth St.; visit the **Matchless Mine Cabin**, E 7th St.; or see the **Tabor Opera House**, Fourth St. at U.S. 24.

● **The Adobe Inn**
303 North Hwy. 24, Buena Vista, CO 81211. (719)395-6340.

$49-65, Oct-May. $65-75, Jun-Oct.

9 AM to 5 PM.
•V, MC.
•**Innkeepers: Paul, Margie & Michael Knox.**
•*5 rms, 5 pb.*
•Full breakfast, featuring fresh fruit or juice, an entree and choice of tea, coffee or Mexican hot chocolate.
•No pets, no smoking.
•On Hwy. 24, 2 blocks from town.

This adobe hacienda provides a taste of the old Southwest. The five guest rooms are dubbed the Indian, Mexican, Antique, Wicker and Mediterranean and are distinctively decorated in the appropriate style.

For dining, you will want to enjoy the Casa Del Sol Restaurant, owned by the Knox family. You might also want to visit the King Charles Inn or the Mt. Princeton Hot Springs.

When you visit you'll want to read or catch sunny rays on the private patios. The large library has a wide assortment of books and guests are invited to play the baby grand piano.

● **Trout City Inn**
PO Box 431, Buena Vista, CO 81211.
(719)495-0348/ Oct-Jun; 395-8433/ Jun-Oct.

$34-42. Discount for groups of eight or more.
Call 3-5 PM, Jun - Oct. Answering machine takes messages.
•V, MC.
•**Innkeepers: Juel & Irene Kjeldsen.**
•*4 rm, 4 pb.*
•Full breakfast, featuring homemade breads and jellies. Each day's menu is posted on the blackboard in the depot office.
•No smoking, no pets, no children under 10, no alcohol served. DC solar power, no AC outlets.
•5 mi. east of Buena Vista on U.S. Hwy. 24/285. 6 mi. from Trout Creek Pass.

An **1880s railroad depot** is reconstructed on its original historic site, with waiting room ticket office and antique telegraph. Guests sleep in a genuine pullman car, caboose or Victorian depot rooms. Your hosts enjoy antique steam trains, horses, antique autos, architecture, swimming, nature, wildlife conservation, and Native American history. Juel is a retired computer systems manager; Irene teaches handicapped children.

For dining, be sure to ask your hosts for the local dining guide.

When you visit you'll discover hiking, biking and riding trails right at the door. Walk to the ghost town or visit the gold or silver mines where you may pan for gold. Walk along Trout Creek and look for the brown trout and beaver lodges. Check out the mountain bike trails, collect rock samples and just enjoy the marvelous scenery. Your hosts will provide hiking and biking maps and free transportation for you and your bike to the head of the trail. If you're back at 5 PM, enjoy apple cider, cheese and crackers with your hosts.

● **The Poor Farm Country Inn**
8495 CR 160, Salida, CO 81201. (719)539-3818.

$41-51.

Call anytime. •V, MC.
•**Innkeepers: Herb & Dottie Hostetler.**
•*5 rms, 2 sb, 2 pb.*
•Homemade country breakfast served family style. It's not unusual for guests to find extra treats of cookies, or even pie or homemade ice cream waiting for them.
•No pets, limited smoking.
•1 1/2 mi from Salida

This three-story brick building, built as a poor farm in 1891, was used for this purpose until the early 1940s. Today it has been converted to "one of the finest and most lovely structures" in the county.

For dining, ask your hosts to recommend one of the excellent restaurants in the area.

When you visit you'll enjoy strolling the lovely grounds. Just out the back door is the beautiful Arkansas River. Enjoy the 100-year-old Library Lounge while relaxing with a glass of complimentary wine or beverage.

Florida
Canaveral National Seashore: Edgewater

This lovely city is on the Atlantic Ocean but is just a short drive away from the Orlando area attractions of Walt Disney World Magic Kingdom, Epcot Center, Sea World, and many other gardens, museums and entertainments.

The **Canaveral National Seashore** encompasses 25 miles of uninhabited beaches, dunes, and lagoons. Rangers lead activities at the **Playalinda Beach**, on the south end of the seashore, and at **Apollo Beach**, at the north end. Adjoining the south end of the seashore is the **Merritt Island National Wildlife Refuge**, on SR 402, near Titusville. **Black Point Wildlife Drive**, off SR 406, is a self-guided driving tour covering 7 miles of major wildlife habitats. Just South of Titusville, on U.S. 1, is the entrance to **Kennedy Space Center**. Spaceport USA, on SR 405, just south of Titusville, includes multimedia presentations, lectures, models, exhibits of spacecraft and moon rocks.

Continue north on U.S. 1 to Daytona Beach , where there are many shopping opportunities, including the **Daytona Outlet Mall**, on South Ridgewood Ave. The **Daytona International Speedway**, on U.S. 92, has races of various vehicles throughout the year. On days without races, 15-minute bus tours of the track are available. The **Museum of Arts and Sciences**, 1040 Museum Blvd., has regional natural history exhibits and early American art, art of Cuba, Florida and Europe. Dixie Queen River Cruises, 841 Ballough Rd., has 2 1/2-hour sightseeing cruises from a sternwheeler. 35 miles north of Daytona Beach, on SR A1A, is Marineland. Here you can see a variety of marine exhibits, including penguins, dolphins, sharks, moray eels and barracudas. Programs are presented throughout the day with performing dolphins and underwater feedings of the fish. A multidimensional movie, a children's playground and a shell museum are also on the grounds.

● The Colonial House

110 Yelkca Terrace, Edgewater, FL 32132. (904)427-4570.

$45/S or D. $59/S or D, in February and major holidays.
Call in the evening.
• No cr cds.
• Innkeeper: Eva Brandner.
• *3 rms, 1 sb, 1 pb.*
• Full breakfast. A sample menu would include choice of beverage, ham and egg omelette, hash browns, toast, butter, jelly, fruit, orange juice, homemade Danish pastry.
• No pets, no smoking, no children under 5.
• 20 miles S. of Daytona Beach; East of I-95.

This white colonial-style home was built in the early 1920s. In a quiet neighborhood, surrounded by oak trees, it is just minutes from the beach. A fruit basket awaits you when you arrive.

For dining, you'll enjoy Riverview Charlie's, the Skyline, Norwood's Seafood or Blackbeard's Inn.

When you visit you'll be able to enjoy the solar-heated whirlpool and swimming pool year-around. Watch the squirrels play and jump from oak tree to oak tree. When you're ready for a little exercise, walk to the nearby beach, where you can relax on the golden sand, enjoy sports or charter a boat.

Georgia

Darien

You'll want to come back repeatedly to this unspoiled portion of the Atlantic coast, where the Altamaha River empties into the Atlantic. Shrimp boats ply the river. Charter fishing trips are available. **Fort George State Historic Site**, east of US 17 of Ft. George Dr., has a reconstructed fort and blockhouse on the original site. Living history demonstrations are given on summer weekends.

Hofwyl-Broadfield Plantation, between Darien and Brunswick on US 17, is a restored 1800s mansion, once a thriving rice plantation. The house has original furnishings. A museum, slide show and self-guided tour allow the visitor to learn about the history of the rice industry in this delta and provide an opportunity to see the animals and plants native to the area.

Jekyll Island, south of Darien and once owned by wealthy East Coast moguls, was dubbed "Millionaires Island." It's now a prominent Georgia resort area. A tour of the historic district, on Riverview Dr., includes a museum, slide show, and open-air tram ride, with stops at selected "cottages" that once belonged to the prosperous owners of the island. An ll-acre water park called **Summer Waves** is also on the island.

Richmond Hill is north of Darien, on US 17. History buffs will be interested in seeing the site of the Revolutionary War **Battle of Kings Ferry**, a few miles north on US 17, and the Civil War **Fort McAllister**, 10 miles east on US 17 to SR 144. Exhibits on the history of the fort are available at the visitor center.

● Open Gates
Vernon Square, Darien, GA 31305.
(912)437-6985.

$43-53. Discounts for families, travel agents and stays of 4 days or more.

Call anytime.
- No cr. cds.
- **Innkeeper: Carolyn Hodges.**
- *4 rms, 2 pb, 1 sb.*
- Full breakfast with orange juice, toast, homemade jams and jellies, and delicious entrees such as Plantation Pancakes, shirred egg and sausage.
- Check with your hosts if you have pets or children.
- In Darien.

This handsome house was built in 1876 after reconstruction. Filled with period furnishings, it was one of the four chosen by the state department of tourism to represent historic Georgia homes in Christmas publications. In 1990 "Southern Homes" magazine included it in its feature on Georgia B&Bs. Carolyn is president of the historical society. She has knowledge of the town (second oldest in Georgia) and provides tours of the Altamaha River, barrier islands and Fanny Kemble's domain (ask your host about her).

For dining, be sure to visit Hunter's Cafe for broiled flounder and crab stew. The Buccaneers Club preserves the atmosphere of an old-time speakeasy. Try Archie's fried shrimp and catfish. If you are crazy about caviar, perhaps you'll want to ask Carolyn about getting some of the "world's best" from the Altamaha River.

When you visit , you're offered your choice of sherry or lemonade. If you're a bird-watcher, you'll want to ask Carolyn about the nearby bird sanctuaries. This is one of the few areas where there are still wood storks.

Sautee

You'll want to revel in the scenery in this secluded mountain setting. You can enjoy hiking along the trails, mountain climbing, horseback riding, and fishing.

Just a few minutes away is the Alpine Village of **Helen**. There you'll find an 18-bell carillon, the **Museum of the Hills**, craft and antique shops. Helen holds many popular special events each year, including the famous Octoberfest during September and October. There are also many recreational opportunities in the nearby **Chattahoochee National Forest** and **Unicol State Park**.

East of Sautee, on US 441, is Tallulah Falls. Tallulah Gorge is the centerpiece of **Tallulah Gorge Park**. A trail runs along the rim of the gorge providing views of the 1,000 foot drop, waterfall and native plants. **Terrora Park**, on US 441, has displays showing the use of water to generate power and depicting the history of the Tallulah Falls.

On US 19, southeast of Sautee, is Dahlonega. This area once was a gold mining center and the site of a federal mint. **The Dahlonega Gold Museum**, on the public square, has a film describing the gold years, exhibits of mining equipment, and photographs of mining activities. Visitors may pan for gold at **Blackburn Park, Old Dahlonega** and **Crisson Mines**.

● **Woodhaven Chalet**
Route 1, Box 1086, Covered Bridge Road, Sautee, GA 30571. (404)878-2580.

$55-65/D.

Call at least two weeks before you plan to visit.
•No cr. crds.
•Innkeepers: Van & Ginger Wunderlich.
•*3 rms, 1 pb, 1 sb.*
•A deluxe continental breakfast, with fresh fruit or juice, homemade natural breads and cereals, and beverages, is served in the dining area. You'll always find a hot or cold beverage available.
•No pets, no children under 10, no smoking except on decks and porches.

This charming chalet in the woods has handpainted original art and china pieces in each room. Van Wunderlich may be willing to play the grand piano on the balcony for an evening sing-along when requested by guests.

For dining, you'll definitely want to visit a German restaurant in Helen. Ask your hosts for recommendations.

When you visit, you'll want to spend time hiking in the area surrounding the chalet. When you take time to relax indoors you'll find two fireplaces radiating warmth in cool weather and cooling air conditioning during warmer weather. Here you'll be able to read or play a game of darts, cards or scrabble.

Senoia

*You'll want to pick up the Historical Society's driving tour of 24 homes. Senoia, founded in 1860, is filled with old homes, some built before the Civil War. If you want to see more old homes, both **Grantville** and **Nowan** also have driving tours of historic homes. There are many antique shops in the area and in nearby **Sharpsburg**. You'll want to visit the old fashioned hardware store and **Moreland's Museum**, in the Old Mill Building.*

*It's a little longer drive, but well worth it, to visit the beautiful **Callaway Gardens**, on US 27, at Pine Mountain. On the 2,500 acres you'll see a large collection of native azaleas, greenhouses filled with native and tropical plants, the **John A. Sibley Horticultural Center**, the **Outdoor Garden**, and the 45-acre **Meadowlark Gardens**. An unusual sight is the **Day Butterfly Center** where 50 species of butterflies can be observed in the conservatory. There are state parks nearby for picnics, hikes and outdoor activities.*

*Atlanta is just 37 miles away and the **Little White House**, on SR 85W, in Warm Springs, is 30 to 45 minutes away. You might choose to visit during one of the annual special festivals, held throughout the area. You'll love this historic old town.*

● The Culpepper House Bed & Breakfast

P.O. Box 462, Broad at Morgan, Senoia, GA 30276. (404)599-8182.

$50-60/D. Discount to senior citizens, families, travel agents.

Call 9 AM to 10 PM. Make reservations 2 weeks in advance.
- No cr. crds.
- **Innkeeper: Mary A. Brown.**
- *3 rms, 1 pb, 2 sb.*
- A full southern breakfast, featuring cheese grits, sweet rolls, bacon or ham, poached eggs and homemade jams and jellies may be served in the country kitchen or, on special occasions, in the formal dining room.
- No children under 10. No pets.
- 13 miles from Fayetteville.

Culpepper's is a large Victorian house with gingerbread trim on the large porch and interior staircases. It has curved walls, stained glass, and is furnished with period furniture. Your host is interested in historic preservation, arts and crafts, cooking, listening to music and reading.

For dining, you'll discover many exceptional restaurants in the area. Especially interesting are the Cross Roads, in Senoia, D. Henry's, in Griffin, 12 Savannah and Something Special, in Newnan, Jasmine Tea Room, Dragon Lady and Shadows, in Peachtree City, and In Clove, in LaGrange.

When you visit you'll want to sit back and rock in the rocking chair on the front porch. Your host has an old record collection that makes interesting browsing. In addition, the B&B has a library full of magazines and books. Try an old-fashioned game of croquet.

Hawaii

Kanoeohe, Oahu

You'll want to luxuriate in the sunshine and the many sandy beaches. Kanoeohe is in a beautiful, quiet mountain valley, on the popular island of Oahu, just a short drive from touristy Waikiki and not far from the Polynesian Cultural Center. It is on the shore of Kaneohe Bay. Just off the Heeia area of the bay are coral gardens which can be viewed from a glass bottom boat. In the immediate area is the **Byodo-In Temple**, a Buddhist religious and cultural center, in Valley of the Temples Park. **Ho'omaluhia Park** is a large recreational facility offering programs and activities to promote environmental awareness. The **Polynesian Cultural Center** is a recreation of authentic South Seas island villages of various cultures, including Hawaiian. Various sports, customs, arts, and crafts are demonstrated throughout the exhibition area. Island food is available for sampling and visitors may learn the hula, mat weaving and other native arts. Canoe rides are available. In the evening, visitors may have dinner and watch a 90 minute performance featuring songs and dances of the islands. Although not inexpensive, it's definitely worth a visit.

While you are here, you should also see the **U.S.S. Arizona National Memorial**. The Navy tour is far better than other more costly trips. Also try to visit **Kapiolani Park**, with the **Kodak Hula Show**, the **Honolulu Zoo** and the **Aquarium**.

● **Emma's Guest Rooms**
47-600 Hui Ulili St., Kanohe, Oahu, HI 96744. (809)239-7248/ Fax: 239-7224.

$45 per night if you stay for three or more nights. $55 if stay is for less than three nights.

Call 8 AM to 10 PM. •V, MC, D, AE.
•Innkeepers: Emma & Stan Sargeant.
•*3 rms, 3 pb.*
•No breakfast is served but guests have their own kitchenette, dining and TV lounge.
•No pets, no smoking, no alcohol, no children under 10. •In Kanohe.

This modern five-bedroom home is clean and tastefully decorated. Your hosts are world travelers, and history buffs. They speak German and English.

For dining, you'll find a multitude of eating establishments, from fast food to gourmet. Discuss your preferences with your hosts.

When you visit you'll enjoy using the lanai for relaxing or snoozing. A large library with a selection of books is available for reading.

Idaho

Salmon National Forest - Shoup

*You'll want to dream of the romance of Lewis and Clark and the early days of our western frontier when you visit this area. In fact, the historic **Lewis and Clark Trail** passes nearby and the forest itself still looks much as it did back then.*

*Because of swift currents, a portion of the **Salmon River** near here was called the "River of No Return." Now, however, jet boats provide transportation on the still formidable waterway. Other parts of the river are less forbidding. Whitewater trips and steelhead fishing can be arranged through several companies in the area. A hot springs is not far away.*

*The **Frank Church Wilderness Area** is popular for big game hunting. Of course, walkers are sure to find plenty of space for walking. And, this is an ideal spot for bird and animal watching.*

*The historic **Gold Hill Mine** offers interesting tours. The **Shoup Store** still has an old-time Pelton wheel for power and hand gas pumps. Many of the residents have kept their crank telephones — the last in the U.S. — even though they are no longer in use. If you visit during the third weekend in July, you'll be able to join the celebration of "Downriver Days."*

This is a perfect spot for those who want to get away from pollution and big cities congestion for a few days.

Smith House Bed & Breakfast

49 Salmon River Road, Shoup, ID 83469.
(208)394-2121/ (800)238-5915 for reservations.

$35-50. Open Mar. 15 - Nov. 30.

Call 8 AM - 10 PM.
- V, MC.
- Innkeepers: Aubrey & Marsha Smith.
- 5 rms, 1 pb, 2 sb.
- Full breakfast with juice, fresh fruit, omelet, sausages, Idaho hash browns, muffins or toast and jam, served in the main house under the skylight.
- No smoking.
- In the forest, 50 miles NW of Salmon on Highway 93.

This log home in the wilderness includes the main house and a guest house. Guests are welcomed with a fruit basket, fresh flowers, mints, choice of beverage and hospitality. Former Floridians, Aubrey (a retired Army Chaplain) and Marsha (a former legal secretary) fulfilled a life-long dream of owning a log home in the forest, when they moved here. They enjoy arts, crafts, reading, gardening and bird watching.

For dining, the Ramshead Lodge is just around the corner and the Shoup Cafe is not very far. Your hosts will direct you to other restaurants that fit your desires after you arrive.

When you visit sit in the hot tub and dream. The Smiths will let you pick and enjoy fresh fruit from their wide selection of trees: cherry, apricot, plum, apple, pear and peach. The garden has an assortment of fresh vegetables and herbs. Peruse the assortment of books and videos, including video games.

Illinois

Carlyle and Highland — St. Louis Area

You'll want to relax and enjoy these lovely old towns. They're also less than an hour's drive from St. Louis so you may want to spend a day of your getaway in the city.

In the Carlyle area you'll find Illinois' largest man-made lake: **Carlyle Lake**. You'll be able to rent a sail boat or pontoon boat, go fishing or swimming. There are two golf courses, tennis courts, a swimming pool, parks, bike and hiking trails. Visit the **Clinton County Historical Museum** or peruse some of the antique specialty shops in the historic shopping district.

Highland is known as "Neu Sweizerland" and is one of the oldest and largest Swiss settlements in the U.S. It has a rich Swiss-German heritage that is carried out in the decor of the homes and businesses. Among the things to see in town are the **Latzer Homestead** and the **Wicks Organ Company**, where you may be able to arrange a factory tour. Visit **Lake Crystal** or browse through the many antique and gift shops.

If you spend a day in St. Louis consider spending it at **Six Flags Amusement Park**, seeing the **Gateway Arch**, the **St. Louis Science Center**, the zoo or the **Missouri Botanical Gardens**.

● The Country Haus Bed & Breakfast
1191 Franklin, Carlyle, IL 62231.
(618)594-8313.

$45-55.

Call 8 AM - 10 PM.
- V, MC, AE.
- Innkeepers: Ron & Vickie Cook.
- *4 rms, 4 pb.*
- Full breakfast served in the dining room. Typical menu might include egg and bacon casserole, homemade muffins, fruit, coffee or tea.
- No pets, no smoking, no children under 3.
- In Carlyle.

This 1890s Eastlake Style home, with original stained glass windows and pocket doors, has been decorated with a country theme. Ron and Vickie will be able to tell you about local areas of interest. They enjoy refurbishing old buildings and travel. Ron loves hunting, fishing and golfing. Vickie collects owls.

For dining, you can make reservations at the Country Haus, Wednesday through Sunday, for home cooking at reasonable prices. The Fin & Feather, specializing in steak and seafood is just 8 miles away.

When you visit sign up for a soak in the whirlpool; ask if you may borrow fishing or golfing equipment for a day; savor an evening cookie or soft drink provided by your hosts; peruse a book or magazine in the library; enjoy a peaceful summer night on the porch swing or deck.

● Phyllis' Bed & Breakfast

801 Ninth Street, Highland, IL 62249.
(618)654-4619.

$40-45/one person; $45-50/two people.

Call anytime.
- V, MC.
- **Innkeeper: Phyllis Bible.**
- *4 rms, 4 pb.*
- Full breakfast might include coffee, juice, cereal, muffins, fruit, coffee cake and quiche or sausage and biscuits served in the breakfast room or on the deck.
- No pets, no smoking, no alcohol.
- 2 blocks from the square in Highland.

Built in the early 1900s, the inn has always had loving care. Each guest room is decorated in a different and attractive style. Your host enjoys crafts, antiques and flowers.

For dining, you'll find several enticing establishments in the area. Ask Phyllis to help you decide which will suit your taste.

When you visit browse through the gift shop; sit on the deck and watch the birds and other small animals; borrow a book from the library; in cold weather enjoy the warmth of the fireplace; relax in a big chair and enjoy visiting with other guests.

Kolache Coffee Rolls

From James E. Wanek, **Wanek's Lodge at Estes**
Estes Park, Colorado.

Roll:
3 rounded tablespoons dry yeast
3 rounded tablespoons sugar
a pinch of salt
2 tablespoons cooking oil
1 cup hot water (110F)
1 cup milk warmed -- no hotter than 110F.
5-6 cups white all-purpose flour
1 egg

Filling: Any fruit pie filling such as cherry, blueberry, peach, apple, etc.

In a large bowl dissolve yeast, sugar and salt in hot water. Add oil and milk. Stir in 2 or 3 cups flour. Then turn onto a lightly floured surface and knead in enough of remaining flour to make a soft dough. Knead dough 8 to 10 minutes until smooth and elastic. Place dough in a greased bowl, turning to coat all sides with oil. Cover with a damp cloth and let rise in a warm place, free from drafts, until doubled in size.

Form into 1 1/2 inch balls. Press balls on greased cookie sheets until in flat rounds about 2 1/2 inch in diameter and 1/2 inch thick. Allow 1 inch or more between rounds on sheet. Cover and let rise until doubled in size. Make a pocket in the center by pushing dough out toward the edges until each resembles a 3 inch pizza. Beat egg lightly and brush edges of roll. Add 2 teaspoons of filling in each center. Bake 10 - 12 minutes, in a 375F. oven until golden brown. Remove from cookie sheets and cool slightly before serving warm. Makes 36 to 40 Kolaches.

Note: These Kolaches may be frozen in a single layer in plastic bags. Bring to room temperature before serving, then warm each of the Kolaches directly on an oven rack (not on a cookie sheet) in the upper 1/3 of a 350F. oven for 3-4 minutes. Serve.

This was developed from an old family recipe.

Galena

You'll want to visit the **Ulysses S. Grant Home State Historical Site**, 510 Bouthillier St., which includes many of Grant's possessions including White House china and silver. The **Old Market House**, Market Square, is one of the oldest remaining city market houses in the midwest.

Vinegar Hill Lead Mine, north on SR 84, is a reminder of this area's flourishing lead mine trade in the 1800s. Guided tours are offered and a museum contains exhibits of early mining equipment. The town is filled with restored 19th century homes and examples of period architecture. 90 percent of the buildings in town are on the Historic Register.

You may visit several homes independently or take guided tours. Among the more interesting choices are the **Dowling House**, Main and Diagonal Sts, said to be the oldest house in Galena; the **Belvedere Mansion**, 1008 Park Ave., an 1857, 22-room, Italionate mansion and garden; and the **Galena-Jo Daviess County History Museum**, 211 S. Bench St., an 1858 mansion containing Civil War artifacts.

There are antique shops, art galleries, pottery and gift shops. You'll find museums to visit, riverboats, hiking, biking, cross country and downhill skiing and an alpine slide. Main Street is preserved much as it looked in the 1850s.

● **Avery Guest House**
606 South Prospect Street, Galena, IL 61036.
(815)777-3883.

$46-55/D. Discounts for senior citizens.

Call 9 AM to 9 PM.
- V, MC, D.
- **Innkeepers: Flo & Roger Jensen.**
- *4 rms, 2 sb.*
- Expanded continental breakfast with muffins, fruit bowl, juice, cheese plate, juice, cereal, coffee.
- No pets, no smoking.
- In Galena, one block from main street.

This pre-civil war home has 10 ft. ceilings and period furniture. Its hillside location gives you a pleasing view. Flo plays the piano and is always ready for sing-alongs. Roger makes stained glass windows.

For dining, you'll enjoy Galena's many fine restaurants, including Kingston Inn, Silver Annie's, Stillman's and the DeSoto House Hotel. There are many excellent casual places with 1850s ambience.

When you visit, table games and many books will always be available in the large library. If you play piano you may use Flo's. Enjoy relaxing on the comfortable porch swing.

Monmouth

You'll want to brush up on the interesting history of the area. Monmouth is the birthplace of Wyatt Earp and has a museum dedicated to his memory. Other museums open to the public are the Minne Stewart Home and the Holt House. Golfers will want to play the Gibson Woods Golf Course. On a sunny day, perhaps you'd like to put together your own picnic and visit Monmouth Park.

Just a few miles away, Galesburg is noted for being an important station on the "Underground Railroad" and as the birthplace and burial site of famed poet, Carl Sandburg. You can visit a restored cottage and museum at the **Sandburg Historical Site**, 331 E. Third St. **Lake Stoney Recreational Area** has swimming pools, a water slide, boat rentals, 18 hole golf course, tennis courts, a playground, and gardens. The **Galesburg Railroad Museum**, Seminary and Mulberry Sts., has a 1912 Pullman car, a 1920 post office car, a caboose, locomotive and other equipment cars and railroad memorabilia.

North from Galesburg on US 34, then 2 miles north is **Bishop Hill State Historical Site**. The five-acre living history museum contains restored buildings with guides reenacting life in the Swedish communal settlement as it was in the last half of the 19th century. The Bishop Hill Museum, within the colony, has an exceptional collection of paintings by American folk artist, Olof Krans.

● Carr Mansion Guest House
416 E. Broadway, Monmouth, IL ZIP [61462. (309)734-3654.

$40/S or D.

Call 9 AM to 9 PM.
- V, MC.
- **Innkeepers: Christopher & Carla Kanthak.**
- *3 rms, 2 sb.*
- Full breakfast of hot entree, home baked bread, fruit, juice, coffee and tea. Your breakfast will be served in the formal dining room, on the lovely china service.
- No pets, no smoking, no children under 12.
- 3 blks from the town square in Monmouth, on Hwys 67 & 34.

This three-story, 20 room, 1877 Victorian mansion is listed on the National Register of Historic Places. It has many unique architectural features with cozy nooks for relaxing and reflection. Christopher and Carla enjoy traveling, history and good conversation.

For dining, you'll want to go to Cerars' Barnstormer Restaurant, Filling Station III, or The Happy Burro.

When you visit you'll find that guests are encouraged to explore the mansion and find the many unique architectural features. During warm weather, you'll love loafing on the veranda, stone-walled terrace or balcony. In cooler weather, the cozy fireside is especially enticing.

Nauvoo

You'll want to take at least one walking tour of this historic town. Settled by Joseph Smith and other members of The Church of Jesus Christ of the Latter-day Saints in 1839, the town flourished until 1844 when a mob killed Joseph Smith and his brother.

Discouraged by the opposition of neighbors, the Mormons began to emigrate from the state in 1846. By 1849 the town was nearly deserted when a French Icarian sect formed a communal society in Nauvoo. That society had disintegrated by 1858. Now the town is filled with restored, 19th century buildings, unique shops and museums.

You'll want to visit the **Nauvoo Restoration Visitor Center** for a movie on the town's history and a suggested tour of some of the old buildings. The **Joseph Smith Historic Center** includes the first home of the Smith family, the mansion Joseph Smith occupied, the store he operated, and his grave.

You'll also enjoy a self-guided tour of the **Nauvoo Mill and Bakery**, Mulholland St.

Visit **Nauvoo State Park** to see a museum containing a room for each stage of the city's history. Although the history of this area makes it especially interesting, it's also a great place for hiking, biking, fishing and golfing.

●Mississippi Memories Bed & Breakfast
Box 291, Riverview Heights, Nauvoo, IL 62354.
(217)453-2771

$49-59/D. Discount to travel agent.

Call 9 AM to 8 PM.
- V, MC.
- Innkeepers: Marge & Dean Starr.
- *4 rms, 1 pb, 2 sb.*
- A full breakfast might consist of fresh fruit plates, ham, eggs, homemade sticky rolls, cereal, juice, coffee and milk. You'll dine in the kitchen, on the deck, or in the dining room.
- No pets, no smoking, no alcohol.
- On Hwy 96, 5 miles from Nauvoo.

On the banks of the Mississippi, this spacious house has two large decks overlooking the river and most rooms have a river view. This is a perfect spot for wildlife watchers. Your hosts enjoy music, farming, rock hunting and reading.

For dining, you'll love your gourmet breakfasts at Mississippi Memories. In the evening you'll find outstanding food at Hotel Nauvoo or more casual dining at Dottie's Red Front.

When you visit you'll find lots of activities right at Mississippi Memories. You're welcome to visit the farm; there is a large library to peruse. In the evenings, there are often sing-alongs. The geode hunting is great for "rock hounds." Or, you can watch the barges, look for wildlife, or go fishing on the river.

● The Ancient Pines
2015 Parley Street, Nauvoo, IL 62354.
(317)453-2767.

$40.

Call 9 AM to 9 PM.
•No cr. cds.
•**Innkeeper: Genevieve Simmens.**
•*4 rms, 2 sb.*
•Full breakfast with fresh baked bread, eggs, sausage, juice or fruit, served in the dining room. A heart healthy meal served when requested.
•No smoking, only small caged pets.
•In Nauvoo.

This turn-of-the-century brick home was preserved within the same family for four generations and few changes were made. It is surrounded by 140 year-old evergreens. It has pressed tin ceilings, stained glass windows, original carved woodwork, oak and pine floors and claw foot tubs. Your host practices organic gardening in her flower and vegetable gardens.

For dining, be sure to have a meal at the famed Hotel Nauvoo.

When you visit you'll find the veranda or side porch are wonderful places to rest after a busy day. From the veranda you can frequently watch workers in the nearby winery. You're welcome to meander through the flower and herb gardens or to play badminton and croquet. In the library you'll find music and books.

Baked Cheese Grits with Tomato Butterfly Garnish

From Mary Brown, **Culpepper House Bed & Breakfast**
Senoia, Georgia

4 cups cooked grits (you may use instant grits)
1 cup grated sharp cheddar cheese
1 small grated onion
1 egg
1 tablespoon butter or margarine
6 tomato wedges

Cook grits to a very soft consistency. Stir into grits, 1/2 cup grated cheese, onion, egg and butter. Pour into baking dish and bake for 20 minutes in 350F. oven. While this is baking, cut a fresh tomato into 6 wedges, no thicker than 1/2 inch at the thickest side, to make 3 butterflies. On a pointed end of each tomato wedge, gently peel back the tomato skin 1/2 the length of the wedge. Sprinkle the remaining 1/2 cup of grated cheese over the entire surface of the grits. Place the tomato wedges on top of the surface for garnish. Arrange two wedges back to back, skin sides facing and loose peel pulled up so you have a "butterfly." Your grits will be garnished with three butterflies. Replace in the oven for about 10 minutes or until the cheese melts and grits are hot. Serve. Makes 6 to 8 servings.

Rock Island

You'll want to view the Mississippi River, possibly by taking a sightseeing or dinner excursion boat or by just driving down the river. Rock Island, with Moline, IL, Davenport and Bettendorf, IA, is a part of the metropolitan area known as "Quad Cities."

The famous Dred Scott Decision that was among the precipitating causes of the Civil War started here with a suit filed by a Rock Island resident. Worth a visit are the **Confederate and National Cemeteries and Rock Island Arsenal**, on Rock Island, where there are a number of restored buildings, a firearms collection, and a show demonstrating lock and dam navigation on the river.

The **Niabi Zoo**, on US 1, in Moline, has a variety of animals. The **Children's Museum**, 533 Sixteenth St., in Bettendorf, has "hands on" exhibits for children including a TotSpot for very young children. See the historic district of **East Davenport**, in Davenport.

In Illinois you may enjoy a narrated riverboat cruise or, in Iowa, enjoy food, entertainment and gambling on a casino riverboat. In the four cities, there is a variety of museums, shopping opportunities, parks, gardens, outdoor recreation and theater. You won't run out of things to see and do while you visit.

● **Top O'the Morning Bed and Breakfast Inn**
1505 Nineteenth Avenue, Rock Island, IL 61201.
(309)786-3513.

$50-60/D.

Call after 5 PM.
- No cr. crds.
- Innkeepers: Peggy Doak.
- *3 rms, 3 pb.*
- Full breakfast with fresh fruit, breads, entree, and beverage.
- No pets.
- In the center of Rock Island.

This prairie-style mansion was built by the president of the Rock Island Railroad in 1912. Originally part of a country estate, it is surrounded by over three acres of oak trees, lawn, orchard and gardens. The Mississippi River runs by the estate.

For dining, exceptional food is available at W.L. Velie's, in a 1920s mansion; The Iowa Machine Shed Co, for Iowa pork; the Jubilee floating restaurant. You can also dine on many of the Casino gambling boats.

When you visit you'll want to stroll the grounds, view the Mississippi River, play horseshoes or pick fruit and berries in season. In the library you may read original letters written during the Civil War. If you're a pianist you can play the lovely grand piano.

Indiana

Knightstown

You'll want to drive or walk through the streets of this Indiana town to see the old homes, visit the local coppersmith factory or take an excursion train ride from Knightstown to Carthage. It's only a short drive from Knightstown to **Old Metamora**, a restored 19th-century canal town, with an operating aqueduct. Also at Metamora on US 52 S is **Whitewater Canal State Historic Site**, which has a restored section of the old waterway that operated between 1836 and 1847. Also see an operating gristmill.

Fifteen minutes away is the **Indiana Basketball Hall of Fame**, (take SR 3 N, and then go E on SR 38) at New Castle. East of Knightstown on US 40 is Richmond, and the **Indiana Football Hall of Fame**. Plan to visit the **Hayes Regional Arboretum**, on Elks Rd, with its woods and plants, a nature trail and a driving tour route. Bordering **Whitewater River Gorge**, is a 3 1/2-mile trail that also passes Richmond historic and scenic sights. Richmond also has an interesting art museum and historical museum.

On the way to or from Richmond, on US 40, stop in Cambridge City to see the **Huddleston Farmhouse Inn Museum**. Here a restored farmhouse barn and smokehouse have been restored to the period of the 1840s. Just north of Indianapolis, and less than an hour away, is Noblesville and the living history museum village of **Conner Prairie**. In the area, costumed guides portray citizens of an 19th century pioneer village.

A half hour away is Indianapolis and the Benjamin Harrison Home, James Whitcomb Riley Home, Eiteljorg Museum of Indian and Western Art, Indianapolis Museum of Art, The Children's Museum and the Indianapolis Speedway. Union Station, in Indianapolis, has been restored as a marketplace with stores, restaurants and entertainment.

● **Old Hoosier House**
7601 South Greensboro Pike, Knightstown, IN 46148.
(317)345-2969.

$55-65. Discount to senior citizens, travel agent and off-season.

Call any time.
- No cr. cds.
- **Innkeepers: Jean & Tom Lewis.**
- *4 rms, 3 pb, 1 sb.*
- Full breakfast, featuring fruit, juice, entree, homemade rolls and beverage, served on the deck or in the dining room.
- No pets, no smoking, no alcohol.
- 1 1/2 miles from Knightstown and 25 miles from Indianapolis.

This historic old brick farmhouse was on the underground slave route. Built in 1836, it was completely restored in 1983. It has central air conditioning and the large rooms are filled with antiques. An 18-hole golf course is right next door.

For dining, your hosts will furnish you with a list of the many nearby restaurants and we'd especially recommend The Port Hole, in New Castle, Welliver's Fabulous Buffet, in Hagerstown, or The Kopper Kettle, in Morristown.

When you visit you'll be just a few steps away from the fine golf course next door. The surrounding woods and rural area are wonderful for bird watching and hiking. Guests enjoy sitting on the front porch or back deck to watch birds, golfers, and other people.

Iowa

Amana Colonies
— Homestead and Marengo

You'll want to tour the colonies first. They are Iowa's largest tourist attraction.

Originally settled in the 1850s by members of a religious sect from Germany, Switzerland and France, the colonies consist of seven villages. The original settlers had a communal system. Self-guided tours include a restored **original home, blacksmith shop, Communal Kitchen** and several museums. You will also want to take tours of the **Amana Woolen Mill** and a **winery**, visit antique shops, and furniture shops. Pick up a map at the Visitors Bureau. While you're visiting, intersperse tours of the colonies with a hike on the nature trail, a game of golf, an evening at the summertime theater, summer biking or winter cross country skiing.

Homestead in one of the original colonies. Marengo is just a short distance west of the colonies and the home of the **Pioneer Heritage Museum**.

Also nearby are the **Herbert Hoover Presidential Library and Museum**, in West Branch; **Plum Grove** (restored residence of the territory's first governor) and the **University of Iowa**, in Iowa City; **Brucemore Mansion**, in Cedar Rapids; the **Kalona Historical Village**, in the Amish community of Kalona; Iowa County Lake and three golf courses.

● Die Heimat Country Inn
Main Street, Amana Colonies, Homestead, IA 52236.
(319)622-3937.

$37-47/D.

Call anytime.
- V, MC, D.
- **Innkeepers: Don & Sheila Janda.**
- *19 rms, 19 pb.*
- Full breakfast, served buffet style. You'll have your choice of juice, beverage, bread, eggs, fruit, fruit soup, muffins, French toast or waffles.
- Limited pets and smoking.
- End of Main Street, in Homestead.

Built in 1854, this country inn was a stopping place for travelers as they crossed the plains. It has now been completely restored and is decorated with Amana traditional walnut and cherry furniture. Many of the rooms have canopies, quilts and heirlooms. Don and Sheila collect antiques, antique cars and information about Amana heritage.

For dining, you'll want to visit Bill Zuber's Restaurant, right on Main Street in Amana, or try some of the other Colony restaurants serving delicious German family style food.

When you visit absorb the wonderful peace and quiet, take time to read and relax. In the summer, try the Amana wooden gliders in the shaded yard. Any time of the year, you are welcome to enjoy the games and puzzles in the sitting room.

● **Loy's Bed & Breakfast**
R.R. 1, Box 82, Marengo, IA ZIP [52301. (319)642-7787.

$50-60.

Call early in the morning and at meal time.
- No cr. crds.
- **Innkeepers: Loy & Robert Walker.**
- *3 rms, 1 pb, 1 sb.*
- A full country breakfast is served on porch, patio or kitchen dining room with juice, entree, fruit in season, hot breads and beverages.
- Pets must be caged, smoking outdoors only, limited social drinking.
- North of I-80, Exit 216. 8 miles from Marengo, close to the Amana colonies.

This B & B is in a contemporary farm home surrounded by a large lawn, cornfields and, depending on the season, beautiful flowers or white snow. The farm is base for a large corn and hog operation. In addition to being farmers, your hosts are community volunteers, substitute teacher, Iowa State U grads and grandparents.

For dining, in addition to the great breakfast, if you request it, Loy may find time to cook a great "Iowa Chop" dinner for you. Other dining choices would include, the eight Amana Colony restaurants, Carnsforth, the old stage coach stop at Victor or the Landmark Truckstop.

When you visit, after a hearty breakfast in the kitchen, you may tour the farm facilities, walk on a country road, help garden or spend the day at the lake. You may play pool or billiards, ping pong, shuffle board or horseshoes. There are toys and a swing set for children.

Honey Glazed Baked French Toast

From Carla Kanthak, Carr Mansion Guest House
Monmouth, IL

1 baguette French bread cut in 1 inch slices
6 eggs
1 cup milk
1 cup light cream
1 1/2 teaspoon vanilla extract
1/4 teaspoon cinnamon
1/4 cup butter, melted
1/4 cup brown sugar
1/2 cup chopped peanuts
1/2 cup honey

Butter a large 9 x 9 baking dish. Arrange bread slices to fill pan completely. Combine eggs, milk, cream, vanilla and cinnamon. Mix well. Pour over bread, cover and refrigerate overnight.

In the morning, preheat oven to 350F. In a small bowl combine butter, brown sugar, chopped nuts and honey. Mix well. Spread evenly over bread, Bake 45 minutes or until puffed and golden. Serve with honey or syrup. Serves 6 to 8 people.

Kentucky

Bowling Green

You'll want to explore a cave when you visit this southern city. Although Bowling Green has a variety of industries and cultural activities, it's also surrounded by famous underground caverns. **Mammoth Cave National Park**, is less than an hour's drive northeast of here. It is one of the longest explored caves. There are a variety of tours, for varying energy levels, but plan to do some walking and wear shoes with good traction. Within the park are several nature trails, two rivers for fishing and boating. One-hour cruises on the Green River are available. Other caves available for touring are the **Kentucky Diamond Caverns**, in Park City, and **Crystal Onyx Cave**, in Cave City. While you are in Cave City, you may also want to visit the **Mammoth Cave Wildlife Museum**, on SR 90. It contains a variety of wildlife specimens.

The city of Bowling Green has a wide variety of activities and entertainment. If you're a sports car enthusiast you will also want to visit the **Corvette Assembly Plant**, just off I-65 at Louisville Rd. Free tours are given at 9 AM and 1 PM, business days (closed mid-July through mid-August). Bowling Green is the home of **Western Kentucky University**. The **Kentucky Library and Museum** at the University has a variety of historic and prehistoric artifacts. The library has many rare books and books on Kentucky history. **Riverview**, in Hobson Grove Park, is a restored Italianate home filled with late 19th century furnishings. Guided tours are available Tues. through Sun. Call for times.

Southwest of Bowling Green on US 68, is South Union, once the home of an active Shaker community. The **South Union Shaker Museum** has displays in an 1824 Shaker home. A **Shaker Festival** is held in South Union the last two weekends in June.

You'll have much to choose from when you visit this area, including concerts, plays, planetarium shows, tennis, golf, state park recreation (boating, swimming, horseback riding, picnics) or commercial tours.

● **Bowling Green Bed & Breakfast**
1415 Beddington Way, Bowling Green, KY 42104.
(502)781-3861.

$44/S; $55/D. Special weekly and family rates.

Call early in the morning.
• No cr. crds.
• **Innkeepers: Dr Norman & Ronna Lee Hunter.**
• *2 rms, 1 pb, 1 sb.*
• A full breakfast of fruit, cereal, milk, muffins, entree and beverage will be served in the dining room.
• No pets, no children under 14, no smoking, limited alcohol.
• Three miles from town square and convenient to highways.

This recently-built brick home is in a new subdivision on a landscaped corner property. The interior, with natural woodwork and skylights, is furnished in antiques. Your hosts are a chemistry professor and a retired nurse and teacher. They enjoy travel, antiques, photography, bowling, hiking, reading, music, theater and writing.

For dining, seek out these unique restaurants: Mariah's, the oldest brick home in Bowling Green, on the site of the spring where first settlers stopped; the Barren River State Park dining room; the Mammoth Cave Dining Room and The Parakeet, downtown.

When you visit you'll delight in relaxing or having a picnic on the deck and patio. Musicians will enjoy playing the organ. If you have any spare time, you're welcome to browse through the large selection of reading material, to watch movies on the VCR, to enjoy the TV or stereo.

Louisiana

New Orleans

You'll want to visit the French Quarter, Preservation Hall and the Old French Market. New Orleans is filled with wonderful, unique attractions. It's especially famed for the Mardi Gras and New Orleans jazz.

Among the many outstanding things to see and do are riding the old fashioned **St. Charles Streetcar**. It travels up and down St. Charles Ave., of course. Take a tour of the famous **Superdome**, 1500 Poydras St. Tours are given daily, except during special events.

Visit **Aquarium of the Americas**, Mississippi River and Canal St. This building houses more than 7,500 aquatic animals. Spend hours at the **Audubon Zoo**, 6500 Magazine St., where there are acres of natural habitats housing many animals. See the **St. Louis Cathedral**, on Jackson Square, one of the oldest churches in the U.S. Walk through the **Musee Conti Wax Museum**, 917 Conti St., where life-size wax figures are depicted in settings significant in New Orleans history.

You'll want to participate in the **National Park Service walking tour** of historic cemeteries and of the **French Quarter**. Tours begin at the Visitor and Folklife Center in the French Market at 916 N. Peters St. Finally, spend an evening at **Preservation Hall**, 726 St. Peter St., where a band plays traditional jazz each evening, 8:30 PM - 12:30 AM.

Also popular are a Cajun Swamp Tour, plantations, riverboat rides, the riverwalk, theater productions, Historic Garden District, Magazine Street Antique Shops, the Canal Street Shopping Mall or Jackson Brewery.

Don't forget to taste a beignet.

● **Essem's House**
3660 Gentilly Blvd. New Orleans, LA 70122.
(504)947-3401.

$55. Seasonal discount.

Call before 8 AM or after 6 PM.
•V, MC, D.
•**Innkeeper: Sarah Margaret Brown.**
•*2 rms, 2 pb.*
•Continental breakfast of breads, juice and beverage, served in the dining room. Guests who wish to sleep in find coffee and pastries in dining room warmer.
•No pets, no smoking, no alcohol, no children under 10.
•One mile from US 90 or US 10.

This large 1930s home is in a beautiful area that is convenient to major areas of interest. It has off-street parking. Your host enjoys gardening, traveling, cooking and sight-seeing.

For dining, there are many wonderful possibilities. Among the choices are Mandinas, and Brunnings at the Lake. Sarah would suggest you try a "Po Boy," "Red Beans and Rice," "Gumbo," "Shrimp Creole" and "Fried Catfish" while you're here.

When you visit you'll find you're in a place that's comfortable for relaxing when you're worn out from "doing" and "seeing." The sun room has a guest TV; there are many books and magazines available for visitors to enjoy; the giant oak, in the garden, provides great shade in summer months; and there's a warm fire in the fireplace for cooler months.

● St. Charles Guest House Bed & Breakfast

1748 Prytania St., New Orleans, LA 70130.
(504)523-6556.

$48-75. Higher rates for special events.

Call 30 days before planned stay.
- V, MC, AE.
- **Innkeepers: Joanne & Dennis Hilton.**
- *36 rms, 24 pb and 4 sb.*
- Continental breakfast of fruit, juice, fresh bakery products, beverage.
- On streetcar line, 1 mile from the French Quarter and River-front, 3/4 mile from Convention Center.

In the historic Lower Garden District, on the streetcar line, this B&B has been a guest house for over 30 years. Your hosts are experts on what to see and do in the area. Dennis is a social worker and therapist. They say their guests are the "most interesting people in the world."

For dining, we'd suggest Commander's Palace, the Versailles, the Caribbean Room in Portchartrain Hotel, Michael's Cajun Dance Restaurant, Mulat's Cajun Restaurant and Dance Hall, Cafe Atchafalayn or Copeland's Cajun American.

When you visit check out books from the extensive library. You might want to loaf on one of the decks while you read. Or, sit among the lush banana trees, by the pool, to catch some tanning rays, or swim in the pool when weather permits (March - November).

Strawberry Slurry

From Sarah Margaret Brown, **Essem's House**
New Orleans, Louisiana

CALORIE WISE

Yogurt cheese made from 1 pound plain nonfat yogurt
1 pint strawberries, washed, stemmed and coarsely mashed
Artificial sweetener to taste
1 teaspoon vanilla extract

OTHERWISE

8 ounces cream cheese softened to room temperature
1 pint strawberries, washed, stemmed and coarsely mashed
Sugar to taste
1 teaspoon vanilla extract

To make yogurt cheese: Put yogurt in a cheesecloth lined strainer. Set strainer over a bowl and put in the refrigerator overnight. In the morning you'll have a nonfat cheese similar to cream cheese.

For either recipe, stir together all ingredients, leaving some lumps of strawberries and the cream cheese. This may be served as a topping for any breakfast bread or as a filling for crepes.

Maine

Bath, Boothbay Harbor, Waldeboro

You'll want to visit the beautiful beaches, take a harbor cruise, and involve yourself in marine-related activities when you visit these towns. Bath has been involved in shipbuilding since the early 1600s. Visit the **Maine Maritime Museum**, 243 Washington St., the site of two former shipyards that built large wooden sailing ships. Here you can observe ongoing construction and repair skills, see a restored Grand Banks schooner and visit a museum. Children will enjoy their special play ship. Cruises are available. After you leave the museum, drive past the **Bath Iron Works**, where large vessels are being built today. See historic old mansions.

Boothbay Harbor is the home of several river and ocean cruises. Trips leave the piers from May to mid-October and vary in length from 1 hour to an entire day. Deep sea fishing trips can also be arranged here. **Boothbay Railway Village**, on SR 27, is a re-creation of an early 1900s Maine village with restored buildings and railroad memorabilia. The **Department of Marine Resources**, on McKown's point, has an aquarium, tidal pool and fish exhibits.

The **Waldoboro Museum**, on SR 220, brings back a taste of the 19th century. It includes a restored school house, farm kitchen, bedroom and country store.**Colonial Pemaquid State Historical Site**, SR 130 has a museum displaying artifacts from the 17th century. Nearby, and with a shared admission, is **Fort William Henry State Historic Site**, with a reconstruction of an early colonial fort. At Lighthouse Park is the **Pemaquid Point Lighthouse**, a fishermen's museum and art gallery.

A must when you visit is Freeport, home of the famed **L.L. Bean store**, open 24 hours a day, every day of the year. Also visit the **Desert of Maine**, an area of sand dunes that is growing larger as the once-fertile top soil is lost. **Popham Beach and Reid State Park** have beautiful scenic beaches. Both are within easy driving distances of these towns.

● **Glad II**
60 Pearl Street, Bath, ME 04530.
(207)443-1191.

$45/S or D. Discount to senior citizen and travel agent.

Call anytime.
- V, MC, AE.
- **Innkeeper: Gladys Lansky.**
- *2 rms, 1 sb.*
- Expanded continental breakfast of juice, fresh fruit, cereals, home made muffins or breads, jam and beverage.
- No pets, no smoking, no children under 12.
- 7/10 mile from US 1 or 8 minute walk to town.

This Victorian home dates from 1851. It is comfortably furnished with the guest in mind. Gladys teaches piano, likes to read, travel, enjoys people and her dog, Nicholas.

For dining, you'll find food you'll enjoy at The Osprey, J. R. Maxwell's, the First Wok, Great Impasta or Taste of Maine.

When you visit you are welcome to browse in the library and when you've found a book, read it on the screened porch or in the living room. Nicholas will be happy to play with you and his Teddy Bears, if you feel like it. Some guests wash their car while they're here, weed the garden, or lay under the willow tree and take a nap. If you are a pianist, you're welcome to play Gladys' beautiful mellow Baldwin Grand Piano.

- **Welch House Inn**
36 McKown Street, Boothbay Harbor, ME 04538.
(207)633-3431.

$55-90/D. These rates apply 4/15-10/15. Discount for stay of 7 or more nights.

Call 8 AM - 11 PM.
- V, MC.
- **Innkeepers: David & Martha Mason.**
- *16 rms, 16 pb.*
- Expanded continental breakfast served buffet style in the glass sunroom, facing the harbor. The buffet usually includes juice, fresh fruit, cereals, homemade muffins and granola, beverages.
- No children under 8, pets only in limited parts of inn.
  - Located in town on top of McKown hill. Right on the harbor.

This 1849 sea captain's home has a rooftop observation deck and a glass-enclosed breakfast/commons room. Many of the furnishings are antiques; everything looks comfortable. Your hosts enjoy chess, needlework, gardening and photography.

For dining, there are several excellent restaurants in the area. We think you might like the Black Orchid, McSeagull's, the Osprey, or the Cabbage Island Clambake.

When you visit climb to the rooftop observation deck for an unsurpassed view of the harbor and ocean, relax with a good book or walk to harbor and town activities from this central location. If you want company when you go for a walk, the dog will be happy to join you.

- **Broad Bay Inn and Gallery**

1014 Main Street, P.O. Box 607, Waldoboro, ME 04572.
(207)832-6668.

$40-70. Senior citizen, travel agent and seasonal discounts.

Call before 9 AM or after 6 PM.
- V, MC.
- **Innkeepers: Jim & Libby Hopkins.**
- *5 rms, 1 pb, 2 sb.*
- Full breakfast with fruit or juice, homemade muffins or rolls, entree, cereal, beverage.
- No pets, no children under 12, restricted smoking.
- In Waldoboro.

This 1830 mid-coast inn is filled with Victorian antiques, paintings and plants. Both innkeepers are commercial artists; their gallery features work by Maine artists and craftspeople. Both are active in community affairs.

For dining, you'll find several excellent restaurants in the area. Ask your hosts to help you select those that fit your taste.

When you visit you'll be just a short walk away from the river, tennis courts, theater, antique shops and restaurants. You'll enjoy relaxing on the sundeck or in a hammock. Browse through the art gallery. Be sure to see the garden which is included in the garden club tour.

● **Tide Watch Inn**
55 Pine Street, P.O. Box 94, Waldoboro, ME 04572.
(207)832-4987.

$50-60.

Call anytime.
• AE.
• Innkeepers: Caty & Mel Hanson.
• *3 rms., 1 pb, 1 sb.*
• Full Maine breakfast. A sample breakfast might include an omelet, fruit, juice, muffins, toast, hash browns and coffee.
• No pets.
• In Waldoboro.

A twin Colonial, circa 1850, the inn formerly housed many of the shipbuilders of the Waldoboro five-masted schooner. It is situated on the Medomak River. Mel is a semi-retired chef and artist. Both are antique collectors.

For dining, look for Moody's Diner.

When you visit bring your own boat or canoe. Watch the birds feeding in the back yard while you eat your breakfast. Sit in the front yard and watch the commercial clam diggers and fishermen go out.

Broad Bay Baked Eggs

From Libby Hopkins, **Broad Bay Inn & Gallery**
Waldoboro, ME

1/4 cup grated parmesan cheese
4 eggs
1/2 cup grated Vermont cheddar cheese
8 small sausages, cooked
Salt and Pepper to taste
1 tablespoon butter
optional: chives, bacon bits, parsley

Grease two shallow individual baking dishes. Sprinkle with parmesan cheese. Break one or two eggs into each dish. Sprinkle grated cheddar cheese around the yolks. Place the cooked sausages on each side of the yolks. Sprinkle with salt and pepper. Dot with butter. Bake uncovered in 350F oven until eggs are set (12 to 15 minutes). Garnish with chopped parsley, chives or bacon bits. Serves 2. Guests will love it.

Eastport

You'll want to wander through this town and look at the old homes and the lovely trees.

The **Barracks Museum**, on Washington St., houses items from the War of 1812. Pack a picnic lunch and take the ferry from here to **Deer Island**, in New Brunswick. Between Deer Island and Dog Island is the largest whirlpool in the western hemisphere. Inquire about festivals and ceremonies at the **Passamaquoddy Indian Reservation**, on SR 190 N. From Eastport you'll find boats available during the summer for whale watching in the harbor. This is also a great area for both fresh water and ocean fishing.

Nearby, on SR 189, is Lubec, the first spot in the U.S. to see the sunrise. Just across Lubec narrows, in New Brunswick, is the Roosevelt Campobello International Park, maintained by Canada and the U.S. On the grounds is the home occupied by Franklin D. Roosevelt, during the summer, until 1921. Also at Lubec is **Quoddy Head State Park and West Quoddy Lighthouse**. Here cliffs rise high above the ocean. The park has hiking trails, a peat bog, and picnic facilities. The lighthouse is open for visitor tours. A delightful place to while away summer days.

North of Eastport, at the end of a scenic drive on US 1, is Calais, an international city. It is connected to St. Stephens, New Brunswick, by an international bridge. Hikers and nature lovers will want to visit **Moosehorn National Wildlife Refuge**, southwest of Calais on Charlotte Road. The refuge contains more than 22,000 acres with many trails. It is a refuge for migratory birds.

MAINE 69

- **Todd House Bed & Breakfast**

Todd's Head Eastport, ME 04631.
(207)853-2328.

$45-80. Four rooms meet our criteria year around.

Call 8 - 9 AM.
- No cr. cds.
- Innkeeper: Ruth M. McInnis.
- 5 rms, 2 pb, 2 sb.
- Expanded continental breakfast with juice, fruit, cereal, homemade muffins, beverage.
- No smoking.
- At the north end of Eastport.

This historic Cape Cod, built in 1775, is on the National Register of Historic Places. It has a center chimney, a large cooking fireplace, and many authentic furnishings.

For dining, you'll revel in the excellent dinners at Rolando's (seafood and Italian) or Flag Officer's Mess (steaks and seafood). Lunches are great at Frank's Pizzeria, Oggie's Bakery, or Wes and Lyn's.

When you visit you may want to spend all of your time here if you're in a relaxed mood. When you sit on the deck you'll have a clear sweeping view of Passamaquoddy Bay; the house library has a lot of interesting reading material; if you're interested in genealogy, you'll want to browse through the old records at the house and the museum; entertainment will be provided by Kitty, the cat; there are lovely sun rises and sunsets, year around; and if you prefer to cook outside, you're welcome to use the large, stone barbecue.

Jonesboro

You'll want to play golf or tennis, go salt water swimming, take whale and puffin watching cruises, tour a cannery, go shopping for antiques and crafts, and attend summer theater and concerts. All of this is available in the immediate vicinity of Jonesboro.

Take a short trip west on US 1 to Columbia Falls and the **Ruggles House**, built in 1818. Furnished in period furnishings, it is noted for its flying staircase and carvings so beautiful that an angel is said to have guided the hand of the carver. East of Jonesboro, on US 1, is Machias, where the **Burnham Tavern Museum** is thought to be the oldest building in Maine. Colonial revolutionaries made plans for war here. South of Machias, on SR 92, is Machiasport and the **Gates House**, built in 1807. Its rooms contain period furnishings and more Revolutionary War memorabilia. South of Machias, on Roque Bluffs Road, is the **Roque Bluffs State Park** with Maine's most eastern beach.

Just a day trip from Jonesboro are Bar Harbor, Acadia National Park and Campobello, coastal areas with boat trips for whale and bird watching, interior Maine wilderness or many historic areas. **Acadia National Park** is filled with ocean, woodland, and mountain scenery. You'll be able to use bicycle trails and hiking trails, swim in salt water or fresh water. Naturalists give guided walks. You can take a ferry to some of the islands, take a narrated bus tour or a naturalist sea cruise. There are also tapes for self-guided auto tours. There is a natural history museum and a museum of stone age antiquities but mostly you'll delight in the spectacular sights of crashing waves, towering mountains and woods filled with wildlife.

At the entrance to the park is Bar Harbor. It is the home of the **Jackson Laboratory**, a international genetics laboratory. Lecture programs are given. The **Mount Desert Oceanarium**, west 8 1/2 miles on SR 3, features guided tours, harbor seals, demonstrations of lobster traps and a visit on board a lobster boat. From Bar Harbor you can also take an excursion on the **Arcadian Whale Watcher** for a four-hour watch for whales feeding.

● **Chandler River Lodge**
Rte. 1, Jonesboro, ME 04648.
(207)434-2651. Sep.-Jun. call (201)679-2778. OPEN ONLY DURING JULY AND AUGUST.

$35/S; $45/D; $10/ex prsn. Discount for extended stay.

Call anytime.
• No cr. crds.
• Innkeeper: Lorna Kerr.
• *5 rms, 2 pb, 1 sb.*
• Continental breakfast, featuring homemade breads and coffee cakes, juice, toast, beverage and cereal, served infcrmally in the dining room.
• Just off Hwy 1 in Jonesboro.

This quiet downeast farm house, was built in the 1889s. It is on 24 riverfront acres, on the banks of the Chandler River. Your innkeeper is an elementary teacher, who enjoys the outdoors, sailing, gardening and photography.

For dining, try outdoor lobster feeds (sloppy but good), church suppers (for basic down-home food and a feel of the area), Micmac Farm (candlelight dining in an old farmhouse), Helens (famous for their pie) or Red Barn (fresh sea food).

When you visit you'll learn all about the area while relaxing or keeping very busy, whichever you prefer. You may snooze or catch some sun on the large wraparound porch, bird watch down by the pond or along the river, help pick raspberries, strawberries or blueberries, wander through the field and pick some wild flowers for your room, spend the evening in the den, sharing experiences with fellow guests.

Stratton

You'll want to visit this area in the Winter. There is great downhill skiing at nearby Sugarloaf USA, and excellent cross-country skiing at Carrabasset Valley Ski Touring Center. There are also many cross-country and snowmobile trails throughout the area.

Summers are wonderful, too. Hikers will want to try some of the many fine trails, including a part of the Appalachian trail. You can go mountain climbing, golfing, swimming and canoeing (no rentals available, though). This area is ideal for a variety of outdoor activities.

Take a drive southeast on SR 16/27 to Kingfield and the **Stanley Museum**, on School Street, where the artistry of the Stanley family is on display. Photographs of rural Maine and steam-powered cars are exhibited.

Continue south on SR 16 to US 201 and then south on 201 to Skowhegan. The town is a town of firsts: Lakewood Theater is said to be Maine's oldest theater; The Skowhegan State Fair, held in mid-August, was the nation's first state fair. The **History House**, 40 Elm St., dates from 1839 and exhibits artifacts and antiques. The **Margaret Chase Smith Library**, on Norridgewock Ave., has information and displays on the life of the famous politician.

Southwest of Stratton on SR 16 is Rangely. Here the **Wilhelm Reich Museum**, on Dodge Pond Rd., is filled with scientific exhibits on the human body and a children's discovery room. The **Rangely Lake State Park** has more than 600 acres of space for hiking, swimming, fishing and boating.

● **The Widow's Walk**
Box 150, 171 Main Street, Stratton, ME 04982.
(207)246-6901.

5/1-10/15: $20/S; $30/D. 12/25-5/1: $32/S; $46/D.

Call 5 PM to 10 PM.
- V, MC.
- Innkeepers: Mary & Jerry Hopson.
- *6 rms, 3 sb.*
- Full breakfast featuring pancakes, French Toast, or eggs, served in the dining room.
- No pets, no smoking.
- On Hwy 27, in Stratton.

A Victorian Steamboat Gothic design, on the National Register, this interesting old home is on the shore of Stratton Brook. You'll enjoy the homey, informal atmosphere.

For dining, you'll want to try Cathy's Place, the Porter House Restaurant or Truffle Hound Restaurant.

When you visit in the winter, you'll be able to go cross-country skiing from the back yard. Ping Pong and many board games are available.

Maryland

Hagerstown

You'll want to think of historic times when you visit this town. Antietam National Battlefield, the scene of the bloodiest day of the Civil War, is 11 miles south of Hagerstown. Just a few more miles to the south is Harpers Ferry, WV, another key town in the history of the Civil War.

Lovers of old houses and history will need to see the **Hagar House and Museum**, 19 Key St., built in 1740, and the **Miller House**, 135 W. Washington St., built in 1820. The **Hagerstown Roundhouse Museum**, 300 S. Burhans Blvd., is filled with railroad memorabilia. The **Washington County Museum of Fine Arts**, on US 11, is worthy of a visit as well. It contains paintings, sculpture, and changing exhibits. **Ft. Frederick State Park** is just south of the city. Here you can find a pre-revolutionary war fort, erected during the French and Indian War.

Take a trip to visit the **Chesapeke and Ohio Canal National Historical Park**. From Hagerstown, you can take I-81, US 11 or SR 65 south toward West Virginia and the Potomac River. Although canal boat trips originate from Georgetown or Potomac, near Washington D.C., portions of the canal can be viewed along the river, between Potomac and Cumberland, MD.

This area is also a fine place for biking, swimming, tennis or skiing. Shoppers will find antique malls and discount outlets. Its really a fine spot for several getaways.

● **Lewrene Farm B&B**
9738 Downsville Pike, Hagerstown, MD 21740.
(301)582-1735.

$45-75. Discount to groups.

Call anytime.
•No cr. cds.
•**Innkeepers: Irene & Lewis Lehman.**
•*6 rms, 3 pb, 1 sb.*
•Full breakfast of juice, entree, homemade breads, jelly and coffee or tea.
•No pets, no smoking. Children are welcome.
•4 miles south of Hagerstown.

This colonial style farmhouse is furnished with antiques. Your hosts enjoy antiques, travel, languages and quilting. They speak Spanish and a "little German."

For dining, you may be able to dine with your hosts in a family-style meal, with advance reservations. There are also several fine restaurants in the area including Railroad Junction and Family Time.

When you visit you'll love being able to roam through the farm lands and woods surrounding the house. Peacocks and roosters are on the property. You're welcome to browse through the library for books, then read them in the gazebo or while sitting on the old-fashioned platform swing. You're also welcome to watch TV or use the VCR, to play the piano, or try putting together some of the puzzles.

Massachusetts
Cape Cod (Brewster, Dennis, Dennisport, East Orleans, Provincetown, Sandwich).

*You'll want to soak up the sunshine, the sea air and the history of this area. It is a recreation paradise. The **Cape Cod National Seashore** is a 28,000-acre park, with homes, dunes, beaches, lighthouses, woodlands, cliffs, trails, ponds and marshes. Here you can enjoy hiking, surfing, horseback riding, shelling, fishing, picnicking and biking. Brewster has nine bayside beaches offering swimming, surfing, sailing, sunbathing and other water sports. It also is the home of the **Cape Cod Museum of Natural History**, other museums, a gristmill, and the **Cape Cod Aquarium**. The **Cape Cod Bicycle Trail** runs less that 1/2 mile away.*

In the heart of Cape Cod, Dennis and Dennisport not only have plenty of recreational opportunities within walking distance but they offer a central location for day trips to scenic, recreational and historic points of interest. Here you'll find the **Cape Museum of Fine Arts** and the summer productions of the **Cape Playhouse**. Orleans and East Orleans, bordered on two sides by salt water and dotted with lakes, are popular spots for boating and fishing. **Nuaser Beach**, said to be one of the finest beaches in North America, has miles of sand dunes. Provincetown, at the tip of the cape, is the site of the first landing of the Pilgrims. Here you'll find the **Pilgrim Monument and Museum**, built to honor the Pilgrims; the **Provincetown Art Museum**, with changing and permanent exhibits; the **Heritage Museum**, with a variety of exhibits, including a large model of a fishing schooner; the **Seth Nickerson House**, built in 1746; and several whale-watching tours. Heritage Plantation, in Sandwich, has gardens, nature trails, a mill and buildings, with historic artifacts, including a military and an auto museum. Sandwich also is the home of the **Glass Museum**, the **Burgess "Peter Rabbit Museum,"** a gristmill, doll museum, nature trail and several historic houses.

● Old Sea Pines Inn
2553 Main Street, Box 1026, Brewster, MA 02631.
(508)896-6114.

$40-85. Seasonal and travel agent discounts.

Call 9 AM to 10 PM.
- V, MC, AE, DC, CB.
- Innkeepers: Stephen & Michele Rowan.
- 21 rms, 16 pb, 3 sb.
- Full breakfast with juice, fresh fruit, cereal, choice of beverages and choice of delicious hot entrees.
- No pets, no smoking in bedrooms, no children under 8, except in family suite.
- On Cape Cod, 90 mi. from Boston.

This **turn-of-the-century mansion** was once an elite girl's finishing school. It has been renovated and decorated with period antiques. Your hosts enjoy antiques, sailing, music, literature, art, and travel.

For dining, the area is filled with exceptional restaurants. Among our favorites are Chillingsworth, Bramble Inn and Tower Restaurant.

When you visit you'll appreciate the escape from a busy schedule offered by the inn. Imagine sipping a beverage by the fireside, reading a book from the library, rocking on the porches or deck, ordering afternoon tea and scones in the dining room or chatting with interesting guests. Take time to learn about the old school that used to occupy the building. A collection of writings and photos are available. You'll have plenty of privacy on the 3 1/2 acres surrounding the inn, yet many activities offered by the area are within easy walking distance.

● **Isaiah Hall B & B Inn**
152 Whig Street, Dennis, MA 02638.
(508)385-9928/ (800)736-0160.

$55-95.

Call 8:30 AM to 10 PM.
- V, MC, AE.
- Innkeeper: Marie Brophy.
- *11 rms, 10 pb, 1 sb.*
- Expanded continental breakfast with fruit, yogurt, homemade breads or muffins, jams and jellies, cereal, coffee or tea.
- No pets; no children under 7, some no-smoking rooms.
- On a quiet street, in Dennis Village.

This 1857 farmhouse was originally the home of Isaiah B. Hall, a builder and cooper. In 1948, the main house and carriage house were converted to an inn. This inn is listed by both the AAA and Mobil guides.

For dining, you'll enjoy Sebastian's Dennis Inn, the Scargo Cafe or the Red Pheasant.

When you visit plan to stroll through the inn's gardens, take time to rock on the porch, play board games or badminton. There is also a TV for watching. All of Dennis is just a short walk away.

● **The Rose Petal Bed & Breakfast**
152 Sea Street, P.O. Box 974, Dennisport, MA 02639.
(508)398-8470.

$40-55. Highest rates mid-June to Mid-September.

Call 8 AM to 9 PM.
● V, MC.
● **Innkeepers: Dan & Gayle Kelly.**

● *4 rms, 2 sb.*
● Full breakfast, featuring fresh ground coffee or specialty teas, home-baked pastries, cereal, fresh fruit and a delicious entree.
● Restricted smoking.
● 1/2 mile to Village Center.

This 1872 home was originally restored as a B&B in 1986. It was redecorated and refinished in the winter of 1992. You'll find an exceptionally clean and neat B&B, with color-coordinated linens and luxury bath robes furnished to guests. Gayle and Dan are former university administrators. Dan is an expert baker and pastry chef. Ask him to share a recipe. Both enjoy landscaping their yard.

For dining, you'll enjoy a variety of specialties at Captain William's House, Clancy's Tavern, the Ebb Tide or Sundae School Ice Cream Parlor.

When you visit unwind on a park bench in the beautiful yard and smell the tea roses; relax in the comfortable parlor while perusing regional magazines and guides; watch TV, play the piano or enjoy a parlor game. Then, take a walk past the lovely old homes to sandy beach.

● **Ship's Knees Inn**
186 Beach Road, P.O. Box 756, East Orleans, MA 02643.
(508)255-1312.

$45-100. Readers may stay in any of the rooms for $55 or under, except during July and August.

Call anytime.
•V, MC.
•Innkeepers: Jean & Ken Pitchford.
•22 rms, 8 pb, 5 sb.
•Continental breakfast of assorted breads and beverages is served buffet style in the common area from 8 to 10 AM.
•No pets. Some restrictions on children, depending on location.
•On the Midcape Highway, 20 miles from Hyannis.

This 170-year-old restored sea captain's home is decorated in nautical and colonial themes with authentic antiques. Some of the rooms have ocean views. Your hosts are a nurse and an artist. Both are natives of England.

For dining, you'll want to ask your hosts for their restaurant list. They'll be happy to talk to you about your preferences.

When you visit you may swim in the inn's pool or play tennis. The lawn and area surrounding the inn are great places to relax and to have a picnic or a barbecue. Nearby are excellent golf courses and bicycle trails.

●Lamplighter Inn and Guest House

26 Bradford House, Provincetown, MA 02657.
(508)487-2529 / Fax: 487-0079.

$50. Seasonal discount and to travel agent.

Call 8 AM to 10 PM.
- V, MC, AE.
- **Innkeepers: Mike and Joe.**
- *10 rms, 8 pb, 1 sb.*
- Continental breakfast.
- No pets, no children under 12, parking for only 1 car per room.
- One block from the beach and 5 minutes from town center.

This sea captain's home was built in the 1800s. It's just a short walk to Cape Cod Bay, which can be seen from the roof-top deck. Your hosts enjoy art, gardening, bonsai, koi, goldfish and cats.

For dining, we're told that Lobster Pot, Ciro & Sals, Mews, Moor's, Sebastian's or Paparazzi's are all excellent.

When you visit be sure to ask about feeding the koi in the water garden and take a stroll through the bonsai collection. Catch some sun on the roof deck or the grounds, then you'll want to visit the many attractions that are just a short walk away.

The Summer House
158 Main Street, Sandwich, MA 02563.
(508)888-4991.

$50-75/D. $40-65, 10/16-5/31. Sr. citizen and travel agent discounts.

Call 8 AM to 10 PM.
- V, MC, D, AE.
- Innkeepers: David & Kay Merrell.
- 5 rms, 1 pb, 2 sb.
- A full breakfast is served in the sunny breakfast room, at tables for two, between 8 and 9:30 every morning. It will undoubtedly include juice, fresh fruit, a hot entree and a home-made pastry or bread.
- No pets, restricted smoking, no children under 6.
- In the historic district of the village.

Featured in Country Living magazine twice, this lovely Greek Revival style home was built in 1835. It has been carefully restored, keeping the seven fireplaces, original window glass and hardware. Genuine 19th century furnishings and hand-stitched quilts have been added to authenticate the restoration. Kay is a quilter, gardener and weaver. Dave likes woodworking, jogging and volleyball. Both enjoy backpacking, travel and reading.

For dining, you'll find nearby and exceptional food at Marshland, Michael's at Sandy Neck or Sandwich's Sandwiches.

When you visit plan to be back "home" in time to enjoy English tea, served at an umbrella table in the garden. Browse through the vegetable and flower gardens, then find a book in the library and find a shady or sunny spot on the lawn to read. For serious relaxation or daydreaming, claim one of the hammocks. For less sunny days visit the parlor and enjoy a newspaper, magazine or the color TV.

Eggs Florentine

From Gayle Kelly, **Rose Petal B&B**
Dennisport, MA

8 English muffins
1 - 10 ounce package frozen spinach or 1 pound fresh spinach
16 eggs
4 ounces shredded cheddar cheese
2 tablespoons butter
2 tablespoons flour
2 cups milk, heated
1/4 teaspoon dry mustard
1 teaspoon worcestershire sauce
salt, white pepper, nutmeg, cloves, minced onion

Saute spinach in a pan, seasoning with butter, salt, pepper and nutmeg. Top toasted English muffin half with spinach, 1 poached egg and about 2 tablespoons cheese sauce. Sprinkle with paprika to garnish and serve immediately.

Cheddar Cheese Sauce
Heat butter and flour together, making a roux. Cool slightly, adding heated milk. Season lightly with salt, white pepper, nutmeg, cloves and minced onion. Stir while bringing to a simmer. Continue cooking, stirring until thickened. If too thick, adjust consistency, by adding more milk. Add shredded cheddar cheese, mustard and worcestershire sauce. Heat until blended.

Prepare spinach and cheese sauce in advance. Prepare eggs to order, allowing about 10 minutes to prepare.

Rehoboth

You'll want to engage in an assortment of activities that are available in the small town of Rehoboth.

While you're in town you might want to tour a restored one-room schoolhouse, enjoy a museum in a replica of an 18th century farmhouse, attend services in an 18th century Baptist church, browse through antique shops, play at several golf courses, bicycle along winding roads, canoe down the Palmer River (if you bring your own canoe) or enjoy a New England clambake.

In nearby Fall River, you can visit nearby **Battleship Massachusetts**, I-95, Exit 5, at Battleship Cove, where you can tour the battleship, see a marine museum, PT boats, a destroyer, and a submarine. **Fall River Heritage State Park**, next to Battleship Cove, has a boardwalk along the waterfront and a visitor center with many exhibits on Fall River history. Another **Marine Museum**, at 70 Water St., traces the history of steamships, including the Titanic. Shoppers will want to bargain hunt in some of the several factory outlets; many are off of I-95, at Jefferson and Quarry Sts.

If you have any extra time — or on your next trip you can use Rehoboth as a home base to visit other cities. You're less than an hour from Boston, Plymouth or Newport, RI; 40 min. from New Bedford and 20 min. from Providence, RI.

Gilbert's Bed & Breakfast
30 Spring Street, Rehoboth, MA ZIP [02769.
(508)252-6416 / (800)828-6821.

$30-32/S; $45-50/D. Lower rates are for two or more consecutive nights. Discount to families and travel agent.

Call 7-8 AM or 5-7 PM.
- V, MC.
- Innkeepers: Pete & Jeanne Gilbert.
- *3 rms, 1 sb.*
- A delicious full breakfast is served in the country kitchen. A typical breakfast might consist of blueberry pancakes, sausage, fresh fruit cup, juice, coffee or tea. Another favorite is Jeanne's bran muffins.
- No pets, no smoking.
- 12 miles from Providence, RI and 8 miles from Fall River.

This 157-year-old farmhouse is furnished with antiques. Your room will have windows with original tiny panes of glass, antique hardware and handmade rugs on wide-board floors. You'll be surrounded by 100 acres of trees. Pete likes rebuilding reed organs, playing banjo, base, piano and organ. Jeanne enjoys horseback riding, ponies, writing and photography.

For dining, there are many superb choices 8 miles or less from the B&B. We'd recommend Captain PJs Seafood Gallery, Venus de Milo, The Country Inn, Leone's on the Waterfront or the Cathay Pearl Restaurant.

When you visit you're invited to swim in the in-ground pool or go hiking in the surrounding tree farm. If you wish you may ride the horses, go for a pony cart ride, help with the barn chores, work in the gardens or bask in the fresh air and sunshine on the stone terrace.

Sudbury (near Boston area)

*You'll want to visit the restored **Wayside Inn**, the grist mill that grinds grain for the inn's bakery and the Little Red School House.*

*The Wayside Inn in Sudbury was the scene of Longfellow's **Tales of a Wayside Inn**. **Great Meadows National Wildlife Refuge** has great bird watching, nature trails and hiking. The **Sudbury River** is popular for canoeing. Sudbury is 20 miles from Boston, only 7 miles from Concord and 11 miles from Lexington with the myriad historical sites.*

*Concord is famous for Minute Men, Ralph Waldo Emerson, Louisa May Alcott and Henry David Thoreau. In Concord you'll find **Minute Man National Historical Park**; **Orchard House**, the home of Louisa May Alcott; the **Thoreau Lyceum** and **Walden Pond Reservation**, with Henry David Thoreau memorabilia; and **Concord Museum**, **Emerson House** and the **Old Manse**, associated with Ralph Waldo Emerson. There are many other familiar and famous associations with the past that you'll discover in Concord. In fact, you'll want to spend several days in the area.*

*Just down the road from Concord is Lexington, the site of the first conflict of the Revolutionary War. You may visit the **Lexington Battle Green**, site of that first encounter. **Historical Society Houses** which date from the 17th and 18th century, the **Revolutionary Monument**, **Museum of Our National Heritage**, **Old Burying Ground**, and **Old Belfry** will bring the early history of our nation to life.*

● **Sudbury Bed & Breakfast**
*3 Drum Lane, Sudbury, MA ZIP
[01776.*
(508)443-2860.

$45/S; $55/D; $10/child.

Call 9 AM to 9 PM.
•No cr. crds.
•Innkeepers: Nancy & Don Somers.
•*3 rms, 1 1/2 sb.*
•Continental breakfast of juice, fruit, homemade muffins and beverage.
•No smoking, no pets.
•1 1/2 mi. from Hwy 20; 20 mi. from Boston.

This lovely colonial home is on an acre of wooded land. In their spare time your hosts enjoy tennis, books and fishing.

For dining, you'll find these excellent restaurants nearby: Lotus Blossom, Wayside Inn, Matt Garrets, Descantos and the 99 pub.

When you visit you'll find the neighborhood surrounding your B & B is quiet and terrific for walking and running. The recreation room has an extensive library for restful reading. Just a short walk away is Sudbury Center, historic sites and Heritage Park.

Ware

You'll want to canoe on the river, go fishing and boating in Spring and Summer when you visit here. In the fall you'll love the magnificent color of the foliage; in the winter go sledding, skating and skiing. Ware is located midway between Boston and the Berkshires on Highways 9 and 32, just a short distance from the Massachusetts Turnpike.

Amherst, the home of Amherst College and the University of Massachusetts is just 20 miles away. Take a day trip to see the **Emily Dickinson Homestead**, the **Jones Library** with its special collections, the **Strong House** and the **Hadley Farm Museum**. Twenty five miles away is Sturbridge, where you can see 200-acre **Old Sturbridge Village**. This living history museum recreates a New England village of the 1830s. Costumed interpreters in more than 40 buildings demonstrate activities of the bygone era. **Bethlehem in Sturbridge** is an automated theater with figures, narration and laser show recreating Bethlehem at the time of Christ's birth. It's 30 miles to Springfield or to Worcester. In Springfield are the **Springfield Library and Museums**. Located at State and Chestnut Streets, it is composed of the **Connecticut Valley Historical Museum**, the **George Walter Vincent Smith Art Museum**, the **Springfield Science Museum** and the **Museum of Fine Arts**. Each could take an hour or several hours of your time. Also in Springfield are the **Naismith Memorial Basketball Hall of Fame**, the **Indian Motorcycle Museum**, **Old First Church** and the **Springfield Armory National Historic Site** (the first armory in the country). **Forest Park**, a 730 acre municipal park, has baseball fields, tennis courts, playground, miniature train ride, lawn bowling, a children's zoo, pony rides and picnic areas. Worcester is home to the **Worcester Art Museum**, with important collections from 50 centuries and 50 countries; the New England Science Center, a 59-acre science park with planetarium, zoo, observatory, and other natural science exhibits; the **Higgins Armory Museum**, exhibiting medieval and Renaissance armor and arms; the **Salisbury Mansion**; and several other entertaining areas of interest.

MASSACHUSETTS

● **The Wildwood Inn**
121 Church Street, Ware, MA 01080.
(413)967-7798.

11/1-4/30: $38-54. 5/1-10/31: $42-56. During Winter holidays guests will be charged summer rates.

Call 6 PM - 10 PM.
- AE.
- **Innkeepers: Fraidell Fenster & Richard Watson.**
- *7 rms, 4 sb.*
- Full breakfast with juice, entree, muffins, cereal and beverage.
- No pets, no smoking, no children under 6.
- 1 mile from town center.

This inn, built in 1880, sits on two acres of field and forest, bordered by a 110-acre park. The inn is furnished in American Primitive antiques. The owners have collections of early cradles and heirloom quilts.

For dining, you may eat Italian at Teresa's, New England at Salem Cross Inn, seafood at Snow's and great desserts at Judie's.

When you visit you'll enjoy reading in the parlor by the crackling fire in winter or on the wrap-around porch in summer. Your hosts have a library of books and magazines which they will lend to you. There are also jigsaw puzzles to work and board games to play. You'll find walking in the woods or sitting under the evergreens peaceful and relaxing.

Michigan

Frankenmuth

You'll want to imagine you're visiting Germany when you come to this town with a Bavarian heritage.

This is the home of the famous **Bronner's Christmas Wonderland**, 25 Christmas Lane, the world's largest display of Christmas decorations — a must see. Among other displays are 260 decorated Christmas trees and a Christmas Lane, which is lighted each evening. The **Frankenmuth Mill**, 701 Mill St., is a reconstructed mill with self-guided tours and video presentations. The **Frankenmuth Historical Museum**, 613 South Main St., depicts this area's interesting history. Crafts are frequently demonstrated. **Frankenmuth Riverboat Tours**, 445 S. Main St., has sightseeing cruises on the river. The **Military and Space Museum**, 1250 S. Weiss St., has exhibits honoring Michigan veterans of foreign wars and state astronauts.

Just 25 miles away, in Censsee County, is **Crossroads Village**, a recreation of an 18th century village, with chapel, one-room school, print shop and railroad train. To get there take I-75 toward Flint to Mount Morris Rd.; then go 5 1/2 miles east to Bray Rd.; go 1 1/2 miles south on Bray.

Shoppers will be delighted to learn that just 7 miles from Frankenmuth is **Manufacturer's Market Place**, and **The Village Shops** with over 150 retail discount stores. Frankenmuth is one of Michigan's top family tourist attractions.

MICHIGAN

- **Bed & Breakfast at The Pines**
327 Ardussi Street, Frankenmuth, MI ZIP 48734.
(517)652-9019.

$30/S; $35/D.

Call anytime.
- No cr. crds.
- Innkeepers: Richard & Donna Hodge.
- 2 rms, 1/2 pb, 1 sb.
- Expanded continental breakfast with fresh seasonal fruits, toast, bagels, jams, Sour Cream Twists, cereal, beverage.
- No smoking.
- 3 blks. W of Main St., in Frankenmuth.

This traditional ranch-style home is within walking distance of the tourist areas. All bedrooms have ceiling fans, heirloom quilts and Victorian antiques. The innkeepers are a former dairy farmer and home economics teacher, interested in agriculture, computers, hunting, fishing, genealogy, flowers, herb gardening and antiques.

For dining, you'll want to try the family-style meals at Zehnders, Bavarian meals at the Bavarian Inn, the Italian cuisine at Gheppeto's, the wild game at the Dixie Inn or pizza at Tiffanys'.

When you visit you are welcome to enjoy the use of the home, watch TV, read or visit with other guests. There is a secluded back yard to use for reading, bird watching and relaxing. A perennial garden attracts hummingbirds and butterflies. The house is just a short walk away from the library, where you'll be able to check out a book or video.

Ithaca

You'll want to come from May through September when the area is busy with festivals and parades. Among the top festivals are the **Highland Festival**, the last weekend in May, the **Antique Steam Show**, the second weekend in August, and the 4th of July parade.

Spend relaxed, lazy (or not so lazy) days in the school swimming pool, on the tennis courts or golf course. There are many gift and antique shops in the area for shoppers and browsers. Ithaca is near the center of the Michigan lower peninsula. It's between Alma, the home of Alma College, and Mt. Pleasant, the home of Central Michigan University, and often provides housing for students and parents.

Saginaw is only 27 miles away. In Saginaw you'll also find a wide choice of things to see and do. The **Rose Garden**, on Rust Ave. west of Washington Ave., is spectacular featuring 60 varieties of roses. The **Japanese Cultural Center**, 527 Ezra Rust Dr., also features a unique and beautiful garden with a tea house. Children will enjoy the small animals and pony rides at the **Children's Zoo**, junction of S. Washington Ave & E. Rust Dr.

The **Saginaw Art Museum**, 1126 N. Michigan Ave., has a variety of permanent and changing exhibits and a formal garden featuring sculpture. The **Historical Museum**, 500 Federal Ave., has exhibits tracing regional history and development. This is also an ideal spot to enjoy hiking, downhill and cross-country skiing.

● Chaffins' Balmoral Farm Bed & Breakfast

1245 West Washington Road, Ithaca, MI ZIP [48847.
(517)875-3410.

$20-40. Open Apr. 15 - Nov. 15.

Call anytime during season.
- No cr. crds.
- **Innkeepers: Bob & Sue Chaffin.**
- 2 rms, 1 sb.
- A full country breakfast featuring Michigan grown products such as blueberry muffins or pancakes, fresh eggs, bacon or sausage and beverage.
- No smoking, no alcohol. Children are welcome.
- 3/4 mi. W of Ithaca.

This B&B is located in a turn-of-the century farmhouse, located on a working farm. The original farm was a 1930's "showplace." The superintendent's house and dairy barn have been restored and furnished. Your hosts like to share information about the farm.

For dining, you'll enjoy the Country Inn, in St. Louis, or Razor's Cafe, in Ithaca. **When you visit** you'll have a whole farm to roam. You'll love hiking in the woods, exploring the barn, checking on field work in progress, and riding the farm tractor. At the end of a busy day, swing on the porch swing.

Manistee National Forest, Cadillac and Ludington

You'll want to visit this area if you like outdoor recreation, woods, sand and water.

In the **Manistee National Forest**, you'll find sand dunes, a wild flower trail, rivers and streams for canoeing and trout fishing, and trails for hiking, cross-country skiing, backpacking, or snowshoeing.

Cadillac is at the east edge of the forest and on the shores of Lakes Mitchell and Cadillac. Among the activities available are swimming, fishing, boating, camping, canoeing, picnicking, hiking, hunting, downhill and cross-country skiing, snowmobiling, ice fishing and ice sailing. **Johnny's Wild Game and Fish Farm**, 46 1/2 Mile Rd., is south off of US 131. At the farm you'll be able to see a variety of wild and tame animals and fish for rainbow trout.

Ludington, on the shores of Lake Michigan, is also very popular with visitors who enjoy lots of water. There is a **ferry** going between Ludington and Manitowoc, WI. At **Ludington State Park** you'll find two lakes and a river: Lake Michigan, Lake Hamlin and the Sable River. Visitors can fish, hike, swim, water ski, climb sand dunes, go boating and biking.

Stearns and Waterworks Parks, on Lake Michigan, have beaches for sunbathing and swimming but also offer shuffleboard, fishing boating, picnicking, a playground and miniature golf.

Fishing is available in Ludington from the breakwall or in chartered boats. For a change of scene, visit **White Pine Village**, 1687 Lakeshore Dr., a reconstructed 19th century village with guides in period dress demonstrating activities and crafts of the era.

- **Essenmacher's Bed & Breakfast**
204 Locust Lane, Cadillac, MI 49601.
(616)775-3828.

$50/S; $55/D. Discount for families.

Call weekends and evenings.
- V, MC.
- **Innkeepers: Doug & Vickie Essenmacher.**
- *2 rms, 2 pb.*
- Expanded continental breakfast. A sample menu might include poached pears with raspberry sauce, Quiche Lorraine, toasted English muffin bread with homemade jam, juice, milk, hot beverage.
- No pets, no smoking, no alcohol.
- On Lake Mitchell, just outside the city limits.

This 100-year-old cottage was built when the city of Cadillac was just evolving from a lumber camp. Vickie enjoys quilting, crafts, traveling and skiing. Doug is interested in sports and boating.

For dining, you can have European food at Hermann's, downtown; dine outdoors beside the lake at Lakeside Charlie's; or enjoy Mexican food at Chico's.

When you visit enjoy your own private access to the lake, relax in the sun on the deck, play croquet, feed the ducks, and watch the squirrels and birds. Ask about lakeside bonfires and perhaps you'll be able to charter a cruise on board Doug and Vickie's boat.

The Inn at Ludington

701 E. Ludington Avenue, Ludington, MI 49431.
(616)845-7055.

$50-85/S or D. Seasonal discount 11/1-4/30.

Call 10 AM to 10 PM.
- V, MC, AE.
- **Innkeeper: Diane Shields.**
- *6 rms, 4 pb, 1 sb.*
- Full breakfast, served family style, featuring locally grown fruits and Michigan products.
- No pets, restricted smoking.
- Within walking distance of Lake Michigan beach and Ludington shops.

This 100-year-old Queen Anne Victorian home has a three-story tower facing the avenue and is surrounded by an English style flower border. It is filled with antiques and cherished collectibles. There are four working fireplaces.

For dining, you'll find something delicious to fit every taste: P.M. Steamers offers contemporary dining and a great view of the marina; Scotty's specializes in seafood and steaks; Gibbs is a good place to bring the family and has a very complete menu; and Grand Hotel has excellent pub food, including homemade soup and giant "wet burritos."

When you visit you'll find a library of books, magazines and games available for every taste. You're welcome to curl up in front of the fire with a cup of tea and your choice of reading or gaming materials. Make reservations for the first weekend in March, April or November for a "Murder Weekend." In December the inn features "Dickens Christmas" weekends with Victorian food and entertainment.

Cape Cod Blueberry French Toast

From David and Kay Merrell,
The Summer House Bed & Breakfast
Sandwich, MA

1 loaf Italian bread
8 ounces cream cheese
1 jar blueberry preserves
3 eggs
1 cup milk
2 cups fresh or frozen thawed blueberries
1 tablespoon butter or margarine
powdered sugar

With serrated knife, cut 12 diagonal slices from the Italian bread, each about 3/4 inch thick. Spread 6 slices with blueberry preserves. Spread remaining 6 slices with cream cheese. Sprinkle 1 cup blueberries evenly over the 6 slices with preserves. Place the 6 slices with cream cheese on top, cheese down, to make a 6 sandwiches. In a pie plate, beat milk and eggs with a fork, just until mixed. Dip the sandwiches into the egg mixture, one at a time until well coated on both sides. Heat a non-stick skillet over medium heat. Add butter or margarine until melted and hot. Cook sandwiches on both sides until golden brown. Sprinkle with powdered sugar and remaining blueberries. Serve immediately, with warm maple syrup, if desired.

Port Sanilac

You'll want to enjoy the popular diversions of swimming and boating on the shores of Lake Huron. Here you'll be able to charter boats, go fishing, swimming or scuba diving.

The **Sanilac Historic Museum**, 228 S. Ridge Rd., has a restored and furnished Victorian home, a dairy museum and a restored and furnished cabin. The **Barn Theater** has seasonal productions of plays and concerts.

Just about 30 miles away is Port Huron, one of the oldest settlements in the state. Visitors enjoy the **Museum of Arts and History**, 1115 Sixth St., where displays include a pioneer log home, Native American collections, marine exhibits and Edison memorabilia. Bring a picnic lunch to Port Huron and visit **Lakeside Park**, for swimming, **Lighthouse Park**, to see one the Great Lakes oldest lighthouses, and **Pine Grove Park**, to see the "Huron," one of the last commissioned lightships. This area is a wonderful spot for water associated recreation.

● **Raymond House Inn**
111 South Ridge Street, Port Sanilac, MI 48469.
(313)622-8800.

$50-70. Sun-Thurs: $50; Fri-Sat, holidays, in Jul and Aug: $70.

Call anytime before 10 PM.
• V, MC, DC.
• **Innkeeper: Shirley Denison.**
• *7 rms, 7 pb.*
• Expanded continental breakfast, featuring hot and cold cereals, homemade muffins, fresh fruit, bagels, orange juice, beverages.
• No pets, no smoking, no children under 10.
• On M-25, in Port Sanilac.

This is an 1871 Victorian house with gingerbread trim, antique furnishings, handmade rugs, and high ceilings. Shirley is a sculptor and potter.

For dining, you'll enjoy the whitefish at Huron Shores Golf Club, the Italian food and the view at Paisano's, and the great food, salad and reasonable prices at the Wayside.

When you visit be sure to look at the antique stereopticons, browse through the library for reading material, find someone to play Monopoly, Scrabble or Trivial Pursuit with you, relax on the patio or under the trees, watch cable TV and movie videos or look at the old photo albums.

Minnesota

Morris

You'll want to visit here for a relaxing, but interesting, getaway. Among the outdoor activities available are golf, at **Pomme de Terre Golf Course**; biking and hiking on special trails; swimming and tennis, at **Pomme de Terre Park**, cross-country skiing or hunting, in the surrounding countryside. For a change of pace, visit the Morris Campus, of the **University of Minnesota**, to see plays and the art gallery.

Drive north on US 59 to Elbow Lake to the **Grant County Historical Museum**. The museum has a variety of antique artifacts.

Drive east on SR 28 to Glenwood. On the banks of Lake Minnewaska are Indian mounds and burial grounds, including the graves of Chief White Bear and Princess Minnewaska. The **Pope County Historical Museum**, 809 S. Lakeshore Dr., has early artifacts. Visit the **DNR Fisheries Headquarters**, on N. Lakeshore Dr. Display ponds of fish are open to visitors.

Take SR 104 north from Glenwood to Alexandria to see the **Runestone Museum**. The museum contains a stone with carvings said to be made by Vikings visiting the area in the 14th century. The exhibit also contain Viking implements dating back to the same era.

● The American House
410 East Third Street, Morris, MN 56267.
(612)589-4054.

$35-40/D.

Call evenings.
- V, MC.
- **Innkeepers: Karen & Kyle Berget.**
- *3 rms, 1 sb.*
- Full breakfast typically including fruit, omelet, rolls, fruit and beverage, served in the dining room on antique china.
- No pets, restricted smoking.
- In the city of Morris, just a block from the University.

This Victorian house, built in 1900, has original stencil designs, parquet hardwood flooring in the dining room, stained glass windows, beaded woodwork and unique brass doorknobs. It is furnished with family heirlooms and antiques. Kyle is a Fifth Grade teacher and Karen is a student at UMM. Both enjoy collecting antiques.

For dining, you'll find fine food at the Diamond Club, in Morris, or the Minniwaska House, in nearby Glenwood.

When you visit you're welcome to borrow your hosts' "bicycle built for two" to ride the Morris bike trails. Enjoy a good book while relaxing on the porch or delight in the stereo-scope and over 100 different cards.

Missouri

Camdenton

You'll want to schedule several days in this area. A tourist Center in the **Lake of the Ozarks Region**, Camdenton, is an ideal spot to stop. The lake has 1150 miles of meandering shore line and excellent fishing, boating and swimming.

You're only minutes away from **Ha Ha Tonka State Park**, where many significant geological features are concentrated. **Bridal Cave**, on Lake Rd., is known for its variety of colors and large onyx formations. There are picnic facilities on the grounds, a boat dock and a nature trail. Anyone interested in antique cars will want to visit **Kelsey's Antique Cards**, on US 54. The museum contains many old cars which have been restored.

Ozark Caverns, in Lake of the Ozarks State Park, is another popular cave with beautiful formations. The **Osage Power Plant**, near Lake Ozark, on US 54, offers free tours from 8:30 AM - 3 PM.

In this area, there are antique shops, gift shops, an outlet mall, unusual shopping centers, water parks, country music shows and fun galore.

MISSOURI

●Ramblewood Bed & Breakfast
402 Panoramic Drive, Camdenton, MO ZIP 165020.
(314)346-3410.

$40/S; $45/D.

Call after 5 PM.
- No cr. crds.
- **Innkeeper: Mary E. Massey.**
- 2 rms, 1 sb.
- Breakfast is a special occasion here. A beautiful fruit plate or compote is the centerpiece for your full breakfast. The rest of the menu often includes homemade breads or Belgian waffles, glazed ham, omelet or casserole. Breakfast is served on china, crystal and linen. Every woman receives a hand-made rose.
- No pets, no smoking, no children under 12.
- In Camdenton.

This home is nestled in trees and is just 6 blocks from the town square. The comfortable rooms are decorated with wicker and roses. Your breakfast is frequently served on the deck overlooking a forest of Dogwood, Redbud and Oak. Your host is likely to pamper you with tea or lemonade and cookies, served when you arrive. Her interests include home decorating, painting, gardening, and hiking.

For dining, have lunch at Peace and Plenty, Kennilworth House or Yankee Peddler Tea Room. For dinner there is a variety of ethnic restaurants to choose.

When you visit you'll have afternoon lemonade on the flower-filled deck. This is a great spot for bird and squirrel watching. Kermit the Frog lives under the begonia pot. More relaxing is at hand on the front porch where you can sit in a swing to watch the world go by.

Independence

You'll want to see the **Harry S. Truman Library and Museum**, on Delaware St., and possibly some of the other sites associated with President Truman.

The library houses personal and public papers associated with the Truman presidency as well as gifts from other countries and exhibits. The **Harry S. Truman National Historic Site** is the house in which the Trumans lived throughout their marriage. Visitors to the Truman Home should arrive early at the Ticket and Information Center, 223 N. Main St. A ticket must be picked up by the person using it and on the day it is to be used. The **Harry S. Truman Courtroom and Office**, in Independence Square, shows a courtroom and office in which former president Truman served as a county judge. Here you may also see the multi-media feature "The Man from Independence."

Although the city is most famous as the home of a U.S. president, it has many other historic and interesting sites. It is the world headquarters of the Reorganized Church of Latter Day Saints. There is a visitors' center, museum, and art gallery associated with the headquarters and an auditorium containing a 6,400-pipe organ. Organ recitals are given daily, at 3 PM, in the summer. Also here are **Fort Osage**, on Sibley Rd. near Sibley, a restoration of an 1808 U.S. outpost; **Valie Mansion**, 1500 N. Liberty, a restored innovative house of the early 1880s; an **1859 Marshal's Home and Jail Museum**, 217 N. Main St.; and the **Bingham-Waggoner estate**, 313 W. Pacific, the 1800s mansion that was the home of artist and political protester George Caleb Bingham, and which was later purchased by a wealthy flour milling family and extensively remodeled.

Worlds of Fun theme park has the roller coaster voted best of 1991. It is just a short drive from the stadiums of the Kansas City Chiefs and Royals.

● **Woodstock Inn Bed & Breakfast**
1212 W. Lexington, Independence, MO 64050.
(816)833-2233.

$45-65. Off-season discounts to senior citizens and for longer stays.

Call in the early afternoon.
•V, MC, AE.
•**Innkeepers: Ben & Mona Crosby.**
•*11 rms, 11 pb.*
•Full breakfast with an assortment of juices, a cold cereal bar, eggs to order served with meat and potatoes, waffles or baked breads and sweets.
•No pets, no smoking.
•In historic Independence, just one mile from the central city and 20 min. from Kansas City.

This friendly, homelike inn is near both the Truman Library and the Church of Latter Day Saints world headquarters. The inn has ramps to make it wheelchair accessible.

For dining, you must try Stephenson's apple orchard, and Gates, famous for barbecue.

When you visit an inn of this size, you'll have more opportunity to chat with other guests than with the owners who have been decorators and owners of art, antique and collectible galleries. The inn is within walking distance of many attractions.

Saint Louis

You'll want to take a tour on an excursion boat, see a floating heliport and a World War II minesweeper, at the river. If you're a sports fan, you'll want to see the Cardinals during baseball season, and the Blues in hockey season. You should drive or walk by the **Gateway Arch**. Inside the visitor center is the **Museum of Westward Expansion**, with programs and displays related to early settlers of the U.S.

The **Missouri Botanical Garden**, 4344 Shaw Blvd., has 79 acres filled with a variety of special gardens. A geodesic dome shelters a collection of tropical plants, including orchids. Visitors can elect to take a 20 minute electric tram ride through the gardens. The **Magic House**, 516 South Kirkwood Rd., is a children's museum with hands-on exhibits. Topics include science, computers, and communications.

Forest Park has an assortment of recreational areas, museums and entertainment centers including the famed **St. Louis Science Center**, 5050 Oakland Ave., and the **Zoological Park**. The science center includes the **McDonnell Planetarium**, the **Monsanto Science Park**, and an **Omnimax Theater**. There are many hands-on exhibits in the center. A miniature railroad provides tours of the grounds. The Children's Zoo has animals in a closer setting where children can get a better view.

The **St. Louis Art Museum**, on Art Hill, in Forest Park, has over 30,000 works of art covering a variety of periods and cultures. If you're a beer drinker you'll enjoy the tour of the **Anheuser-Busch Brewery**, Lynch & 13th. In St. Louis, there are splendid theaters, the St. Louis Symphony, art museums, historical museums, specialty museums, industrial tours, historical houses, parks and recreational activities, most of which are exceptional and well worth a visit. Contact the St. Louis Visitor Information Center, 10 S. Broadway, St. Louis 63102, (314)869-7100 for a more complete list of things to see and do.

● **The Winter House**
3522 Arsenal Street, St. Louis, MO 63118.
(314)664-4399.

$55-75/D. Discount travel agent.

Call 7 PM to 10 PM.
• V, MC, DC, CB, AE.
• **Innkeepers: Sarah & Ken Winter.**
• *2 rms, 3 pb.*
• Expanded continental breakfast. A sample menu might include fresh squeezed orange juice, gourmet coffee, baked apple, cinnamon toast and muffins, served in the dining room on antique china, crystal and silver, perhaps with piano accompaniment.
• No pets, no smoking, no children under 12.
• One mi. S of I-44 and 1 mi. W of I-55. 3 mi from downtown.

This B&B is an 1897 red brick Victorian home, with a pressed tin ceiling, a turret and a balcony. The house is complete with a dog named Sam. Your hosts' interests include photography, travel, bed & breakfasts and Tower Grove Park.

For dining, you'll find a wide array of wonderful dining in the city, but excellent choices in the area would be the Cafe de Manilla, the King & I, PHO Grand, Tony's, Zia's or Hodaks.

When you visit you'll be within walking distance of Tower Grove Park, with tennis courts and a fitness trail. The park is next to the Missouri Botanical Gardens. If the weather is cool enjoy the gas log in the parlor fireplace. Enjoy live piano music at breakfast. If you crave additional company, Sam (the dog) loves to be petted.

Warrensburg

You'll want to celebrate your citizenship in this town in the heart of the U.S. It's a place to observe, enjoy and relax.

*Drive east on US 50 to Sedalia. Travel north of Sedalia on US 65, for 6 miles, to **Bothwell State Park**, and **Bothwell Lodge**. The lodge was the country home of a businessman from 1897 to 1929 and is furnished as he left it. While you're here, continue south on US 65 to **Truman Reservoir** and its visitor center. The reservoir has many recreational opportunities including excellent fishing.*

*From Warrensburg you may go east on US 50 and then north on SR 291 to Independence, where there are many more things to see and do (See the listing for Independence in this book). When visiting the Warrensburg area, shoppers will want to make stops in Amish stores and antique spots. **Central Missouri State University** has frequent concerts, theater and an excellent athletic program.*

*Come in August to visit the **State Fair**, in Sedalia, with top entertainment and agricultural displays. In June, Sedalia has the **Scott Joplin Ragtime Festival**. Nearby attractions include **Knob Noster State Park, Bothwell State Park, Whiteman Air Force Base**, historic sites and civil war battlefields. If you're looking for still more to do, just an hour away is Kansas City for shopping and major league sports.*

● **Cedarcroft Farm Bed & Breakfast**
Route 3, Box 130, Warrensburg, MO 64093.
(816)747-5728 (800)368-4944.

$43-47. For special events, $46-50. Travel agent discount.

Call 7 AM - 9 AM, or after 7 PM.
•V, MC, D.
•**Innkeepers: Sandra & Bill Wayne.**
•*2 rms, 1 sb.*
•Full breakfast of homemade biscuits and sausage gravy, honey butter, assorted spreads made by local Amish, other homemade baked items, juice and fruit in season.
•No pets, no smoking indoors.
•Southeast of Warrensburg. Free pickup from Warrensburg Amtrak station or KATY trail extension.

This renovated 1867 farmhouse, on 80 acres of secluded woods, meadows and streams, was built by Sandra's great grandfather, a Union veteran and pioneer soil conservationist. Sandra and Bill are retired air force veterans, who have taught college courses.

For dining, make arrangements with your hosts to have the special Cedarcroft roast beef country dinner. Visit the Dinner Bell, in LaMonte, and the Feed Lot, in Windsor, for country cooking.

When you visit you'll be amazed at the quiet and privacy. Walk the natural trails and you might see turkey, deer, coyote, quail, owls or hawks. Help with horse care (but your hosts can't offer riding) or try catch and release farm pond fishing. Peruse the collection of books and magazines from the 1840s to 1870s. If you're interested in the Civil War, you'll be delighted with your hosts' knowledge of events and equipment and their collection of videos reenacting battles.

Montana

Bozeman

You'll want to explore the **Museum of the Rockies**, south of the Montana State University campus at S. 7th St. and Kagy Blvd. It has great dinosaur exhibits as well as a planetarium and other interesting displays relating to the history of the Rocky Mountains.

Pick up a map of the **South Wilson Historic District** at the museum and give yourself a tour of the interesting buildings in this area. A smaller museum, but with interesting pioneer artifacts, is the **Gallatin Pioneers Museum**, in the Courthouse. Computer hobbyists will want to visit the **American Computer Museum**, 234 E. Babcock St., with exhibits detailing the evolution of computers.

Just a few miles away, in Livingston, is the **Depot Center Museum**. It houses interesting historic exhibits and paintings by western artists, including C.M. Russell and Frederic Remington.

A must for visitors to this wonderful area is exploring the outdoors. If you visit in the winter, you'll never be far from excellent cross-country skiing. If you prefer downhill skiing, Bridger Bowl is just 15 miles north and Big Sky is 45 miles south. When the weather is warmer, visit **Kirk Hill Nature Center** for great hiking, rent a mountain bike to see the mountains or try one of the three blue-ribbon trout streams in the area. If you can, of course, you must drive the 1 1/2 hours to Yellowstone National Park.

● **Torch and Toes Bed & Breakfast**
309 South Third Avenue, Bozeman, MT 59715.
(406)586-7285.

$45-55. Discounts for senior citizens and travel agents.

Call 9 AM to Noon.
• V, MC.
• **Innkeepers: Ronald & Judy Hess.**
• *4 rms, 2 pb, 1 sb.*
• Full breakfast, featuring fresh fruit, muffins, eggs, juice and coffee.
• No pets, no smoking.
• On I-90.

This 1906 Colonial Revival style house has oak woodwork, fireplace, leaded windows, and turn-of-the-century antiques. It's filled with many interesting collections, including dolls, old post cards and mouse traps. Ron is on the historic preservation committee and knows much of the area history. Judy is an weaver, interested in sharing stories and ideas.

For dining, in Bozeman, you'll find excellent continental cuisine at O'Brien's, John Bozeman's Bistro or Sir Scott's Oasis.

When you visit you'll have a great time exploring the main floor and finding the collections your hosts have gathered. The swings on the front porch or the deck in back are wonderful places to relax — perhaps with a book or magazine from the library. You're welcome to help pick raspberries in the back yard. Your hosts enjoy visiting with guests and telling about the history of the area or sharing hobbies.

Nebraska

Elgin

You'll want to be prepared to get away from the city hustle and bustle to relax in this quiet Nebraska town.

That doesn't mean that you won't have anything to do, though. You can take a walking tour of the town and countryside, swim, play volleyball, horseshoes, tennis or basketball in the city park.

It is just a short drive to **Ashfall Fossil Beds State Historical Park**, near Royal, where you can watch fossils being unearthed. **Neligh Mills**, at Neligh, is one of the few remaining water-turbine powered flour mills. Although it is not operating, there are exhibits on the flour milling industry throughout the three-story building. Much of the mill is restored.

Fort Hartsuff State Historical Park, at Elyria, has restored buildings from this 1870s fort. The grounds and the buildings are open daily throughout the year. There is a **trout hatchery** on Grove Lake, near Royal. If you like to fish, bring your gear because Grove Lake and Flober Springs, near Elgin, both offer good fishing. If you want even more activities, you can drive to the nearby larger cities of Norfolk, Columbus, O'Neil or Grand Island where you'll find excellent shopping and many things to see and do.

Plantation House

RR 2, Box 17, Elgin, NE 68636-9301. (402)843-2287.

$35-50. Seasonal and commercial discounts.

Call anytime.
- No cr. cds.
- **Innkeepers: Merland & Barbara Clark.**
- *5 rms, 2 sb, 2 pb.*
- Breakfast is served family style in the formal dining room. A typical breakfast would include juice, eggs, sausage, toast, jam, homemade muffins or rolls and beverage. However, guests may request special diet breakfasts.
- No pets, no smoking. Bedrooms are on second floor.
- In Elgin, near the junction of SR 14 & 70.

This rambling home, with more than 25 rooms, and 5 fireplaces, is more than 100 years old. It has two circular stairways, beautiful oak woodwork and some of the original furniture blended with other antiques, memorabilia and locally produced crafts. Merland is a farmer and Barbara is a homemaker and amateur artist. They enjoy computers, history, genealogy, oil painting, eggeury, farming and antiques.

For dining, you'll be able to choose from several choice restaurants, including the L Bar B Steakhouse, in Clearwater; the Imperial Steakhouse, in Neligh, the Branding Iron or the Center Street Bakery, in Tilden, and the Villa Inn or the Artists' Arbor, in Albion.

When you visit you might want to talk in the living room, watch TV or play games in the family room, drink lemonade in the gazebo, plan a trip on the computer, or play games on the lawn. Take a ride in one of the unique vehicles, go for a long walk and explore the area, or read in solitude.

New Hampshire

Franconia Notch: Littleton / Franconia

You'll want to visit Franconia Notch, said to be the most widely known and most visited of mountain gaps. It has been a favorite spot for tourists since the 1800s. One breathtaking view is from the **Cannon Mountain Aerial Tramway** which takes you to a summit observation platform. From there, foot trails lead to other extraordinary points of view. Among the other best known scenic spots are **The Flume**, a narrow chasm through which tumbles waterfalls and pools. A free bus will take you to within 1/2 mile of the gorge but there are some steep grades which must be walked. **The Profile** appears to be the head of a man naturally formed by five ledges of rock. The best view is from the eastern shore of Lake Profile. **Echo Lake** is surrounded on three sides by mountains and is best known for (what else) echoes. The **Crawford Notch**, on US 302, is the site of the Arethusa Falls, one of the highest waterfalls in the state and, at the north end of the notch, the Silver Cascade, 1,000 feet of rushing water.

At Littleton, the **Ammonoosuc River** falls 235 feet as it goes through the town. Just 8 miles west of town on SR 18 is the **Samuel C. Moore Station**, the largest hydroelectric plant in New England. A visitor center has exhibits. The town itself was a station on the underground railway during the Civil War. The Chamber of Commerce has a flyer describing a walking tour of Main Street and the historic sites. In Franconia, the **Frost Place** is the house that poet Robert Frost lived in for some time. The visitor may view two rooms containing Frost memorabilia, a narrated slide show, an 1859 farmhouse and a 1/2 mile nature trail. The **New England Ski Museum**, near the Cannon Mountain Aerial Tramway, has art, photographs, clothing, equipment, slide and film presentations detailing the history of skiing.

● **Blanche's B & B**
351 Easton Valley Rd., Franconia, NH 03580. (603)823-7061.

$55-60. Discount for week's stay.

Call before 9 PM.
- V, MC, AE.
- **Innkeepers: Brenda Shannon, John Vail, & Blanche, the dog.**
- *5 rms, 2 sb.*
- A full breakfast is served at individual tables in the dining room. An example might include fresh fruit salad with maple yogurt dressing, spinach omelette, homefries, honey-nut Rolls, Juice, Coffee or Tea.
- No pets, no smoking.
- 5 mi from Franconia & I-93; 25 mi from I-91.

This 1887 farmhouse is in a quiet, rural setting, at the base of the Kinsman Ridge. It has been restored to a perfection that may be better than its original glory. John is a carpenter, with a special interest in old houses and especially this old house; Brenda is a decorative painter and floorcloth maker.

For dining, you really must try Tim-Bir Alley, in Littleton. The WestLake Chinese Restaurant, in Lincoln, and the Rabbit Hill Inn, in Lower Waterford VT, are highly recommended.

When you visit you'll want to curl up with a book from your hosts' collection, relax in the yard, doze in the hammock, play croquet, watch Brenda make her floorcloths, or ask your hosts to arrange for a hayride with their farmer neighbor.

● The Beal House Inn
247 West Main St., Littleton, NH 03561. (603)444-2661.

$45-85. Rates may be slightly higher during fall foliage season. Discounts to groups, with extended stays.

Call 10 AM - 10 PM.
- V, MC.
- Innkeepers: Catherine & Jean-Marie (John) Fisher-Motheu.
- *13 rms, 9 pb, 2 sb.*
- Expanded continental breakfast. An example might include Belgian Waffles, made by Jean-Marie, plus muffins, breads, cheese, fruit, cereal, juices and hot beverages.
- No pets, no smoking.
- 1 mile from I-93; 3 hrs. from Boston or Montreal.

This 1833 Federal Renaissance Farmhouse has been an inn since 1938. It has a cupola and glassed-in front porch. There are down comforters on all of the beds, some of which are canopied. There are antiques throughout the building. Most of the furnishings are for sale — a Beal House tradition. Jean-Marie played professional soccer in Belgium, is a connoisseur of wine; Catherine is an antique and toy collector.

For dining, you may enjoy dinner in the former carriage house, now the evening dining room, at the Beal House. Littleton also has a variety of other restaurants.

When you visit if the weather is warm, be sure to find the open air deck, on the hill, for a serene spot from which to view the mountains and village activities. The game room has billiards, board games, puzzles, and lots of books. Catherine has an antique toy collection and guests frequently enjoy browsing through it. A pleasant spot to enjoy, in comfort.

Golden Squash Raisin Bread

From Donna Hodge, **Bed and Breakfast at the Pines**
Frankenmuth, MI

1 cup milk
1 cup cooked, mashed winter squash
1/4 cup oil
1/4 cup honey
2 teaspoons salt
1 teaspoon cinnamon
1 teaspoon nutmeg or other spices
2 packages dry yeast
1/2 cup warm water
6 1/2 cups all-purpose flour
2 eggs
1 1/2 cup raisins

Scald milk. Stir in cooked squash, oil, honey, salt and spices. Cool to lukewarm. Dissolve yeast in water. Stir. Add to milk mixture. Add 3 cups flour, eggs and raisins, and beat until batter is smooth. Add enough of the remaining flour to make the dough leave the sides of the bowl. Turn out onto a floured board and knead about 10 minutes until the dough is elastic and smooth. Place in a greased bowl. Cover and allow to rise until doubled in size, about 1 hour. Punch down and turn onto a board. Divide in half and shape into loaves. Place in two greased 8 x 4 bread pans. Brush tops with melted margarine. Cover and let rise until doubled, about 1 hour. Bake at 375F. for 40 minutes or until golden brown. Remove from oven, let cool for 5 minutes, remove from pans and cool completely before slicing.

Lyme

You'll want to make winter reservations for a ski vacation in this area.

Visit **Dartmouth College**, in Hanover, at Main & Wheelock Sts., the nation's ninth oldest college. The college guide service offers tours. Highlights of a visit would include **Dartmouth Row**, with many of the oldest buildings on campus; **Baker Memorial Library**, holding almost two million books and frescoes by Mexican artist Jose Clemente Orozco; **Hood Museum of Art**, with ten galleries presenting changing exhibits of notable art; and, **Hopkins Center for the Arts**, a major cultural center housing presentations of theater, music, film, and dance.

Webster Cottage, 32 N. Main, was the residence of Daniel Webster when he was a student. The **League of New Hampshire Craftsmen**, 13 Lebanon St, shows work by exceptionally talented men and women. Leaving Hanover and browsing the countryside, you'll find several entertaining sites.

Paradise Point Nature Center, on SR 104 between Hebron and Bristol, is owned by the Audubon Society and has live animal exhibits, day camps, workshops and three nature trails. **La Salette Shrine and Center**, on SR 4A, at Enfield, offers a Rosary Walk, a Pilgrim's Way and a Peace Walk. On Stinson Lake Road, near Rumney, is the **Mary Baker Eddy House**, where Mrs. Eddy lived in the 1860s.

The resort community of Sunapee, offers **boat cruises** around Lake Sunapee and **Mount Sunapee State Park** with chairlifts to the top of Mount Sunapee, hiking, skiing, swimming and picnicking.

Loch Lyme Lodge

RFD 278, Rt. 10, Lyme, NH 03768.
(603)795-2141.

$45-74/D. Highest rates mid-Jun. to mid-Sep.

Call mornings.
- No cr. cds.
- Innkeepers: Paul & Judy Barker.
- *4 rms, 2 sb. There are several cabins available during the summer.*

- Full breakfast of fruit, juice, cereal, eggs, meat, breads, and beverage served family style on the sun porch.
- No pets. Children are always welcome.
- 1 mi. from Lyme.

This 1784 farmhouse, overlooking a lovely lake, is on 125 acres of fields and woods. The rooms are upstairs in the lodge and families have been coming here for years. Make early reservations. Paul and Judy enjoy soccer, skiing, wreath making, singing, children and cooking.

For dining, you may eat right at the lodge. Modified American Plan rates are available late June to late August. Other excellent restaurants include nearby D'Artagnan, the Ivy Grill, at the Hanover Inn, or Peter Christian's, in Hanover.

When you visit you'll find plenty to do at the lodge and on its surrounding property. The lodge overlooks Post Pond, a spring-fed lake. You can get boats, canoes and kayaks from the inn. You'll be able to go hiking, fishing, cross-country skiing, ice fishing, skating, snowshoeing and sliding right on the inn's property. The public rooms include a fireplace, piano room and large living room.

Monadnock Region: Jaffrey

You'll want to climb a mountain, even if you only take a few steps. Jaffrey is at the foot of the Grand Monadnock, the second most climbed mountain in the world, and you'll be able to see a superb view of surrounding states from the 3165 ft. summit. To get to the mountain go 2 mi. W on SR 124, to **Monadnock State Park**, where there are miles of trails. While there are many things to do in this region, you'll definitely need transportation to go from one site to another. One of the delights of travel around the area is the opportunity to view the many picturesque New England villages.

The **Cathedral of the Pines**, in Rindge, is a nondenominational shrine to all U.S. citizens killed in wars. There are flags of states, rocks from each state, art objects and war relics to see. The **Friendly Farm**, in Dublin, has farm livestock that may be fed and petted. The **Barrett House**, in New Ipswich, dates from 1800. It has period furnishings and antique musical instruments. Peterborough is the site of **Miller State Park**, on SR 101, with a scenic drive, foot trails, picnic facilities and Pack Monadnock Mountain, with a 2,288 ft. summit. The **Peterborough Historical Society**, on Grove St, has a museum and the **Sharon Arts Center** has an exhibit and store showing hand crafted items.

Keene is the largest city in the region and is less than 1/2 hr. drive from Jaffrey. The **Keene State College** is the scene of plays and concerts during the school year. If you are interested in old houses with appealing furnishings, visit the **Horatio Colony House Museum**, 199 Main St. The **Horatio Colony Wildlife Sanctuary**, on SR 9, has nature trails for hiking, cross-country skiing, and snowshoeing while observing the wildlife of the area. Shop at the **Colony Mill Marketplace**. A little more pricey, but fun, is **Silver Ranch**, on SR 124 near Jaffrey, offering airplane rides, horsedrawn carriage and sleigh rides. There are lakes and streams for water sports, tennis courts, golf courses, and stables for horseback riding. Four summer theaters offer summer evening entertainment. In the winter, cross-country ski trails are everywhere and there are four downhill areas within 30 minutes drive.

● The Galaway House

247 Old Peterbrorough Rd, Jaffrey, NH 03452. (603)532-8083.

$40/S; $50/D. OPEN SEPT - JUNE. CLOSED JULY & AUG. Seasonal discount may be available.

Call evenings.
- No cr. cds.
- Innkeepers: **Joe & Marie Manning.**
- *2 rms, 1 sb.*
- A full breakfast of cereal, eggs, pancakes, bacon, muffins, grapefruit and beverage is served in the dining room.
- No pets, no smoking.
- Midway between Jaffrey and Peterborough.

This colonial home is on an old prerevolutionary road. Your hosts are dedicated to bringing the warmth and hospitality of Irish B&Bs to New England. Although the house is "new" by local standards, it has original pine floors. Joe and Marie enjoy skiing, boating, reading, hiking, bird watching, history and New England lore.

For dining, there are few chain restaurants but choices run from pizza to gourmet, including Italian, Chinese, Japanese, Macrobiotic, Old New England, and seafood. All are within 15 min. drive and your hosts will be happy to help you choose a restaurant that you'll enjoy.

When you visit you'll want to sit by the fireplace on cool nights and walk the woodland trails during the day. Your hosts enjoy the intimacy they can offer because they are small. They'll be happy to tell you about the history of the area, the hidden glens and byways that most tourists can't find.

North Woodstock

You'll want to drive the **Kancamagus Highway**, which begins here and goes east through the forest and mountains. It is one of New Hampshire's most scenic drives.

North Woodstock, in the center of the **White Mountain National Forest**, is an ideal place from which to explore this popular forest area. The mountains and forest are noted for outdoor recreation and the beauty of the area. Among popular outdoor activities are hiking and fishing in the spring, summer and fall, and skiing in the winter. Visitor information centers at Lincoln, Campton and near Conway are open all year. Many of the ski resorts are world famous. **Clark's Trading Post**, 1 mile north of town on US 3, offers fun in the form of a train ride in an old logging train, antique fire fighting equipment, trained bears, and a haunted house.

Lost River Gorge is 6 miles west of North Woodstock on SR 112. In Kinsman Notch, the river winds through narrow passages, caverns and potholes to get "lost" only to reappear again. Finally, it appears at the bottom of the gorge as beautiful Paradise Falls. A trail leads over or through several caverns and a nature garden is filled with native plants.

Just across the Pemigewasset River from North Woodstock, is Lincoln. The **Whale's Tale Water and Amusement Park** has a clown show, a children's pool, flume rides, speed rides, pony carts and amusement rides. The **Loon Mountain Skyride**, 2 miles east of Lincoln on the Kancamagus Highway, offers a gondola ride from the base to the summit of the mountain and a spectacular view of the surrounding forest.

● **Wilderness Inn Bed and Breakfast**
Rts. 3 and 112, North Woodstock, NH 03262. ((603)745-3890.

Summer!: $50-85. Spring, Fall: $40-60. Discounts: Seasonal, travel agent.

Call 7:30 Am to 10:30 PM.
- V, MC, AE.
- Innkeepers: Rosanna and Michael Yarnell.
- 7 rms, 4 pb, 1 sb.
- Full breakfast. Your choice of delectable pancakes, crepes, French toast, omelets, or eggs served with juice, home baked breads and muffins, fresh fruit salad and beverage served on the front porch or in the dining room. Or, if you prefer, continental breakfast served in your room.
- No pets.
- On the Kancamagus Highway. 1/2 mile from I-93, at the junction of Rts 3 and 112.

This German cottage was built in 1912 by the owner of a lumber mill. Mountains rise at the front of the cottage and Lost River flows in back. The guest rooms are furnished with oriental carpets as well as original and reproduction antiques. Michael is a ski instructor at Cannon Mountain Ski Resort and Rosanna is a French teacher.

For dining, if you're visiting on a winter weekend, make a reservation for the 5 or 6 course dinner served at the inn. Other fine places for excellent food include the Woodstock Inn (Clement Room), in North Woodstock, and the Common Man, in Lincoln.

When you visit you'll be able to go to the back yard for swimming and sun bathing. Guests are welcome to help pick the back yard raspberries and, if you like cats, the inn's cat will be happy to play with you on the porch.

New Jersey

Ocean City

*Y*ou'll want to *enjoy all of the advantages of Atlantic City, but without the crowds, when you visit here.*

Ocean City has a boardwalk, a music pier with band concerts throughout the summer, and two amusement parks. Marinas are filled with colorful yachts and charter boats for fishing and sightseeing. The **Ocean City Arts Center** has monthly art exhibits. Museum lovers will want to visit the **Historical Museum**. When you visit, especially during the summer, you're likely to find excitement created by a special event such as a parade, pageant or race.

Historic Cape May, one of the oldest seashore resorts in the area, is just 30 minutes away. The entire community has been designated as a national historic landmark. Trolley tours, carriage tours, guided and self-guided walking tours are available. The city also has several annual events, including "Christmas in Cape May." Rock hounds love to hunt for the famous "Cape May Diamonds," quartz pebbles found at Cape May Point. At **Cape May State Park**, visitors can climb the staircase of the lighthouse to look out over the bay and ocean. A ferry runs from here to Lewes, Delaware. **Cold Spring Village**, just north of the ferry, is a restored 19th century farm village with demonstrations, craft shops, a marine museum and narrated horse and buggy tours. **Lemings Run Gardens**, has many small themed gardens and nearby **Colonial Farm**, depicts whaling in the 1700s.

Just 20 minutes from Ocean City, is Atlantic City. This old resort city is now the home of several casino hotels offering gambling and entertainment. Atlantic City is also the home of the legendary rolling chair — an early and unusual form of boardwalk transportation. In addition to casinos, Atlantic city has long been known for its boardwalks, ocean breezes and sandy beaches. Boating and bicycling are popular pastimes.

● **Enterprise Bed & Breakfast Inn**
1020 Central Avenue, Ocean City, NJ 08226. (609)398-1698.

$55-85. Highest rates are charged weekends during June, July and August. During the rest of the year, there is a discount of two nights for the price of one Sun-Thurs, Sept-June.

Call after 5 pm or anytime on weekends.
•V, MC.
•**Innkeepers: Steve & Patty Hydock.**
•*10 rms, 1 sb, 7 pb.*
•A full breakfast, featuring such specialties as Eggs Benedict, Quiche, stuffed French Toast Strata and several other wonderful items. Breakfast may be served outside on the porch or in the formal dining room.
•No pets, no smoking, no children under 10.
•In Ocean City.

Built as a small hotel at the turn of the century, this air conditioned B&B, with Gingerbread trim is a fascinating place. Patty is a realtor specializing in B&Bs; Steve is a baseball card enthusiast and avid fisherman.

For dining, Steve and Patty recommend their own dining room, although there are other fine restaurants in the area.

When you visit you'll be just 2-1/2 blocks from the beach and the boardwalk and 5 blocks from the amusement pier.

New Mexico

Las Cruces

You'll want to drive to the Rio Grande, just a few miles from downtown.

But then return to Las Cruces for a wonderful getaway. Visit the **Las Cruces Convention and Visitors Bureau**, 311 N. Downtown Mall, to learn about a self-guided tour of the city's two historical districts. Visit **Fort Selden State Monument**, north on I-25 to Exit 19, then 1/4 mile W. Although the fort has not been reconstructed, large remnants of the old fort remain. Pictures are posted along your walking tour to help you restore the fort in your imagination. A museum displays artifacts from the period. Art lovers will enjoy a visit to the **Branigan Cultural Center**, 106 W. Hadley. The center features local artists.

La Mesilla State Monument, a historic restored village, with a wide plaza and 19th century Spanish-style buildings is just a short drive away, south on I-10. Interesting day trips include the **Gila National Forest and Cliff Dwellings**. To get there follow US 180 west and north to Silver City, and the entrance to the forest. The forest has mountains, canyons, and ghost towns. A scenic 110 mile loop drive, starting at Silver City, includes the Cliff Dwellings.

Take another trip northeast on US 70/82 to Alamagordo. The **Alamagordo Space Center** and **Alamagordo Zoo** are entertaining. The space center includes a theater with a laser light show and planetarium, a Space Hall of Fame, an outdoor display of space vehicles and gardens. The Zoo has an outstanding Primate Center. You'll want to stop at **White Sands National Monument**. See huge white sand dunes, Lake Lucero, and a visitor center that explains the history and origin of the sand.

If you have any additional time be sure to see the **Carlsbad Cavern** (21 miles of spectacular surveyed caves). Juarez, Mexico is an easy drive away, with its interesting Mexican markets.

● **Lundeen "Inn of the Arts" B&B**
618 South Alameda Boulevard, Los Cruces, NM 88005. (505)526-3326/ Fax: 526-3355.

$55-85.

Call at least a week before reservation.
•V, MC, D, AE.
•Innkeepers: Linda & Gerald Lundeen.
•15 rms, 15 pb.
•You'll get an expanded continental breakfast. The menu may include taste treats like Swiss Breakfast Parfait, Dutch Babies or Strawberry and Banana French Toast. Frequently guests gather in the kitchen for hot Jamaican coffee and pastries fresh from the oven. They may take a tray breakfast to their room, a balcony or garden.
•No smoking, no alcohol. Check with your hosts if your family includes a child.
•In the downtown historic district.

This Mexican-Territorial adobe home has graceful arched windows, mission tile, fireplaces, balconies and brick patios. Each of the fifteen guest rooms is named and decorated in the style of an American artist and often contains original art works. A living-dining room has an 18-foot-high ceiling and is a showcase for art works provided by the adjoining art gallery. Linda owns the gallery and Gerald is an architect.

For dining, be sure to find the Double Eagle Restaurant, in Old Mesilla.

When you visit explore this dramatic and unusual inn. Ask Gerald about his architectural tours. Learn about Indian dancing and Indian bread making. Make friends with the "love bird," Fairsea. Return from your day-long excursions in time for afternoon beverages, a gallery stroll and good conversation.

New York

Bolton Landing

You'll want to visit the **Sembrich Opera Museum** in Bolton Landing, open July through September. Then venture on to the other exciting possibilities in the Lake George area. There are marinas, public beaches, hiking trails, lake cruise ships, antique shops galore, tennis courts and golf courses. You can rent a boat, jet ski or go parasailing. Get on the **Lake Shore Drive**, which follows the west side of Lake George, to take a beautiful drive to the **Village of Lake George**. Find the factory outlet centers near the village, just off of I-87 on SR 9. At Lake George you can also take cruises that last from 1 to 4 1/2 hrs. **Fort William Henry Museum** is in the center of the village. This reproduction of a key 18th-century British fort has tours and audio-visual shows for visitors. Just off of US 9 is the **Prospect Mountain Veterans Memorial Highway** a scenic drive to a spot overlooking the lake.

Just south of Lake George on US 9 or I-87 is Glens Falls. If you like amusement parks, be sure to plan to spend a day at **The Great Escape Fun Park**. In addition to 100 rides, this park has puppet and magic shows, a ghost town, petting zoo, and jungle world. In Lake George, the **Hyde Collection**, is a mansion containing famous art works from the 15th to the 20th centuries. The **Lake George Opera Festival** is held here every year, running from late July to mid-August. The **Chapman Museum** contains historical exhibits on the immediate area. This is a popular area for hot-air balloons and a balloon festival is held in late September. Reservations can be made for rides, which take off daily May to Oct.

If you still have time or prefer other entertainment, take the **Lake Shore Drive** north to Ticonderoga, at the north end of the lake. Just 1 mi. NE of the town on SR 74, is **Fort Ticonderoga**, built by the French in 1755. It has been restored on the original foundations. There is a museum, daily guided tours and fife and drum demonstrations during July and August, and history oriented cruises on Lake Champlain.

● Hilltop Cottage B & B

Box 186, Lakeshore Dr., Bolton Landing, NY 12814. (518)644-2492.

$45-55/D. Seasonal discount Nov-May.

Call anytime.
- No cr. crds.
- Innkeepers: Anita & Charlie Richards.
- *3 rms., 1 pb, 1 sb.*
- An ample, full breakfast includes homemade jams and breads and is served on the vine-shaded screen porch when weather is nice.
- No pets.
- On route 9N, 8 mi. from I-88.

This 1926 farmhouse was built as the caretaker's cottage for the Stengel-DeCoppet Estates on "Millionaire's Row" along Lake George. It was across the road from the summer estate of Marcella Sembrich, Metropolitan Opera diva, and she boarded her vocal students from Julliard in the cottage. Charlie is a retired high school guidance counselor and Anita was a teacher of German. Anita is executive director of the Sembrich Opera Museum and provides off-season and after hours tours to her guests.

For dining, you'll want to try the Omni-Sagamore Hotel, a four-star restaurant. Within 1/2 mile of Hilltop there are three recommended restaurants: the Ryefield, the Algonquin, and the Char Steer.

When you visit be sure to take advantage of the opportunity to tour the Sembrich Museum. The cottage sits on two acres. Lakeshore Drive runs right in front of the property. The property and surrounding area provides a lot of space from strolling or hiking.

Cattaraugus Indian Reservation

You'll want to observe or participate in many of the activities on the reservation.

In the summer there are 10K races, Lacrosse games, raft races, canoe races, and fishing (you need to get an Indian license). In the winter there is the special javelin throwing sport called Snowsnake. In September the **Seneca Fall Festival** is held with arts, crafts, exhibition dancing and Indian food. In November there is an Indian Foods Dinner and in December there is a Christmas bazaar.

Take a tour of the two Seneca Indian Reservations. You may visit the **Seneca Indian Museum**, go bicycling, swim in Lake Erie and have a noon meal with the Indian Senior Citizens.

The area surrounding the reservation also has interesting attractions. A 20-mile old-fashioned **train ride** leaves from Gowanda, June through October. Take a **raft trip** between Springville and Gowanda, visit antique and flea markets or arrange for a hot air balloon ride.

Festivals and special events include the **July 4th** celebration, the **Eden Corn Festival** in August, the **Silver Creek Grape Festival** in September, the **Hidi Hose Fishing Derby** and the **Pumpkin Festival** in October.

Niagara Falls is just about an hour's drive from here. The **Chautauqua Institute** is 45 miles away. **Amish communities** are nearby and welcome the reservation guests into their shops and homes. Three ski areas are just 25 miles away: Holiday Valley, near Ellicottville, Cokaigne, near Cherry Creek, and Kissing Bridge, near Colden.

No matter when you visit, you're sure to have a wonderful time visiting this area.

● **The Teepee**
RD 1, Box 543, Gowanda, NY 14070.
(716)532-2168.
$30/S; $40/D.

Call anytime, use answering machine.
•No cr. crds.
•**Innkeepers: Max & Phyllis Lay.**
•*4 rms, 2 sb.*
•Full breakfast, including such items as orange juice, bacon and eggs, Indian fry bread, jam and jellies, and beverage.
•No pets.
•1 1/2 mi. from Gowanda; 30 mi. south of Buffalo.

This lovely 4 bedroom home is on the Cattaraugus Indian Reservation. Phyllis and Max are full-blooded Seneca Indians, who built their home themselves because mortgage money was not available to Indians. Max is a Shrine clown, political town chairman, counselor for the Seneca Indian tribe and a retired alcohol and drug abuse counselor. Phyllis is a tour guide for a travel agency, hot air balloon crew, cookie factory tour guide, hostess on excursion train and tourism representative. She has done literacy volunteer work in a nearby prison.

For dining, visit the Haus Talblick, with an excellent menu and German Master Chef; the Olympia, for Greek family cuisine; or the Colony, which is 11 miles away but worth the trip.

When you visit ask Phyllis or Max to give you a tour of the reservation. Ask to see the videos and books about the tribe. They say you'll also find "white man's" magazines and books. Ride their bicycles, go on hikes or, in the winter, use the cross-country skis.

Cooperstown

You'll want to spend more than one getaway in this picturesque town. It is where baseball was said to have begun and is the home of James Fenimore Cooper.

Almost everyone who has ever attended a baseball game wants to see the **National Baseball Hall of Fame and Museum**, where the history and development of baseball is chronicled with exhibits, films and tape recordings.

Fenimore House has James Fenimore Cooper memorabilia and a large folk art collection. The **Farmers' Museum** is a living history museum, depicting rural life in the early 1800s, with exhibits and craftspeople demonstrating early trades. The **Glimmerglass Opera House** offers performances during July and August. It is in a state park with adjacent nature trails for hiking or cross-country skiing.

Narrated **Lake Otsego Boat Tours** are given aboard a wooden boat May through mid-October. The village, itself, has preserved many of its historic homes and buildings. Antique shoppers will find many interest shops and shows throughout the area.

If you ever run out of things to see and do, it is just a short drive to Oneonta where you'll find the **National Soccer Hall of Fame** and the **Hanford Mills Museum** with an operating Gristmill.

There are several interesting museums on the Hartwick College Campus, in Oneonta. The **Science Discovery Center**, in the Physical Science building, at State University College, Ravine Parkway, provides hands-on science exhibits for children.

- **Litco Farms Bed & Breakfast**

P.O. Box 1048, Cooperstown, NY 13326-1048. (607)547-2501.

$55-75. $95/Family Suite. Family discount.

Call after noon.
- No cr. cds.
- **Innkeepers: Jim & Margaret Wolff.**
- *4 rms, 2 pb, 1 sb.*
- Full breakfast of juice, fresh fruit, homemade granola, homemade coffee cakes, French toast, bacon or sausage, beverage, served family style.
- No pets, no smoking.
- 3 mi. NW of Cooperstown, on SR 28/80.

This 1820s farm house has the original wide-plank floors and is decorated with country antiques and quilts. Look for the glass candlesticks that your hosts collect. Margaret is a placement director for the regional vocational schools and an avid quilter. Jim is the local magistrate and sells computer software to automate courts. His hobby is woodworking.

For dining, you'll find restaurants galore in the area. Ask Jim or Margaret to show you their collection of menus and help you make a choice.

When you visit you'll have 70 acres of private grounds, with nature trails, surrounding the B&B on which to roam. There is a beaver pond covering 8 acres. What could be more interesting? There is also a 20-by-40 foot in-ground pool for swimming or sunning. Margaret has a quilt fabric shop and guests are welcome to browse through the shop. And, if you want a book to read, you'll find an extensive library available for guests.

Fingerlakes Region: Canandaigua, Skaneateles

You'll want to spend several getaways in the Finger Lakes Region. There are many wineries to visit in this area, boat rides to take, beautiful parks for recreation, hiking, walking, picnicking and fishing on the lakes. There are art galleries, boutiques, sightseeing, lake cruises (some include lunch or dinner), biking and cross-country skiing.

Two lovely lakefront parks are in the village of Skaneateles. Visitors may take a 32-mile cruise around the lake, a mailboat cruise, sightseeing lunch or dinner cruises. The little village of Elbridge is a pretty community to visit. Nearby is Auburn, where the **Cayuga Museum of History and Art** has several interesting collections. **William Seward House** contains original family furnishings and memorabilia. Canandaigua is home of the **Finger Lakes Performing Art Center** and the lovely **Sonnenberg Gardens**. The gardens are on 50 acres and have several restored gardens (each with a different theme), a greenhouse, fountains, streams, ponds, statues and an 1887 mansion. The mansion is open to the public and food is available. It is the summer home of the **Rochester Philharmonic Orchestra**. Geneva has a historic area where there are some lovely old homes, including **Rose Hill** mansion and garden. This is a wonderful area for an assortment of scenic drives and walks.

The campuses of **Hobart and William Smith Colleges** as well as a branch of **Cornell** are in the vicinity and have maps available for self-guided walking tours of the campuses. Naples is home of the **Bristol Valley Theater** which has plays throughout the summer months; the **Cumming Nature Center**, an outdoor branch of the Rochester Museum and Science Center; and of **Windmer's Wine Cellars**, offering guided tours and wine tasting.

● Lakeview Farm B&B

4761 Rte. 364, Rushville (Canandaigua), NY 14544. (716)554-6973.

$40-45/S; $50-55/D. Highest rates Jun-Oct.

Call anytime.
- AE.
- **Innkeepers: Betty & Howard Freese.**
- *2 rms, 1 sb.*
- Full breakfast of juice, fresh fruit, breads, beverage and entree of eggs and bacon, pancakes or French toast, served in the dining room with a window wall overlooking Canandaigua Lake.
- No pets, no smoking, no children under 8 unless prior arrangements are made.
- On East side of Lake Canandaigua, 5 1/2 mi. South of the town of Canandaigua.

This bright and airy home is situated on 170 acres of woods, pond, and ravine. Howard is a mechanical engineer and Betty is a retired librarian. They have a machinery sales business. They enjoy travel and gardening.

For dining, you'll especially enjoy Thendara Restaurant, Lincoln Hill Inn or the Naples Hotel.

When you visit you'll be able to spend hours exploring the 170 acres surrounding your B&B. The beautiful ravine has many fossils. In winter there are trails for cross-country skiing. You may sit beside the pond, relax in a hammock, play horseshoes or badminton. There are books everywhere, which guests are welcome to borrow. If you're interested, your hosts will undoubtedly be willing to give you a sightseeing tour of the nearby area, including Spook Hill and sites of Native American legends.

- **Cozy Cottage Bed & Breakfast**

4987 Kingston Rd., Elbridge (Skaneateles), NY 13060. (315)689-2082.

$35-40/S; $45-50/D. Highest rates 5/1-11/15.

Call 10 AM - 6 PM. two or more weeks before planned stay.
- No cr.crds.
- **Innkeeper: Elaine Samuels.**
- *2 rms., 1 1/2 sb.*
- Expanded continental breakfast of juice or fruit, cereal, muffins, coffee cake or toast and beverage served in the dining room.
- No smoking, no children under 10. Will accept cats.
- 2 mi. from Rt 5 in Elbridge. 5 mi. from Rt 20 in Skaneateles.

A ranch home, on 4 1/2 acres, in the country, this B&B is run by an experienced B&B operator. Since she purchased the house, the main bath has been completely rebuilt and the rest of the house has been painted, sanded and refinished. In her spare time Elaine enjoys art, theater, animals and B&Bs. She also owns a B&B reservation service.

For dining, there are many choices. Some of the best include, in Skaneateles: Kreb's; in Elbridge: Weber's Wayside Inn; in Camillus: The Inn Between, Top of the Hill, Greengate Inn, in Syracuse; Park Circle, Pasquale's, Grimaldie's, Captain Ahab's, Johnathan's Broiled Seafood, Scotch & Sirloin, Nikki's and Regency Grille.

When you visit you will find this B&B to be clean, quiet, cozy and comfortable. The atmosphere is casual and friendly. It is on 4 1/2 acres and there is a pond, space for nature walks, sunbathing and bird watching. It is central to area attractions. You're welcome to read any of the many books and magazines. Elaine has lived in the area for over 30 years and will be happy to help you with directions.

Bacon and Potato Pie

From Judith Hess, **Torch & Toes Bed & Breakfast**
Bozeman, MT

1 pound bacon
1 medium onion, chopped
8 eggs, beaten
1 pound russet potatoes, peeled and grated
2 1/2 cups grated sharp cheddar cheese
1/2 teaspoon pepper

Preheat oven to 350F. Grease a 9 x 13 baking dish. Cook bacon and onion for about 8 to 10 minutes. Remove from pan and drain well on paper towels. Combine eggs and rest of ingredients. Pour into the prepared baking dish. Put into preheated oven and bake for 45 minutes. Cut into squares.

If you wish, you may cook the bacon and onion, mix the eggs and grate the cheese the night before. Don't grate the potato until morning or it will turn black.

Lake Placid

You'll want to visit the **Olympic Center** and engage in outdoor recreational activities. This town was the site of the 1980 Winter Olympics. During the summer there are miles of well-marked hiking trails in the Adirondack Mountains. Lakes abound for fishing, swimming and boating. There are bridle paths for horseback riding, tennis courts, ice skating in the Olympic arena and golf courses. In the winter there are marvelous facilities for downhill and cross-country skiing, snowshoeing, ice skating and snowmobiling. The Olympic Center is open for visitors and may be toured in both summer and winter, including the ski jump, ice arena and Mount Van Hoevenberg Recreational Area.

This was the home of abolitionist John Brown and the **John Brown State Historical Site** contains his monument, restored farmhouse and a hiking trail. The **Historical Society Museum**, on Averyville Road, has exhibits detailing the last 200 years of the region. There are narrated 1-hour boat cruises from the marina and sightseeing tours from the major motels and hotels. The **Cornell University Uihlein Sugar Maple Research Facility** is open on a varying schedule Mar-Apr. and July-mid Oct, giving demonstrations. This is a wonderful area for an assortment of scenic drives and walks.

Nearby **Sarnac Lake** was a tuberculosis treatment center in the late 19th century and the Chamber of Commerce will provide a self-guided walking tour. Of note is the cottage of Robert Louis Stevenson, who lived here in 1887 while undergoing treatment. North of Sarnac Lake, at Onchiota, just off SR3, is the **Six Nations Indian Museum**, portraying life of the Native American in indoor and outdoor exhibits. Then go on to the Whiteface Mountain Memorial Highway, on SR 431 for 3 1/2 miles west. A toll road will take you to the mountain; a short trail or electric elevator will take you to the summit. The Whiteface Mountain Chairlift, south on SR86, provides a summertime ride to the summit of Little Whiteface Mountain. **Santa's Workshop**, west on SR431, has children's rides, parades, reindeer. All at the North Pole, of course.

● **Highland House Inn**
3 Highland Place, Lake Placid, NY 12946.
(518)523-2377.

$55.

Call 9 AM to 9 PM.
•V, MC.
•**Innkeepers: Teddy & Cathy Blazer.**
•*7 rms, 7 pb.*
•A full breakfast, served to order. A typical meal might include an entree (blueberry pancakes, French toast, sausage, eggs) toast or English muffins, juice, cereal and beverages. In the summer you'll eat on the glass enclosed garden porch.
•No pets, no smoking in bedrooms or dining room.
•In the center of Lake Placid.

A **3-story, 1910 inn**, clean and charming, in a central location. Decor is built around an Adirondack theme. Furnishings are a mixture of restored antiques and fine quality wood furniture. Teddy is General Manager of Whiteface Mountain Ski Area. Cathy is active in the Chamber of Commerce and works on many community events.

For dining, some of the restaurants you can enjoy include Lake Placid Manor, Mirror Lake Inn, The Cottage, The Boathouse, and the Alpine Cellar.

When your visit during the summer, you may enjoy lounging on the deck and having breakfast on the porch. In the winter the woodstove is always going. Mountain bikes are available for rent during the summer and fall. Hikers will find a large library of hiking books and other books on the region but your hosts are also experts on the area and can provide you with information. The deck is a romantic spot to sit in the evening, with the moonlight shining through the birch trees.

Rochester / Lake Ontario Area: Brockport, Fairport

You'll want to see more than it is possible to see in one getaway when you visit this area. Brockport is 15 miles west of Rochester and 12 miles south of Lake Ontario. Fairport is less than 10 miles east of Rochester and about 15 miles south of the lake.

Rochester is noted for its beautiful parks and gardens. The **George Eastman House and International Museum of Photography** are worth a visit. The **Rochester Museum and Science Center** is a science museum featuring natural science, history and anthropology. Children's activities are featured during the summer and on weekends. The **Strong Museum** is a history center with an interactive exhibit for children.

In Mumford, a southern suburb of Rochester, is the **Genessee Country Museum**, a living history museum, with guides dressed in period dress demonstrating life in a 19th century New York village. Other interesting spots include the **Susan B. Anthony Memorial House** and the **Seneca Park Zoo**. Other interesting houses, open to visitors, include the **Campbell Whittlesey House** (Greek Revival architecture and early 19th century), **Woodside Mansion** (Greek Revival, period paintings and furnishings), and the **Stone-Tolan House** (Federal style farmhouse, pioneer life in late 1700s). **Seabreeze Park** is an amusement park with over 70 attractions. **Brown's Race Historic District** has been renovated to show the buildings of early Rochester businesses. It's worth a walking tour and includes a laser and light show and interpretive center. The University of Rochester houses the superb **Memorial Art Gallery** with art from 50 centuries. Also on the campus is the **Eastman School of Music** — one of the best in the U.S. In addition to all of this, there is excellent fishing on Lake Ontario, hiking, bicycling, boat trips, wineries to visit, wildlife refuges, shopping, and skiing in winter.

The Portico Bed & Breakfast

3741 Lake Road, Brockport, NY 14420. (716)637-0220.

$55.

Call anytime, but well in advance of visit.
- No cr. cds.
- Innkeepers: Anne & Ronn Klein.
- *3 rms, 2 sb.*
- Full breakfast, including juice or fruit, pastry, hot entrees, cereals and beverage. A full Victorian breakfast is served on fine china, crystal and silver from 5 to 11 AM.
- No pets, no children under 12.
- 1 mile from Brockport.

This 1850 Greek Revival house is a historic landmark. Your hosts promise you'll find soft music, antiques, relaxation. They provide aroma therapy, to help you relax, thick terry robes, for your comfort. There are three fireplaces, a cupola and a blend of antiques and fun furnishings. Ann and Ronn enjoy cooking, travel, antiquing, reading and people.

For dining, visit the Four Cats Cafe & Bakery, the Dockside Cafe, on the Erie Canal, Tillman's Historic Village Inn or Brown's Berry Patch.

When you visit play games: horse shoes, croquet, indoor Dutch shuffleboard, other games and videos. Take a historic walking tour of nearby homes, soak in an oversized pewter claw-foot tub filled with floral or herbal bath salts, curl up in a cozy chair to read by one of the three fireplaces, picnic in the yard or talk to other guests.

● **Woods Edge Bed & Breakfast**
151 Bluhm Road, Fairport, NY 14450. (716)223-8877.

$50-60/D. $75-90/guest house. Discount to travel agent.

Call 8 AM to 6 PM.
•No cr. cds.
•Innkeepers: Betty & Bill Kinsman.
•2 rms, 1 guest house, 3 pb.
•Full breakfast of juice, fruit salad, muffins, Dutch pancake, beverage, served on screened porch in nice weather.
•No pets, no smoking.
•20 minutes from downtown Rochester.

This secluded country hideaway is nestled in a pine woods. The country theme is carried out with country pine and barn beams, contrasting with the white walls of the house. Bill is a college professor, teaching mechanical engineering. Betty enjoys making stone mosaic pictures and hooking rugs; Bill likes to woodwork. They both enjoy travel.

For dining, try Rundi's Periwinkle Pub and ask Betty and Bill to tell you about some of the 8 other restaurants within two miles of the B&B.

When you visit take a walk in the woods, see the wildlife and enjoy the woodland. Or, sit on the screened porch and enjoy the birds, deer and raccoons that come into the yard.

Muffins Croque Monsieur

From Catherine Fisher-Motheu, **The Beal House Inn**
Littleton, NH

2 cups flour
2 1/2 teaspoons baking powder
1/2 teaspoon salt
2/3 cup Vermont cheddar cheese
2/3 cup diced Canadian bacon or baked ham
paprika
1 egg, well beaten
1 cup milk
1/4 cup butter, melted

Mix together flour, baking powder and salt. Then add cheese and ham. Mix evenly. Mix egg, milk and butter in a small bowl. Add liquid mixture to the dry and stir only until moistened. Do not overmix. Spoon into well-greased muffin tins, filling 2/3 full. Sprinkle paprika over the top of each muffin and bake at 400F., 20-25 minutes. Makes 12 muffins

Rome and Vernon

You'll want to see as much as possible of this area. It offers many small pleasures and is very convenient to the Adirondacks, the Mohawk Valley, the Catskills and the Inland Waterway system of canals and lakes.

Explore **Fort Stanwix National Monument**, where costumed guides interpret military life in the 1800s; the **Erie Canal Village**, a restoration of an 1840 community; and visit **Griffiss Air Force Base**, the home of the Strategic Air Command. Francis Bellamy, author of the "Pledge of Allegiance to the Flag" is buried in the Rome cemetery.

Just a short drive away is **Adirondack Park** with over 6 million acres of mountains, cliffs, meadows, plains, swamplands, lakes, ponds, brooks and streams. Much of the park is wilderness but the scenery is extraordinary and the recreation possibilities are almost limitless.

You might attend **Vernon Downs Harness Racing** events, or enjoy the **stock car races** at the speedway. There are also many Revolutionary/Colonial historical sites, old cemetery visits, picturesque villages, brewery tours and the **Harden Furniture** tour.

Shoppers will certainly want to visit the **Oneida silver outlet**, the china outlet, the pewter, antique and craft shops. If you like outdoor recreation there are numerous state parks for hiking, walking, swimming, boating and fishing. At various times throughout the year there are many special events.

A fabulous area and so many things to do that you won't know where to start.

● **Maplecrest Bed & Breakfast**
6480 Williams Road Rome NY 13440. (315)337-0070.

$40-55. Discounts for families, travel agents and long-term stays.

Call anytime.
•No cr. crds.
•**Innkeeper: Diane Saladino.**
•*3 rms, 1 pb, 1 sb.*
•Full breakfast served in the dining room, on the deck overlooking the garden. Menu includes fruit or juice, bacon or sausage, eggs or egg dish, pancakes, muffins, beverage.
•No pets, no smoking, no children under 2 years.
•3 miles from Rome and 3 miles from Griffis Air Force Base.

A modern split-level ranch home with a king size room, double room and single room.

For dining, you'll find a variety of restaurants. Your host will be happy to help you select an establishment that fits your tastes.

When you visit you'll enjoy watching TV or a movie on the VCR in the comfortable family room. You'll want to relax on the deck, and if you wish, you're welcome to use the grill for cooking.

● **Wright Settlement Bed & Breakfast**
Wright Settlement Lane, RR 7, Box 204, Rome, NY 13440. (315)337-2417.

$40-60.

Call evenings.
• No cr. crds.
• Innkeepers: Steve Wright.
• 3 rms. 1 sb.
• Continental breakfast or full breakfast from an interesting menu, presented at your choice of sites.
• In Rome.

A 130-year-old, brick Victorian farmstead on 55 acres of land which has been owned and used by the Wright family since 1789. Lt. Ebenezer Wright walked with his family from Connecticut and founded the Wright Settlement. Steve is especially interested in history, antiques, gardening and travel.

For dining, delectable options include Savoy Restaurant, Beeches and the Unwind Inn in Rome; the Hulbert House, in Boonville, and the Horned Dorset, in Leonardsville.

When you visit you'll find on the spacious 50 acres, an in-ground pool, gardens, trees, a hiking and cross-country ski trail. New additions to the family are five playful Angora goats. They'd love to meet you and have you pet them. As you stroll the paths of the acreage, if you move quietly, you'll probably spy many varieties of birds and some deer, as well. There are quiet corners and porches with rocking chairs beckoning for reading or writing.

● Lavender Inn B & B
RD 1, Box 325, Vernon, NY 13476. (315)829-2440.

$55-65. Discount to senior citizens.

Call after 4 PM.
- AE.
- Innkeepers: Rose Degni, Lyn Doring.
- *3 rms,3 pb.*
- Full breakfast served family style in the guest dining room and featuring granola, meat entree, main dish, fresh baked pastry, fruit or juice and beverage.
- No pets.
- On SR 5.

This refurbished 1799 Federal farm house has 2 working fireplaces and sits on 5 acres filled with perennial flower gardens. Your hosts enjoy weaving, quilting, woodworking, gardening, floral arranging, flower drying and cooking.

For dining, it is possible to have meals at the inn, if you make advance reservations. There are many other excellent, reasonably priced restaurants and some superb gourmet dining. Among our recommendations are: Town & Country Restaurant, Jeremiah's Squat & Gobble, Top 'O the Hill or Captain John's.

When you visit the inn is ideal for relaxing in a secluded rural setting with its beautiful gardens, and green lawns. Take a walk around the property, enjoy the country air. Enjoy the TV and the VCR in the parlor, if you must be reminded of the present day. If you want to carry it farther, you'll have meeting room facilities and a computer available. Come for a craft study weekend.

North Carolina

Asheville area: Mars Hill, Black Mountain

You'll want to visit the **Biltmore Estate**, on US 25, a 250-room French Renaissance-style chateau, surrounded by 35 acres of gardens and a winery producing champagnes, white, rose' and red wines. You'll also want to see the childhood home of **Thomas Wolfe**, 48 Spruce St., and the birthplace of **Zebulon B. Vance**, US 19/23, a reconstructed log home with six farm buildings.

Asheville is the site of scenic **Chimney Rock Park**, nature and wildlife centers. Nearby is the extraordinary **Blue Ridge Parkway**, **Craggy Gardens** and **Mount Mitchell State Park** with unbelievable scenery. This is a wonderful spot for hiking and walking. The quality of the folk art that's exhibited and/or offered for sale is exceptional. And, if you like to shop there is some fine discount shopping as well.

Mars Hill is in Madison County. The **Appalachian Trail**, with clearly marked access points, goes through the county and the mountains ring Mars Hill. After the mountains, the attractions include waterfalls, fishing, golf courses, and craft fairs. There are opportunities to view clogging and hear mountain music.

Black Mountain has a golf course, hiking trails, fishing opportunities, antique shops and craft shops. It is just a few miles off of the Blue Ridge Parkway.

● **Bed & Breakfast Over Yonder**
433 North Fork Rd., Black Mountain, NC 28711. (704)669-6762.

$45-60. OPEN MAY - OCT.

Call 10 AM - 4 PM.
- No cr. cds.
- **Innkeeper: Wilhelmina K. Headley.**
- 5 rms, 5 pb.
- Full breakfast of fresh seasonal fruit, juice, homemade bread or muffins, beverage, and entree of eggs, waffles, pancakes or mountain trout served on the deck overlooking gardens and mountains.
- No pets, restricted smoking, children restricted to cottage.
- 2 mi. N of Black Mountain.

This 1920's American Craftsman House is situated on 18 acres of private property, with superb mountain views. The property has terraced wild flower gardens, a little spring and a gazebo for comfortable reading.

For dining, you will enjoy Pepper's Sandwich Shop, in Black Mountain, the Biltmore House Deer Park Inn, the dining rooms at the Grove Park Inn, Page 23 or The Greenery, in Asheville.

When you visit you'll be thrilled to have a whole mountainside of your own. This quiet, peaceful spot is wonderful for relaxing, hiking, climbing or catching some mountain sunlight.

Baird House Ltd.
P.O. Box 749, 41 S. Main St., Mars Hill, NC 28754.
(704)689-5722.

$42-53. Allowed rate to NC state employees.

Call 8 AM - 10 AM. Answering machine at any time.
- AE.
- Innkeeper: Mrs. Yvette Kalfayen Wessel.
- 5 rms, 2 pb, 1 1/2 sb.
- Full breakfast of orange juice, homemade granola with bananas or puddings, homemade quick breads, beverage. When possible breakfast is served at 8:30 AM in the dining room.
- No pets, no smoking.
- 18 mi. N. of Asheville.

This 1905 two-story brick house was built for a beloved doctor by his grateful patients. It is furnished in beautiful antiques and oriental rugs. Your host is a history buff, volunteer and traveler.

For dining, you'll enjoy tasty but affordable food at Papa Nick's Italian Restaurant, Weaverville Milling Company, or the 4 Cent Cotton Cafe.

When you visit you'll want to browse through the library of 1,000 books and a wide range of magazines. The marble patio, at the back of the house, is equipped with wrought iron furniture and bordered by a perennial garden. The large front porch has many rockers for comfortable sitting. The narrow second story porch overlooks the patio. Guests like to play cards or Scrabble in the dining room or to sit and talk in the living room. The inn makes a marvelous home base for exploration of an interesting Appalachian county.

White Mountain Crepes

From Michael Yarnell, **Wilderness Inn Bed & Breakfast**
North Woodstock, NH

1 cup flour
1 1/2 cups milk
3 eggs
4 tablespoons melted butter
1 teaspoon sugar
1/2 teaspoon cinnamon
Applesauce with cinnamon
(homemade is best)
sour cream
chopped walnuts

Mix flour, sugar and cinnamon. Add milk gradually to flour mixture, mixing with a whisk until the consistency of heavy cream. Heat an 8 inch omelette pan and melt butter. Add 3 eggs to the batter and mix well. Then add melted butter and mix again. Wipe the pan of excess butter, heat and add about 1/4 cup of batter in pan, swirling until batter covers bottom of pan. Cook until edges begin to brown. Flip crepe and cook 10-20 seconds more on uncooked side. Slide out onto a plate and repeat the process. If you stack one crepe on another, slip a sheet of waxed paper between crepes. Heat applesauce. Spread 1 tablespoon on each crepe, add 1 tablespoon sour cream and sprinkle on some walnuts. Then roll up crepe and sprinkle with powdered sugar. Serve.

Boone

You'll want to see the outdoor historical drama, **Horn in the West**, that portrays the struggles of Daniel Boone and his men during the Revolutionary War, at the Daniel Boone Theater, E of US 421. **Daniel Boone Native Gardens**, adjacent to the theater, displays native plants. **Appalachian State University** has summer concerts and art exhibits throughout the year. The famous **Blue Ridge Parkway** is just a few miles away.

Nearby is **Blowing Rock**. The town got its name from an area 2 mi. south of town on US 321. In this area, wind currents will send light objects thrown over a cliff back to the sender. It is also said to be the only spot in the world where snow falls up instead of down.

A "must" when visiting this area is the **Tweetsie Railroad**, north on US 321. Passengers on this narrow gauge steam train may experience mock robberies and attacks during their train ride. There is a railroad town with 1880s buildings and frequent music and craft shows. A chairlift will take visitors to a mining town where children can pan for gold, pet animals or ride their own small train.

Also on US 321 is **Mystery Hill** and the **Appalachian Heritage Museum**. The museum has antique artifacts and demonstrations of mountain crafts. The Old Mystery House has puzzling optical illusions that appear unexplainable. **Blowing Rock Stables** offers guided trail rides through **Moses Cone Park**. Cone Park has hiking trails; **Price Park** offers boating and picnicking.

You'll want to explore the region to find all the things we forgot to tell you about. Have fun!

● **Grandma Jean's Bed & Breakfast**
209 Meadowview Dr., Boone, NC 28607. (704)262-3670.

$45-55. OPEN APR. - NOV.

Call before 10 AM or after 7 PM.
- V, MC.
- **Innkeeper: Dr. Jean Probinsky.**
- 4 *rms*, 2 *sb*.
- Expanded continental breakfast with fresh seasonal fruit or juice, homemade preserves, homemade breads and muffins, and beverage. Breakfast may be served in your room or in the family dining room.
- No children under 6.
- 2 blocks from the center of town.

This 1920s two-story renovated country home is within a few minutes of most attractions. Grandma likes to make her guests feel comfortable. She speaks Spanish and has traveled extensively.

For dining, you'll find great Southwestern and Mexican food at the Tumbleweed Grille and wonderful seafood at the Speckled Trout.

When you visit Grandma wants you to "relax, relax, relax." One of her favorite activities is sitting around the breakfast table visiting with guests from all over the world.

Clinton

You'll want to wander through town and see the many lovely old homes; play golf at the country club; play tennis on some of the public tennis courts. Just 25 miles away is **Bentonville Battleground State Historic Site**. To reach the Civil War battlefield, take US 701 past Newton Grove, toward Smithfield, then turn 2 1/2 mi. E. One of the last engagements of the Civil War was fought here. On the grounds are the **Harper House**, used as a hospital during the war, battle trenches, history trail, cemetery, and visitor center with exhibits and slide presentation. This area is well known for its produce market — the largest market on the eastern coast is just 12 miles away — and for its tobacco markets. In September through December, the rapid chants of the tobacco auctioneer draw many visitors as well as buyers to the markets.

Just west on SR 24 is Kenansville, with many restored old homes and churches. Open to visitors and worth seeing is **Liberty Hall**, built in the 1800s. Most of the furnishings are original and the wallpaper, upholstery and drapery were recreated, to look like the originals, from historical documents. **Cowan Museum** is in a restored Greek-Revival home and contains more than 2,000 items dating from the 13th Century.

The state capitol of Raleigh is only 60 miles from Clinton. Among the top attractions are a self guided tour of the executive mansion, state capitol, the legislative building and the Victorian neighborhood of Oakwood. Maps are available in the **Andrews-London House**, 301 N. Blount St. Other interesting spots to visit are the **North Carolina Museum of Art**, 2110 Blue Ridge Blvd., with eight major collections of paintings, and the **North Carolina Museum of History**, 109 E. Jones St., covering state history from the Roanoke colonies through the present day. The **North Carolina State University Arboretum**, on Beryl St, near US 1/64 beltline, has more than 5,000 different plants from around the world. Whether you visit Raleigh or stay in Clinton and surroundings areas, you're sure to find many things to see and do during your stay.

● **The Courthouse Inn**
*226 McCoy St., Clinton, NC 28328.
(919)592-3933.*

$45-60. Discount for senior citizens or for business people visiting local plants.

Call anytime.
•V, MC.
•**Innkeepers: Juanita G. McLamb, Glenn McLamb, Anita Green.**
•*8 rms, 8 pb. Wheelchair accessible.*
•Continental self-serve breakfast of juice or fresh fruit, sweet roll, assorted cereals, milk, coffee or tea. Visitors with special diets should talk to the innkeeper when making reservations.
•No pets.
•2 blks from Courthouse Square.

This Greek Revival House, built in 1818 was originally the Sampson County Court House. After 86 years as the official building, it was turned into a private residence. In 1991 it was purchased by the owners of The Shield House and totally renovated as a bed and breakfast inn.

For dining, you'll enjoy the Sandpiper for seafood, Josef's for relaxed dining by the meadow, or Country Squire for English decor and steaks.

When you visit you'll have direct dial phones and cable TV in your air conditioned room. Every room has a private bath. Read a book in the sitting area at the top of the stairs or relax on
one of the porches.

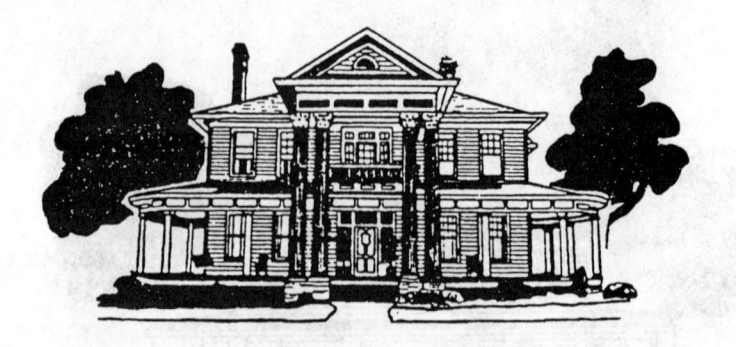

● **The Shield House**
216 Sampson St., Clinton, NC 28328. (919)592-2634. Toll-free reservations (no information) at (800)462-9817.

$45-75. Discount for senior citizens or for business people visiting local plants.

Call anytime.
- V, MC, AE.
- Innkeepers: Anita Green, Juanita G. McLamb, Glenn McLamb.
- 6 rms, 6 pb. Some wheelchair accessibility.
- Continental self-serve breakfast of juice or fresh fruit, sweet roll, assorted cereals, milk, coffee or tea. Visitors with special diets should talk to the innkeeper when making reservations.
- No pets.
- 1 1/2 blks from Courthouse Square.

This **two-story classic revival style house** was built in 1916 and was considered one of the most lavishly decorated homes in the county. Your hosts are antique collectors and have filled the house with authentic period furniture. Anita and Juanita are twins who were formerly registered nurses, now retired from health care. They enjoy reading and their antique collection.

For dining, you'll enjoy the Sandpiper for seafood, Josef's for relaxed dining by the meadow, or Country Squire for English decor and steaks.

When you visit you'll relax on secluded decks and birdwatch or see the squirrels playing in the huge pecan tree. The second floor balcony is wonderful for catching cool breezes, watching the sun set and the moon rise over the church next door. Read a book in the comfortable lounge or visit with a friend in the elegant parlor. Each room has a private bath, cable TV, phone and air conditioning.

Blue Corn Ham Crepes

From Linda Lundeen, **Inn of the Arts**
Las Cruces, NM

1 cup flour	1 teaspoon pepper
1 cup blue cornmeal	1 teaspoon garlic, finely chopped
4 eggs slightly beaten	1 teaspoon ground cumin
1/2 teaspoon salt	1 tablespoon Dijon mustard
1/3 cup melted butter	1/4 cup flour
1 cup water	2 cups skim milk
1 cup milk	1 1/2 cups diced green chile (serve on side if you prefer mild food)
3 cups cooked, diced ham seasoned with your favorite seasoning	Sour cream and cilantro
2 cups mild Monterey Jack cheese, shredded	

Make crepes as follows: Mix liquid ingredients. Stir in salt, flour and cornmeal. Let sit for 2 hours or more in the refrigerator. Heat small 5 to 6 inch skillet, over medium-high heat. Butter lightly. Pour in 2-3 tablespoons batter, quickly rotating pan to spread batter evenly over bottom of pan. Cook over medium heat to brown lightly about 1 minute on each side. Slide onto plate. Stack with 2 sheets of wax paper between each crepe. Can be refrigerated up to 2 days or frozen up to 2 weeks.

To make sauce: Saute chile, with pepper, garlic, cumin and mustard. Or if served with chile on side, cook chile alone. Then saute pepper, garlic, cumin and mustard. Stir in flour and add 1/2 cup of milk at a time until sauce is right consistency.

Assemble crepes: Fill crepes with ham and Monterey Jack cheese. Roll them up, place in pan, seam side down. Spoon the sauce over the crepes. Place in a moderate oven (350F) for 10 minutes to melt the cheese. Top each serving with a spoon of sour cream. Garnish with cilantro.

Glenville

You'll want to enjoy the beauty of the mountains, the clean, fresh air and the clear mountain streams. Drive north from Glenville on SR 107 to Cullowhee. Then continue 3 1/2 miles south on SR 107, then 3 miles east on Caney Fork Rd. to **Judaculla Rock**. The soapstone boulder is covered with Indian pictographs. Also at Cullowhee is **Mountain Heritage Center**, on SR 107, in the H.F.Robinson Administration Bldg. It chronicles the migration of the Scotch-Irish in opening the frontier.

On another day, drive south on SR 107 to Cashiers. **Whitewater Falls Scenic Area**, is an exceptionally beautiful spot. Go south on SR 107 into SC, then north on SR 413 and 171 back into NC. The Whitewater River drops more than 400 ft. in a series of falls and cascades. On the same trip or another expedition, from Cashiers drive west on US 64 to its junction with SR 28 and the Village of Highlands. The **Cullasaja River Gorge** is an exceptionally deep canyon. Drive west toward Franklin along US 64 and SR 28. There are spectacular views of five waterfalls.

At Franklin pan for rubies at the **Cowee Ruby Mines**, 5 miles north on SR 28. Gems found at the mine have ranged from chips to 206 carats. This area is also a wonderful place to see mountain flowers. **Horseshoe Bend**, 20 miles north on SR 28 along the Little Tennessee River is a beautiful place from which to see the countryside and it is often covered with flowers. **Standing Indian Mountain**, is 12 miles west on US 64 then 2 miles east on US 64 and 2 miles south on FR 67. In the Nantahala National Forest, it is noted for purple rhododendron and fine views. **Wayah Bald**, at over 5,000 ft. has a wonderful display of flowers in May and June. From the John B. Byrne Memorial Tower can see four adjoining states. From Glenville go south on SR 107, then east on US 64 to Brevard. At the entrance to the Pisgah National Forest, the area surrounding Brevard is filled with waterfalls, plants, trees and wildlife. After a day of enjoying nature, stay to enjoy the concerts presented at the **Brevard Music Center** every night late June through mid-August.

● Mountain High
200 Big Ridge Rd., Glenville, NC 28736. (704)743-3094.

$45. OPEN JULY TO OCTOBER.

Call any time.
- No cr. cds.
- **Innkeepers: Mr. & Mrs. George M. Carter.**
- *2 rms, 2 pb.*
- Full breakfast. A sample breakfast might include a choice of two fruits, fried apples and waffles, cereal and beverage.
- No pets, no smoking, no children under 12.
- On a mountain side, five miles from town.

Situated at 4,200 ft. above sea level, the house is built into the side of a mountain. You'll have your own spring water and a private lake. There are no houses nearby.

For dining, you'll find exceptional food at Hildeard's Bavarian Restaurant, Cornucopia, Leah's, The Frog and the Owl or Dillard House.

When you visit enjoy the privacy of your own mountain cottage. You'll find many books to read and your own private swimming area. Perhaps you'd like to pack a picnic lunch to eat at the top of your own mountain.

Hertford

You'll want to take time to visit the **Newbold-White House**, thought to be the oldest house in North Carolina. It has been restored by hand and furnished with 17th century furnishings.

Take the **Hertford historical tour** to see other historical buildings. The **Perquimans River** is a good place for fishing. This town is very close to Albemarle Sound so you'll be able to indulge in a variety of water oriented recreation. Nearby **Edenton** is one of the oldest communities in the state. A map of a self-guided walking tour of the area can be obtained at the **Barker House Visitor Center**, on S. Broad St. Guided walking tours also depart from the center. There are several exceptional examples of period architecture.

Elizabeth City is located at the Narrows of the Pasquotank River, just inland from Albemarle Sound. Because a canal connected the Pasquotank with the Elizabeth River, in Virginia, Elizabeth City became a busy port in the 1800s. A walking tour map to historic homes and buildings is available from the Chamber of Commerce, 502 E. Ehringhaus St. The **Museum of the Albemarle**, on US 17, displays artifacts connected with the history of the region. This area might also be used as a central point from which to drive to **Fort Raleigh National Historic Site**, on Roanoke Island, home of the ill-fated "lost colony."

Or, one might drive to **Historic Halifax State Historic Site**, a town filled with houses and buildings dating from the 1700s. And, it's just 65 miles to the **Outerbank Beaches**.

● **Gingerbread Inn**
103 S. Church St., Hertford, NC 27944. (919)426-5809.

$35/S; $45/D.

Call 9 AM to 8 PM.
•V, MC.
•Innkeeper: Jenny & Hans Harnisch.
•*3 rms, 3 pb.*
•Full breakfast of fresh fruit, juice, eggs and bacon or sausage or pancakes, toast and beverage.
•No pets, no smoking.
•On Business US 17, S of Elizabeth City.

This restored Colonial Revival Style home, circa 1904, is included on the Hertford Historical Tour. The rooms are spacious and comfortable. The home is air conditioned and has a wrap around porch for summer comfort.

For dining, be sure to seek out Anglers Cove, in Bethel, for seafood.

When your visit relax and be comfortable. You're welcome to watch cable TV, but it's going to be hard to resist the wonderful smells coming from the bakery, especially when you are handed your own famous gingerbread boy souvenir as you leave.

Salisbury

You'll want to visit the historic sites in this city, once the largest metropolitan area in North Carolina.

During the Civil War, many Yankee prisoners were housed here and you can still visit the old prison site. An audio tape for a driving tour of the **Confederate Prison** site is available from the Rowan Library, at 201 W. Fisher St. There are many significant historic homes. Maps are available at the Rowan County Visitor Center, in the restored Salisbury Depot. Especially note the **Dr. Josephus Hall House**, 226 S. Jackson. This large antebellum house has many of its original furnishings. The **Old Stone House**, southeast on US 52, built in 1766 of granite, is one of the oldest in the state. The **Grimes Mill**, 600 N. Church St., once a commercial mill, built in 1886, houses original intact machinery. The **Spencer Transportation Museum**, northeast on I-85, is housed in an old railway repair shop and has a visitor center, railroad yards and shops. The equipment includes engines, private cars, freight cars, trolleys and coaches; you may purchase rides on some of the trains; there is a visitor center and exhibits. There are public golf courses and tennis courts, walking trails in **Hurley Park**, a nature center, volleyball, horseshoe pits, tennis and miniature golf in **Nicholas Park**.

Southwest of Salisbury, is the town of Kannapolis, founded late in the 19th century around the Cannon Textile Mills. **Cannon Village** is filled with the original, reconstructed or renovated buildings. There is a visitor center that serves as a beginning for a guided tour of the present day **Fieldcrest Cannon manufacturing plants**. The buildings also house a number of factory outlets for major manufacturers.

If you should have any additional time or energy, this area is less than an hour's drive from Charlotte, Greensboro and Winston-Salem where, of course, there are many more things to see and do.

● The 1868 Stewart-Marsh House

220 S. Ellis St., Salisbury, NC 28144. (704)633-6841.

$40-50/S; $50-55/D. Discount for stay of 3 days or longer and to travel agent.

Call 8AM - 10 AM or 7 PM - 10 PM.
- V, MC.
- Innkeepers: Gerry & Chuck Webster.
- *2 rms, 2 pb.*
- Expanded continental breakfast. A sample menu might include baked pineapple with pecans, country grits & sausage casserole, poppy seed bread and cowboy coffee cake. Your breakfast will be served on china and crystal in the dining room.
- No pets, no smoking, children at innkeeper's discretion.
- 4 blocks from the center of town. 1.5 mi. from I-85.

This restored federal style home, was built in 1868. It is on a quiet, tree lined street in the West Square Historic District, of Salisbury. Furnished in antiques, the rooms are comfortable and air-conditioned. One of the guest rooms has a penciled note on the window frame from 1888. The home has been featured on Historic Homes tours.

For dining, we think you'd like the Four Seasons Chinese restaurant, Las Palmas, Miss Lucy's or Sweet Meadows.

When you visit Gerry is an artist who paints in oil and watercolor. Chuck is a wood worker and a history buff, especially interested in the Civil War. They are active in the Historic Foundation and provide personalized walking tours of the historic district, acting as your guide. They invite you to enjoy the history books in their library, to listen to the inn's personal mockingbird and watch the squirrels play.

Ohio

Akron

You'll want to sample the best of Akron while you're here.

This is a city of eclectic charm, with something of interest to almost everyone. For the lover of big old houses and gardens, there is the **Perkins Mansion**, Copley Rd. and S. Portage Path, **Hower House**, on Fir Hill from E. Market St, at the edge of the University of Akron campus, and the outstanding **Stan Hywet Hall and Gardens**, 714 N. Portage Path. Art lovers will want to visit the **Akron Art Museum**, 70 E. Market St., to see works of regional, national and international art. Music lovers will want to attend a performance at the summer home of the Cleveland Orchestra, in the wooded pavilion at **Blossom Music Center**, NW on Steel Corner Rd. The **Akron Zoological Park**, 500 Edgewood Ave., is for you if you like to see wild animals; and if you like outdoor recreation you're sure to find something in the Akron metropolitan parks. Of exceptional interest is **Quaker Square**, 120 E. Mill St., the refurbished Quaker Oats factories, now a combination of museum-like displays, restaurants and shops; and **Goodyear World of Rubber**, 1201 E. Market St., with exhibits showing the history of rubber, including a rubber plantation replica, and a reproduction of Charles Goodyear's workshop.

If you have time, drive northwest of the city limits to Bath, to visit the **Hale Farm and Village**, where crafts people demonstrate daily life in a small village and a farm in the 1800s, Jun. through Oct. There are performing arts and sports and many more attractions than we have space to mention.

● **Portage House**
*601 Copley Rd., Akron, OH 44320.
(216)535-1952.*

$30/S; $35/D. Discount for stays of 2 or more nights.

Call 8 AM to 11 PM.
- No cr. crds.
- **Innkeeper: Jeanne Pinnick.**
- *5 rms, 1 pb, 2 sb.*
- Full breakfast, featuring juice, bacon, toasted homemade bread, beverage and entree of eggs, strata, pancakes, French toast, hot or cold cereal.
- No smoking.
- Near downtown, in the historic district.

This large tudor-style home was built in 1917 on a half-acre of land, originally a part of the farm of the Perkins family, founders of Akron. Your host uses the third floor and leaves five second-floor bedrooms and two baths for guests.

For dining, you'll have a wide array of choices, including: The Depot, Taverne in the Square and Schumacher's, all at Quaker Square. Other excellent food is offered at The Diamond Grill, the Bangkok Buffet, the Hibachi Inn, Carnaby Street Inn and Lou and Hy's.

When your visit you'll find you're in a historic, park-like area. The original Perkins Mansion and the John Brown Home are at the corner of the block and open for daily tours. Guests like the spacious living room for lounging, reading, listening to the stereo or watching TV. There are a number of things for young children here, with a swing and basketball hoop, puzzles, and a friendly dog named Nike.

Circleville, Chillicothe

You'll want to fall in love with lovely and historic Circleville, a small city that has its own historical museum, a genealogy library, the **Ted Lewis Museum** and several nature preserves. Indian mounds are in the vicinity, and Circleville was originally laid out within a circular mound. It is also host to the annual Pumpkin Show and has many antique shops.

Less than 20 minutes away is Chillicothe, where **Mound City Group National Monument**, 3 miles north on SR 104, preserves 23 ancient burial mounds, on a 13 acre site. There are marked trails, trailside exhibits, an observation deck and a visitor center.

Chillicothe's most famous entertainment is the outdoor drama, **Tecumseh**, presented at the Sugar Loaf Mountain Amphitheater, 6 1/2 mi. NE on Delano Rd, E of SR 159, mid-June to mid-Sept. The historical drama depicts the life of Chief Tecumseh of the Shawnee Nation. **Adena**, on Adena Rd., W of SR 104, is a Georgian stone mansion, built in 1806 by Thomas Worthington, governor of Ohio. It is furnished with antiques and surrounded by reconstructed outbuildings. The **Chillicothe Gazette**, 50 W Main St., is the oldest newspaper West of the Alleghenies. The building it occupies is a replica of the first statehouse and wall cases display printed matter since Babylonian times. The **James M. Thomas Museum** exhibits telecommunication equipment chronicling the history of the telephone.

Hocking Hills State Park, between Circleville and Chillicothe and west, off of SRs 374 and 664, covers more than 2,000 acres and is divided into six areas. The most popular is the **Old Man's Cave**, with one large cave, smaller caves, waterfalls and gorges. Each of the other areas feature natural rock formations, cliffs, trails, rare plants and have picnic areas.

● Castle Inn
610 S. Court St., Circleville, OH 43113. (614)477-3986/ (800)477-1541.

$45-85/D. Sr citizen and midweek discount.

Call 9 AM - 9 PM.
- V, MC.
- Innkeepers: Jim & Sue Maxwell.
- *6 rms, 4 pb, 1 sb.*
- Full elegant breakfast, served buffet style, in ornate dining room overlooking the Shakespeare Garden. A weekend buffet might include breakfast pizza, Royal Hash, Castle Quiche, fresh fruits, homemade cinnamon rolls, muffins, and beverage.
- No pets, no children under 8, no smoking inside.
- On the "Street of Old Mansions," near downtown Circleville.

This **16-room mansion**, built in 1900, features castle-like architectural details such as towers, battlements, arches and flying buttresses. An outstanding feature is the stained glass window on the stairway landing depicting "The Four Seasons." The Maxwells have restored the walled garden into a popular Victorian Shakespeare Garden.

For dining, the food is excellent at J.R. Hooks or Alexander's Deli, in Circleville; at Shaws, in Lancester; or at Fox Farm Inn or Harvester, in Chillicothe.

When you visit you will like the large rooms, decorated in Victorian antiques. Be sure to see the Shakespeare Garden, very popular in the Victorian era, which uses only flowers and herbs mentioned in Shakespeare's plays. Enjoy the collection of "Castle" toys, games and books. And, have your photo taken with the suit of armor.

● The Old McDill-Anderson Place

3656 Polk Hollow Rd., Chillicothe, OH 45601. (614)774-1770.

$50-65. Discounts for longer stays, and off-season. Readers of this book are guaranteed a price of $55 or less if the book is mentioned when making advance reservations.

Call 8 AM - 10 PM.
- No cr. crds.
- Innkeepers: The Meyers, Del, Ruth and Anne.
- *5 rms, 2 pb, 2 sb.*
- Full breakfast featuring fresh squeezed juice, fruit, homemade breads made with Ohio Grist Mill flour, entree featuring eggs, sausage or meat, and beverage.
- No pets, no smoking.
- 3 miles from center of Chillicothe.

This 19th Century brick pioneer farmhouse is decorated with period furniture. Each guest room has a rocking chair. Some have hypo-allergenic featherbeds and a woodstove or fireplace. There is a choice of central air conditioning or window fans. Your hosts are interested in historic preservation, architecture antiques, blacksmithing, woodworking, 18th and 19th Century

For dining, you may want to make reservations for an open-hearth meal or a pre-20th Century meal at the Old McDill-Anderson Place. The Fox Farm Inn also is excellent.

When you visit make reservations to attend one of the winter workshops in 18th and 19th Century open-hearth and woodstove cookery, period crafts or historic house renovation. Enjoy strolling through the two acres of property, read books or magazines from the inn's library, or, enjoy the rocking chair in the screened porch.

Elaine's Cozy Cottage Cobbler

From Elaine N. Samuels, **Cozy Cottage**
Skaneateles, NY

6 apples, peeled and sliced
3/4 cup sugar
1 teaspoon cinnamon
1 1/2 cups baking mix (Jiffy or Bisquick)
1/2 cup milk
1/2 cup raisins
1/2 cup chopped walnuts
1 egg
3 tablespoons melted margarine or butter

Heat oven to 400F. Grease a 1 or 1-1/2 quart baking dish. Mix apples, raisins, sugar, cinnamon, nuts and pour into baking dish. Mix remaining ingredients until blended and spoon over the fruit. Bake 15 minutes at 400F, then reduce heat to 350F. and bake 10 minutes or until batter is golden brown and a toothpick inserted in the center comes out clean.

Serve warm. For breakfast serve with cream. For a snack or dessert serve with whipped cream, whipped topping or vanilla ice cream.

When you eat this cobbler at Cozy Cottage, the apples usually come from the orchard on the property.

Old Washington

You'll want to go to see the **National Road-Zane Grey Museum** while you're here. Between Cambridge and Zaneville on US 22/40, it celebrates both a road and an author. The National Road was the nation's first highway from Cumberland, MD, to Vandalia, IL, and Zane Grey was, of course, the well-known author of westerns.

Visit Cambridge, famous for its glass making, see the **Glass Museum**, 812 Jefferson Ave., or **Degenhart Paperweight and Glass Museum**, Highland Hills Rd., at junction of US 22 & I-77, and then inspect a glass factory. **Boyd Crystal Art Glass**, 1203 Morton Ave., or **Mosser Glass**, US 22 E. offer tours. Spend time in **Salt Fork State Park**, 9 mi. NE on US 20, for swimming, fishing, boating, hiking and golf. See **The Living Word**, an outdoor drama, portraying the life of Jesus, at the amphitheater, NW on SR 209.

East of Cambridge on I-70/ US 22/40, is Zanesville, a famed pottery-making center. To learn more about pottery, see the **Ohio Ceramic Center**, 12 mi. S on SR 93, near Roseville, then take a self-guided tour of the nearby **Robinson-Ransbottom Pottery Co.** Enjoy a one-hour cruise on the Muskingum River, in the **Lorena Sternwheeler**. Go over the unique **Y-Bridge**, which divides the city into three parts.

Visit the **Zanesville Art Center**, 620 Military Road. Bird watch at a nature center. Go swimming, fishing or boating on one of the fresh water lakes.

● **Zane Trace B & B**
Box 115, Old Washington, OH 43768. (614)489-5970.

$40-45; $65/Suite OPEN 5/1 - 10/31. Discount to travel agent. Call about 8 PM or leave a message on the machine.
•No cr. crds.
•**Innkeepers: Ruth and Max Wade.**
•4 *rms*, 2 *sb*.
•Continental breakfast of juice, fruit cup, pastries, beverage, served on china, with sterling silver.
•No pets; no children under 12 unless they're good swimmers.
•3/4 mi. from I-70, exit 186, on Old National Road, in village of Old Washington.

This brick Italiante Victorian home was built in 1859. The high ceilings, beautiful woodwork and chandeliers give a feeling of spaciousness. Your hosts enjoy gardening, swimming, antiques.

For dining, there are several excellent restaurants in Cambridge, including the J&K Restaurant, Coney Island and Long Branch.

When you visit you'll want to swim in the heated pool. This is also a wonderful spot for picnicking, suntanning, reading a good book. The antique parlor is a great place to relax in an old fashioned atmosphere, but there's also a card and reading room and a large screened porch overlooking the pool.

Oregon

Myrtle Creek

You'll want to go fishing, if you ever enjoy the pastime. The many rivers in this area are filled with steelhead and salmon. Go rafting on the Umpqua River or take the scenic drive from Roseburg to Diamond Lake, along the river.

The **Umpqua National Forest** is a wonderful spot for outdoor recreation, including hiking, fishing and horseback riding in warm weather, cross-country skiing and snowmobiling in the winter.

It's only a short drive to **Wildlife Safari**, south of Roseburg on I-5, a drive-through zoological park. Here hundreds of wild animals roam free in a natural environment and visitors view them from their autos. Animal programs, train rides and elephant rides are also given. While you are near Roseburg, drive north on I-5 to the **Douglas County Museum** at Exit 123, and then on to Exit 125 and the **Hillcrest Winery**. You may bring a picnic lunch to eat at the vineyard. Tours and wine tasting are available.

South of Myrtle Creek is Grants Pass, a departure point for several raft trips down the Rogue River. Several companies offer a variety of trips: two hour, 1/2 day, full day, two days or three days in length. The **Grants Pass Growers Market**, on First St. between 6th and 7th, is open Tuesdays and Fridays, July through late November. In addition to fruits and vegetables, the market features baked goods, crafts people, artists and musicians. The **Museum of Art**, in Riverside Park, has exhibits of American Art. It is open noon to 4, Tuesday through Saturday.

● **Sonka's Sheep Station Inn**
901 NW Chadwick Lane, Myrtle Creek, OR 97457. (503)863-5168.

$50-60. Discount for extended stay.

Call anytime.
- Innkeepers: Louis & Evelyn Sonka.
- V, MC.
- 5 rms, 3 sb.
- Full ranch breakfast of juice, muffins or coffee cake, fresh fruit, entree of egg casserole, French toast, or waffles, and fresh ground coffee.
- No pets, no smoking inside.
- Five miles to Myrtle Creek.

This **large ranch home** and guest house are on a working sheep ranch. Your hosts are ranchers and enjoy entertaining guests. A quiet country setting provides an opportunity to get away from the city with plenty of interesting activities to observe.

For dining, you'll want to try the steak house or German restaurant in Myrtle Creek. There are several excellent restaurants in Roseburg. Talk to your hosts about your options.

When you visit you can watch ranch activities. These change according to the time of the year but are always busy and interesting. The Border Collies will demonstrate herding the sheep. There are many lawn games available: croquet, volleyball, badminton, horseshoes.... An exciting and different getaway!

Newburg

You'll want to visit a winery and learn about Oregon history when you visit this area. Some of the state's oldest and largest wineries are in the area — at least 20 are within a 20 mile radius of Newberg. Many offer tours and wine tasting.

The **Champoeg State Park**, on the Willamette River, has exhibits on the history and origins of Oregon government. Also on the grounds are an old jail, a pioneer school, the Pioneer Mothers' Memorial Cabin, furnished with pioneer articles, and the Robert Newell House, a replica of an 1852 home, containing other antique artifacts. The **Hoover-Minthorn House** Museum, is the oldest house in Newberg and is where Herbert Hoover spent 5 years as a child. The house has original furnishings and Hoover mementos.

Just 30 minutes away is **Portland**, the largest city in Oregon and another beautiful place to visit. Although there are many things to see and do here, among the top choices would be the **Metro Zoo**, 3 mi. W on US 26. It is noted for its rare and endangered species. **Washington Park**, at the head of Park Place, has International Rose Test Gardens, Japanese Gardens and facilities for a wide variety of outdoor activities.

The **Oregon Museum of Science and Industry**, should have moved to new facilities at 1945 SE Water St., by the time this book is published. It has hands-on exhibits and demonstrations, a planetarium, and an Omnimax Theater. The **Portland Art Museum**, 1219 SW Park, is worth a visit. It has European, Asian and American art and a media arts center. Other superb, entertaining spots to visit in Portland include two sites for the Pendleton Woolen Mills, The Peninsula Rose Garden, the Hoyt Arboretum, Leach Botanical Gardens, Crystal Springs Rhododendron Gardens, the Children's Museum, Pittock Mansion, and boat tours. Visit the Visitors Association, 26 SW Salmon Street, for walking tours and more information about the city.

● **Secluded Bed & Breakfast**
19719 NE Williamson Rd., Newberg, OR 97132. (503)538-2636.

$40-50.

Call 8 AM - 8 PM.
•No cr. crds.
•**Innkeepers: Durell & Del Belanger.**
•*2 rms, 1 pb, 1 sb.*
•Full breakfast, served at a formal table setting with china, crystal and silver. A typical menu might include, Dutch Babies, lean bacon, apples with huckleberries, fresh pears and bananas with peach syrup, whipped cream, maple syrup, juice and coffee.
•No pets, no smoking.
•4 mi. from Newberg and 30 mi. from Portland.

This country home is on 10 wooded acres. Birds, squirrels, deer and other creatures live in the woods. Your hosts are environmentally concerned hobbyists who enjoy flower arranging, gardening, violin making and stained glass window making. Don't be surprised if there are fresh flowers in your room.

For dining, drive 5 minutes to Dundee, where Tin's or Alfie's Wayside Inn are recommended. McMinnville, is 20 minutes away, for Rogers' Seafood or Umberto's Italian Cafe.

When you visit take advantage of the wooded setting for long country walks, hikes or observation of wildlife. Browse through the gardens or find reading material in the library.

Tillamook

You'll want to come to this spot for a getaway if you like water, beaches and all that go with them. Located at the southern end of **Tillamook Bay**, where the Wilson and Trask Rivers converge, this is a popular spot for fresh water and deep sea fishing, crabbing, clamming, beachcombing, sailing, hiking, hang gliding, scuba diving, wind surfing and canoeing.

But, there are other activities to keep you busy. You may travel **Three Capes Road**, making a 38 mile loop to the towns of Oceanside, Netarts, Tierra del Mar, Pacific City, Capes Meares, Cape Lookout and Cape Kiwanda. A shorter loop, of only about 20 miles, follows Bay Ocean Rd. to Cape Meares, S on Loop Rd to Cape Meares State Park, S on Loop Rd through Oceanside and Netarts, NE on Tillamook-Netarts Road to Tillamook. Train lovers will want to take the **Oregon Coastline Express** from the Southern Pacific depot on East Third St. The train takes a scenic trip along the coast, through several towns and past blimp hangers, the world's largest wooden structures. The **Tillamook Cheese Factory**, said to be one of the world's largest, 2 miles N on US 101, has an observation area and audiovisual. The **Pioneer Museum**, Second and Pacific, has a blacksmith shop, mineral room, old steam engine and three floors of exhibits.

This is near winery country and you won't have to travel far to find a winery for touring and tasting. Shoppers will find antique shops, a factory outlet mall and many other interesting shops.

A stay in Tillamook promises to be interesting and fun. You're sure to wish you had more time here.

● **Blue Haven Inn**
3025 Gienger Rd., Tillamook, OR 97141. (503)842-2265.

$50-60.

Call 11 AM - 10 PM.
•No Cr. Cds.
•**Innkeeper: Joy Still.**
•*3 rms, 1 pb, 1 sb.*
•Full Breakfast of sausage, egg souffle, buttermilk biscuits, grits, gravy, homemade jams, juice and coffee.
•2 mi. South of Tillamook.

This country home, built in 1916, is furnished with antiques and collectibles. It is surrounded by tall evergreens and gardens. Your host enjoys cooking, gardening, collecting antiques, miniatures and dolls.

For dining, you may choose to make reservations for a Blue Haven candlelight dinner. Other excellent choices are Roseanna's (in Oceanside) or Hadley House.

When you visit you'll have a full acre of woods, lawn and garden for strolling; an old fashioned porch swing for relaxing; games of croquet and lawn tennis to play; old movies to view on the VCR; birds to watch; and books to read.

Pennsylvania

Clearville

You'll want to find time to visit the nearby historic area of Bedford.

Old Bedford Village, north on US 220, is a reproduction of a colonial village. It contains 40 buildings, many actually built in the period between 1750 and 1850. Crafts are demonstrated and special events are held throughout the year. **Fort Bedford Park and Museum** *has displays of Indian and Colonial artifacts. It also has a large replica of the original fort.*

There are several old and historic buildings throughout the town. Stop at the **Bedford County Courthouse**, *on Juliana St., to see an unusual hanging spiral staircase, dating from 1828.* **Bedford Springs** *are said to have medicinal qualities and it has long been a resort area. Special events include the Great Bedford County Fair, held in August, and the Fall Foliage Festival, held in October. Twelve miles northwest of Bedford on SR 56 is the* **Reynoldsdale Fish Culture Station**. *Here you can see mountain trout in varying stages of development.*

Raystown Lake, *north of Clearville on SR 26, offers swimming, boating, hunting and fishing. If you travel northeast to Breezewood, on US 30, you may want to visit the* **Crawford Wildlife Exhibit**. *About 300 animals are mounted and displayed in natural habitats. In the winter, skiing is great. Shoppers will enjoy outlets, antique stores and the many country auctions.*

● Conifer Ridge Farm
Rt. 2, Box 202A, Clearville, PA 15535. (814)784-3342.

$25/S; $45-50/D. Cabin: $25/day for up to 4.

Call anytime.
- No cr. crds.
- **Innkeepers: Myrtle Haldeman & Dan Haldeman.**
- *2 or 3 rms, 2 pb, 1 sb.*
- A full country breakfast, of home-grown food, is served to guests in the main house. The menu usually includes orange juice, scrambled eggs, sausage, muffins, fruit and coffee.
- Pets and smoking are restricted.
- In Bedford County; 8 mi. from Hwys. 40 & 48; about 10 mi. from Clearville.

This contemporary design passive solar farm home is in a rustic mountain setting on 126 acres of woodland and pasture. Christmas trees and other crops are growing on the property. There is a one-acre pond for swimming, fishing and boating. From your window, you will look out on a mountain and a 100-year-old barn that is still used for farm activities.

For dining, you may want to arrange to have a delicious country gourmet dinner right at Conifer Ridge. Other recommended dining spots include the Coach Room, in Bedford, and Ed's Steak House.

When you visit you'll enjoy going down to the pond, fishing, boating or swimming. There is a rippling stream for wading or catching crayfish. If you're an early riser you'll want to get outside to see the mist rise over the mountain. At dusk you may find a herd of deer grazing at the foot of the mountain. Bird watching is a favorite pastime here. You're welcome to explore the farm fields, the barn or the old cemetery. Enjoy the sunroom, perhaps with a book from the collection available.

Strasburg

You'll want to learn more about the Pennsylvania Dutch, here in the heart of their countryside. This area is noted for the Amish people who live nearby, their wonderful food, arts and crafts.

Be sure to visit a farmers' market and an Amish quilt shop. The **Amish Village**, north on SR 896, has a house and other buildings furnished in typical Amish style and tour guides to explain how the Amish live. The **Strasburg Country Store**, Center Square, is an old restored general store. Strasburg is also a town for railroad buffs. The **Railroad Museum of Pennsylvania**, on SR 741, has restored cars and locomotives dating from the 19th-century to today. The **Strasburg Railroad Co.**, east on SR 741, provides a scenic round trip through "Amish country." The **Choo Choo Barn**, east on SR 741, has 13 operating toy trains, automated figures and vehicles, in a miniature display of the surrounding countryside. The **Toy Train Museum**, on Paradise Lane, has antique and 20th century model trains in five operating layouts. The **Galt Classic Car Exhibit**, north on SR 896, has 50 autos ranging from early to recent models. Several are rare, classic or famous.

Should you have any spare time, plan a trip to Lancaster, just a short drive away. It, too, has Amish and Mennonite model homes and farms, an information center explaining both religions, farmers' markets with wonderful Dutch foods, an amusement park, historic homes, a restored colonial mill village, museums and a winery. Try also the **Landis Valley Museum**, north on Oregon Pike, an 100 acre complex demonstrating the lives of the Pennsylvania Dutch in the 19th-century. Wheatland, 1120 Marietta Ave, is the mansion of President James Buchanan. The **Amish Farm and House**, east on US 30, shows a typical Amish farm in operation. Three farmer's markets are especially enticing: the Bird-in-Hand, on SR 340, the Central, on Penn Square, and the Meadowbrook, on SR 23. Be sure to drive into the country, off the main highways, to see the thriving farms and observe Amish buggies traveling the same routes as modern day autos.

● The Decoy
958 Eisenberger Road, Strasburg, PA 17579. (717)687-8585.

Memorial Day thru 11/30: $50-60. $10 discount off-season.

Call 9:30 AM - 10 PM.
- No cr. crds.
- Innkeepers: Debby & Hap Joy.

- *5 rms, 5 pb.*
- Full breakfast featuring beverage, juice, fruit, entree of eggs and bacon, pancakes, waffles or similar foods.
- No pets, no smoking.
- 4 mi. south of Strasburg in the Amish farmland.

Formerly an Amish home, this B&B is furnished in family antiques. Debbie and Had say they are informal and like to treat guests "like family." Debby is an avid quilter and loves to share information about the best places to shop for fabric and frames.

For dining, you will surely enjoy the Hershey Farm Restaurant or the Iron Horse Inn.

When you visit you'll want to take a walk around the block — that's 2.8 miles at The Decoy. But, you may also loll in the yard, enjoying the spectacular view. Perhaps you'll have a chance to visit with the Amish neighbors.

Wrightsville

You'll want to spend weeks in this lovely area, enjoying historic sites, entertainment and the beautiful countryside.

Just southwest of Wrightsville on US 30 is the historic city of York. It was our nation's capital in 1777 and 1778, during the Revolutionary War. A map of a historic walking tour can be obtained from the Convention and Visitors Bureau, 1 Market Way E. The Golden Plough Tavern, General Gates House and Bobb Log House, 157 W. Market St., are restored 18th century buildings open to the public. The Bonham House, 152 E. Market St., has a museum, a Victorian Parlor, a 20th-century library and a Federal dining room. Other historic buildings of special interest include: a Friends Meeting House, 135 W. Philadelphia St., built in 1766 and still in use; and the York County Colonial Court House, W. Market & Pershing Ave., which has a media presentation and exhibits of colonial artifacts and documents. The Fire Museum of York County, 757 W. Market St., has exhibits of fire fighting equipment from the 19th & 20th centuries. The Bob Hoffman Weightlifting & Softball Hall of Fame, I-83N, Exit 11, has exhibits honoring Olympic weightlifters and softball history. Tour the Harley Davidson Plant at 1425 Eden Rd., Mon-Fri (no children under 12). There are also a number of excellent outlet malls and shopping areas in York.

East of Wrightsville on US 30 is Columbia. Anyone vaguely interested in timepieces will want to visit the **Watch and Clock Museum**, at 5th and Poplar Sts. The museum has more than 9,000 items dating from the 1600s to the present. **Wright's Ferry Mansion**, 2nd and Cherry Sts., is a restored 1738 English stone house. It contains early 18th-century Philadelphia furniture and reflects life in a Pennsylvania Quaker household in the early 1700s.

It's just a short drive north from Wrightsville to Marietta and the **Nissley Vineyards Winery**. You may tour the winery and also watch seasonal activities such as harvesting and bottling. Special events and concerts are held on the lawn of the winery.

PENNSYLVANIA

*Continue northeast from Marietta to Mount Joy. The **Donegal Mills Plantation** is southwest of town on Musser Rd. Costumed guides provide tours of the 100-year old mansion, bake house, mill, garden, wildlife area and nature trail. **Bube's Brewery**, 102 N. Market St., is a 19th-century brewery. Tours are given daily.*

● Roundtop Bed & Breakfast

Box 258, RD 2, Wrightsville, PA 17368. (717)252-3169.
$50-75.

Call anytime. Make reservations 2 to 4 weeks before needed.
- V, MC.
- Innkeepers: Jodi & Tyler Sloan.
- 6 rms, 5 sb, 1 pb.
- Your breakfast will be cooked by your host, a graduate of the Culinary Institute of America. A sample menu would include fresh squeezed orange juice, fruit bowl, herbed hash browns, pineapple banana muffin, spinach and feta omelette, bacon and beverage.
- No pets.
- Only 20 min. from York.

This 100-year-old stone mansion is isolated on 150 acres of woodland. The house has been renovated to take advantage of the view of the spectacular countryside. From the rooftop observatory you can see 20 miles of countryside on a clear day. You'll also be able to get a tan and see the neighboring Bald Eagles. It has two comfortable common rooms with fireplaces. Your host is a professional cook who is writing a cookbook.

For dining, you'll enjoy the Accomac Inn, in Wrightsville; the Railroad House, in Marietta, or Bully's, in Columbia.

When you visit you'll love the sense of isolation and still be able to enjoy public entertainment that is just a few minutes away. This property has hiking trails and a fishing pond. You'll love being surrounded by nature, browsing through the library of old books, games and puzzles. There is a piano for the use of guests. You'll love your hospitable, friendly hosts.

Rhode Island

Middletown, Newport

You'll want to consider a visit to Middletown to be a visit to Newport as well, since they are so close. At Middletown, the **Norman Bird Sanctuary**, on Third Beach Rd., is a 450-acre refuge with 7 miles of trails through a variety of natural settings. At **Whitehall Museum**, 311 Berkeley Ave., you can view an early 18th century home with furnishings dating from the 1600s and 1700s. Visit **Prescott Farm**, north on SR 114, to see a museum featuring colonial artifacts. It has a working 19th century windmill. Just a mile or two away are the famous Newport mansions. The **Newport County Convention and Visitors Bureau**, 23 America's Cup Ave., offers taped walking and driving tours. Be certain to take the 10-mile ocean drive offering views of the Atlantic coast, with many large summer houses. Among the favorite mansions to visit are **The Breakers**, on Ochre Point Ave, a 72-room house built in 1895 for Cornelius Vanderbilt; **Hammersmith Farm**, on Ocean Dr., a 28-room mansion built in 1887 and the site of the wedding reception for Jacqueline Bouvier and John F. Kennedy; and **Hunter House**, 54 Washington St., built in 1748, the headquarters of the commander of the French naval forces during the Revolutionary War.

Mariners will want to visit the **Museum of Yachting**, in Fort Adams State Park., The **Naval War College Museum**, on Coasters Harbor Island, at the Naval Education and Training Center, has exhibits on the history of naval warfare. **Boat tours**, offer one-hour narrated cruises of the harbor and Narragansett Bay. Many depart from America's Cup Ave. and sail past the mansions. Also in Newport is the **International Tennis Hall of Fame and Museum**, 194 Bellevue Ave., where visitors can watch court tennis being played as it was in the 15th century. Tournaments are in July; the rest of the year visitors may use the indoor and grass courts for a fee.

And finally, Fall River, Massachusetts, is also close to Middletown. This is the site of the **Battleship Massachusetts** and other famous naval vessels. Even more exciting, for shoppers, are the many factory outlets.

- **Lindsey's Guest House**
6 James St., Middletown, RI 02840.
(401)846-9386.
10/15-5/15: $40. 5/15-10/15: $55.

Call 3 weeks in advance.
- V, MC.
- **Innkeepers: Anne Lindsey.**
- *3 rms, 1 pb, 1 sb.*
- Expanded continental breakfast. A sample menu might include juice or fruit, cereal, bagel, English muffin, or homemade muffin, homemade jam, beverage served in style in the dining room.
- No pets, no smoking.
- 2 mi. from downtown Newport.

A split level home, with a large deck and yard, in a quiet residential area. There is off-street parking and it is just a 5 min. walk to the beaches. One of the rooms has a handicapped accessible entrance and bath. Anne enjoys visitors, gardening and her children and grandchildren.

For dining, you'll like the Greenhouse Restaurant, the Casino or the Rhumb Line.

When you visit you'll enjoy having a leisurely breakfast in the dining room or on the deck overlooking the garden. Your hostess has cassette tapes for a self-guided auto tour of Newport and a VCR tape of Newport that guests like to see. The B&B is just a 10 minute walk away from the beaches and many wonderful restaurants. It's two miles from downtown Newport and one mile from Bellevue Avenue's famous mansions, Ocean Drive and Cliff Walk.

South Carolina

Georgetown

You'll want to visit some of the many historic buildings and homes. The first settlers began living here in the early 1700s. You can tour by bus, train, boat, or you may drive or walk. Free self-guided tour maps are available from the visitor center, at the Days Inn on US 17.

The **Hopsewee Plantation**, 12 miles south on US 17, is a restored plantation house, built in 1740. It is the home of Thomas Lynch, delegate to the Continental Congress. His son, Thomas, Jr., signed the Declaration of Independence. The house has been restored and has period furnishings. Open Tues.-Fri., 10-5. The **Harold Kaminski House**, 1003 Front St., was built in 1760. This pre-revolutionary house is furnished with antiques dating from 1760 to mid-1800s. **Prince George, Winyah Church**, at Broad & Highmarket Sts., dates from colonial times. It is still in use. **Rice Museum**, is in the Market Building, Front and Screven Sts. It has exhibits illustrating the growth of the rice industry in the U.S. It also has a model of a rice mill.

Drive south from Georgetown about 20 miles, on US 17, to McClellanville. The **Hampton Plantation State Park**, 1950 Rutledge Rd., is a restored 18th-century mansion that was on a large rice plantation.

Drive north from Georgetown about 18 miles on US 17, to **Brookgreen Gardens**. It has some of the most beautiful gardens in the South, and it also has a wildlife park and an art museum on the site of an old southern plantation. Not far away is Huntington Beach State Park, where you can swim, fish, hike, walk the nature trails or explore the marsh boardwalk. There are fishing boats available for charter. Georgetown is also just 10 minutes away from Pawley's Island and an hour away from either Myrtle Beach or Charleston.

● **The Shaw House**
8 Cypress Court, Georgetown, SC 29440. (803)546-9663.
$50/S or D; $10/ex prsn.

Call very early.
- No cr. crds.
- Innkeeper: Mary & Joe Shaw.
- *3 rms, 3 pb.*
- A full southern breakfast, including grits, fresh hot biscuits, egg, sausage, fruit juice and your own pot of coffee.
- No pets.
- 1 blk off Hwy 17.

This white 2-story southern style colonial has spacious rooms furnished with antiques. A glass wall overlooks a beautiful marsh, filled with birds, foxes and rabbits. Your hosts enjoy golf, fishing, reading, bird watching and piano playing.

For dining, you may choose among many wonderful restaurants in Georgetown and at Pawley's Island. Some recommended choices are Rice Paddy, River Room, and Daniels.

When you visit you'll find your B & B overlooks beautiful Willowbrook Marsh, a bird watcher's dream. Breakfast is usually served in the den with picture windows all around. There is a large front porch with rocking chairs or a swing under the live oak overlooking the marsh. You'll enjoy the books you find in the library. The Shaw House is within walking or biking distance of famous historic buildings. Also close by, are golf courses, tennis courts, two marinas, antique and gift shops and museums.

● **Ashfield Manor**
3030 South Island Rd., Georgetown, SC 29440. (803)546-0464/ (803)546-5111. **Sep.-Mar. $40; Apr.-Sep. $55.**

Call 9 AM - 11 PM.
• V, MC, D, AE, DC.
• **Innkeepers: Carol & Dave Ashenfelder.**
• *4 rms, 2 sb.*
• Expanded continental breakfast of juice, muffin, bagel or pastry, homemade jam, cream cheese, fruit cup and beverage.
• No pets, no smoking, no alcohol.
• 4 miles from the center of Georgetown.

This southern colonial style home offers the atmosphere of a southern mansion. It is furnished in period antiques and the bedrooms have four-poster beds. The backyard pond offers a habitat for waterfowl and birds. Guests have their own private entrance. Each room has a color TV with remote control.

For dining, ask your hosts for their recommendations. They especially enjoy the many seafood restaurants that are nearby.

When you visit you'll discover a small boat for fishing is available in the back yard. Bird watching in the back yard and pond is excellent. The oak rockers on the 57 ft. porch provide exceptional relaxation.

Baked Fresh Pineapple with Pecans

From Geraldine P. Webster, **The 1868 Stewart-Marsh House**
Salisbury, NC

4 slices fresh pineapple
1/2 cup pecan halves
1/4 cup raisins
1/4-1/2 cup brown sugar
butter or margarine

Peel and core fresh pineapple. Slice into 3/4" thick slices. Cut slices in half and place in a buttered baking dish. Sprinkle with brown sugar. Add pecans and raisins. Dot with butter. Cover and bake about 20 minutes at 350F. To serve, arrange 2-half slices of pineapple on a plate. Spoon pecans and raisins on top and garnish with lemon balm leaves. Serves 4. Can be increased to serve any number.

Laurens

You'll want to relax and enjoy the beauty of a small southern town. Or, use Laurens as a base from which to explore in several directions.

Drive south out of Laurens to SR 72 and Greenwood. Drive six miles north on SR 254 to the **George W. Park Seed Co.**. This mail order nursery and seed company has display plots that are open to the public. In Greenwood, **The Museum**, 106 Main St., has reconstructions of a Victorian parlor, an early drug store, a doctor's office, and a general store. It has a variety of articles from the late 1800s.The **Callie Self Memorial Carillon** has 37 bells cast in Holland. It is next to the Callie Self Memorial Church on US 25. From Greenwood continue west on SR 72 to Abbeville. The first organized meeting of the Confederacy and the last Confederate cabinet meeting were held in Abbeville. A map and instructions for a self-guided tour of the town are available from the Chamber of Commerce, 104 Pickens St. Be sure to see the historic **Abbeville Opera House** on the town square. Many famous actors and actresses appeared on the stage.Return to Greenwood and then head east on SR 34 to the Village of Ninety Six. **Ninety Six National Historic Site** is two miles south on SR 248. It was the site of a strategically important battle of the Revolutionary War. Visitors can explore a reconstructed fort, a log cabin, earthworks, traces of an old village and other signs of the people who lived here.

Take a day trip to Greenville, the City of Parks. It is the home of **Bob Jones University**, at the junction of US 29 and SR 291. The university has an outstanding collection of religious art. The **Art Gallery and Biblical Museum**, has paintings by European artists from the 13th through the 19th centuries. The **Greenville County Museum of Art**, 420 College St., has a collection of U.S. art from colonial times through today. Both the B. Jones Art Gallery and the Greenville Museum of Art are open Tues.-Sun. The **Greenville Zoo**, 1200 E. Washington St., in Cleveland Park, is very popular. It has exhibits of wild and domestic animals.

Two Sisters Inn
814 South Harper, Laurens SC 29360 (803)984-4880
$35/S; $50/D. Discount for sr. citizens, longer stay.

Call 7 AM - Noon, 4 PM - 10 PM.
- No cr. crds.
- **Innkeepers: Julie Snider & Alyis Wade.**
- *2 rms, 1 pb, 1 sb.*
- Expanded continental breakfast. A sample breakfast might include Fruit & Granola Parfait, Stuffed Croissants, fresh fruit and beverage.
- No pets, restricted smoking.
- Within walking distance of downtown Laurens. 4 1/2 miles from I-385.

This 1930s red brick inn has a red tile roof. It has two large porches with comfortable chairs. The rooms are filled with antiques or reproductions of antiques. Your hosts enjoy genealogy, computers and music.

For dining, you'll want to walk to the famous Graystone Restaurant and enjoy true Southern dining. Other enjoyable places to dine include Andrea's, The Square, Springer's, Carlucci's, Fish & Steak or Hickory Hills Bar BQ.

When you visit enjoy cool drinks on a porch, sleep in the hammock under the 100 year old oak trees, play croquet or badminton or read a book picked from your room or the parlor. If you really want to use up extra energy, your hosts will be willing to let you hoe the garden.

Myrtle Beach

You'll want to come to Myrtle Beach for a relaxed weekend, week or even longer. There are miles of open beach, hundreds of fine eating places.

Myrtle Waves Water Park, US 17N Bypass and 10th Ave. N., is a 20-acre water park with 24 rides and other attractions. **Waccatee Zoo**, southwest on SR 707 and Enterprise Rd., is a 500-acre wildlife farm. It has exotic and domestic animals in natural habitats. This is the home of the **Carolina Opry**, in Surfside Beach, 8 miles S. via US 17. It presents family country music entertainment. The **Dixie Jubilee** is in North Myrtle Beach, 12 miles N. via US 17. It features country, rock 'n roll, gospel and bluegrass music and comedy on a family variety show.

You'll be just minutes from more golf clubs than you can play in a month; a short drive from Calabash, the seafood capital of the world; and less than 2 hours to Charleston, the most beautiful city in the United States. Lovely Brookline Gardens, at Murrells Inlet, is midway between Myrtle Beach and historic Georgetown. Georgetown is only 30 miles away. To reach Murrells Inlet, Georgetown or Charleston, you only need to head south on US 17.

Myrtle Beach is on the **Grand Strand**, 60 miles of beach that extends from the North Carolina border to Georgetown. It has a boardwalk and amusements line the walk and other streets.

Barefoot Landing, 1/4 mile south of North Myrtle Beach is a marketplace on the Grand Strand with more than 80 shops and restaurants. Excellent fishing and surfing are available on the Strand. Myrtle Beach celebrates **Canadian-American Days** in mid-March and **Sun Fun Festival** for four days in early June. The **Christmas Connection** is a holiday celebration on the Grand Strand.

SOUTH CAROLINA

● **Serendipity, an Inn**
407 North 71st Ave., Myrtle Beach, SC 29572. (803)449-5268. **$50-85.** Seasonal, travel agent, and commercial discounts. Highest rates are 6/10-8/23.

Call 8 AM - 10 PM.
● V, MC, AE.
● **Innkeepers: Cos and Ellen Ficarra.**
● *12 rms, 12 pb.*
● Expanded continental breakfast. A sample menu might include juice, fresh fruit, cold cereal, hard boiled eggs, homemade muffins and breads.
● No pets.
● In Myrtle Beach, 1/2 block from I-17.

A small Spanish mission style complex, Serendipity is surrounded by tropical vegetation. The air-conditioned building, is only 1 1/2 blocks from the beach, has a heated pool and whirlpool. Your hosts are enthusiastic collectors of civil war memorabilia, religious antiques, japanese porcelains and potteries and art.

For dining, excellent and nearby restaurants include Villa Romana for Italian, Parsons Table for American and the Outrigger for wonderful seafood. The Grand Strand has over 1,000 restaurants.

When you visit you'll find spacious air conditioned rooms, each furnished and decorated individually. A color TV is in every room. The complex has a heated pool and whirlpool, and outdoor gas grill for guests and a brick patio with comfortable furniture and a fountain. There are free bikes, a soft-cover library, shuffleboard and ping-pong for your use.

South Dakota

Chamberlain

You'll want to visit this area if you enjoy hunting and fishing. Chamberlain is on the Missouri River and is an ideal spot for outdoor recreation. It's also a superb place to learn more about the Great Plains and its first inhabitants, the Native Americans. The **Old West Museum**, on US 16 and I-90 business, has displays from the historic past. **St. Joseph's Indian School**, at I-90, Exit 263, is a school and mission for Lakota Indian children. On the grounds of the school, the **Akta Lakota Museum** has displays on the Sioux past and its culture. The **Great Plains Resource Center** is 2 miles north on SR 50 in the Crow Creek Indian Reservation. It has two walking trails. The Wildlife Loop goes through the wildlife sanctuary and the Upland Prairie Loop goes through a half-mile of typical prairie land. Wear boots and watch out for rattlesnakes. **World Wildlife Adventures**, at I-90, Exit 260, has mounted animals that are native to the area and from around the world. You may want to take the **Native American Loop**, a driving tour. It includes two Sioux Indian reservations, the Great Plains Resource Center, the Akta Lakota Museum and the Big Bend Dam. Call the Chamber of Commerce at (605)734-6541 to learn where you can pick up the self-guided tour cassette tape.

If you like to fish, you'll want to take SR 50 north to Fort Thompson. The **Big Bend Dam and Lake Sharpe** on SR 47, has a shoreline of 200 miles and is noted for its walleye fishing.

Take a day to spend in Mitchell. Its east of Chamberlain on I-90. The **Corn Palace**, Sixth and Main Sts. may be one of the world's wonders. The entire building has a Moorish design and parts of the inside and outside are covered with kernels of corn, grains and grass seeds. Every year thousands of bushels of grains of various colors and types are used to redecorate the palace. The **Enchanted World Doll Museum**, 615 North Main St., is across from the Corn Palace. The museum is designed to look like a castle. It has more than 4,000 dolls in 400 scenes.

Prehistoric Indian Village, on Indian Village Rd., is a mile north of the Corn Palace. A 1,000-year-old village was originally on this site. The area includes a museum, visitor center, a scale model of a prehistoric lodge, and the Patton Galley Exhibit of Prehistoric Farmers/Hunters of the James River Basin. During the summer there are weekend activities that include spear throwing, pottery making and leather tooling. *Oscar Howe Art Center*, 119 West Third Ave., has a permanent collection of works by Sioux artist Oscar Howe and changing exhibits of other art. **Friends of the Middle Border Museum of Pioneer Life and Case Art Gallery**, 1311 S. Duff St., 4 blocks south of I-90 business, has the American Indian Gallery, the Case Art Gallery and several restored buildings from late 1800s and early 1900s. The museum has displays of pioneer businesses and artifacts.

● Riverview Ridge Bed & Breakfast

HC 69, Box 82A, Chamberlain, SD 57325. (605)734-6084.
11/1-5/1: $40-45. 5/1-10/31: $50-55. Family discount.

Call mornings or evenings.
- No cr. crds.
- Innkeepers: Frank & Alta Cable.
- 3 rms, 1 pb, 1 sb.
- A full breakfast is served on crystal dishes. A sample breakfast might include homemade caramel rolls, homemade wheat bread, homemade jellies, entree and beverage. Entrees might include eggs, French toast, pancakes, bacon or sausage.
- 3 miles north of downtown Chamberlain.

This is a modern ranch-style home in a country setting with a beautiful view of the Missouri River. Frank and Alta are retired ranchers. Frank does custom farm work and builds model airplanes. Alta collects crystal, likes reading and cake decorating. They both enjoy traveling and people.

For dining, you'll find excellent food at Al's Oasis, Charlie's, American Creek Marina, and the Western Inn.

When you visit sit on the patio overlooking the river to watch sunsets or just to catch some sun. The view from here is beautiful. This is a lovely area for walks in the rolling hills. You're welcome to choose from the family's many books or to watch the 39 inch TV, with satellite programs and VCR.

Webster

You'll want to visit this area to enjoy the quiet calm of prairie life. There are several area lakes for swimming, boating and fishing. In the summer, the country surrounding Webster is wonderful for biking, walking and jogging. In the winter, it is great for cross-country skiing and snowmobiling. The Dakotah Factory, a manufacturer of bedding, quilts and other bed and bath furnishings, has an outlet store in Webster.

From Webster drive east on US 12 to Waubay, then go north 7 miles on CR 1 to **Waubay National Wildlife Refuge**. It has over 4,500 acres of lakes, marshes, woods and prairie. Many birds and mammals make this area their home. There are hiking trails, an observation tower and a visitor center with displays.

Leaving Waubay, drive east on US 12 to I-29, north on I-29 to SR 10. Turn west to the town of Sisseton. Stop here at the **Tekakwitha Fine Arts Center**, 4015 South Eighth Ave. W., to see displays of artwork by Native American artists. Continue west on SR 10 to Lake City. Historic **Fort Sisseton State Park**, at Lake City, covers 45 acres. It is 10 miles southwest of Lake City, just off SR 25. It contains stone fort buildings and breastworks built in the 1860s. From Lake City you can take SR 25 south back to Webster.

On another day, drive west from Webster on US 12 to Aberdeen. In Aberdeen, visit the **Dacotah Prairie Museum**, at First and Main Sts. Rooms house photographs, artifacts and displays from South Dakota's past. Also see **Storybook Land**, at Wylie Park. It has fairy tale characters in lifelike settings. There are also compounds housing prairie animals that native to the area. You may want to spend the day enjoying the city of Aberdeen. Another interesting option is to head north on US 281 and then east to Columbia. Drive north on CR 16 to the **Sand Lake National Wildlife Refuge**. Every spring about 300,000 snow geese arrive here. They can be observed from a 108-foot observation tower or from a 15-mile driving tour of the refuge. From Columbia drive south back to US 12, then go east to your home base of Webster.

● Lakeside Farm Bed & Breakfast

RR 2, Box 52, Webster, SD 57274-9633. (605)486-4430.

$25/S; $40/D.

Call anytime.
- No cr. crds.
- **Innkeepers: Glenn & Joy Hagen.**
- *2 rms, 1 sb.*
- Full breakfast featuring juice, homemade cinnamon rolls, fruit, omelet, bacon or sausage, beverage. In the evening enjoy tea or coffee with homemade dessert or cookies.
- No smoking, no alcohol, pets restricted.
- 6 miles north of Webster on Hwy 25.

This farm home is on a working farm on the north side of Waubay Lake. It is a farm with wide open spaces, clean fresh air, an abundance of wild life, quiet cool sleeping. Glenn has a toy tractor and machinery collection.

For dining, you'll pick among small, old fashioned cafes. Some may feature Norwegian specialties but they always serve fine, hearty food.

When you visit you'll meet an enthusiastic South Dakotan. Joy says, "most folks think there is nothing in South Dakota. They leave feeling differently." You'll also learn about the pleasures of farm life. In the morning, you can enjoy sleeping in until you're awakened by the smell of Joy's homecooked breakfast or you can wake up early and join the family for the morning chores. The Hagens welcome observers as they go about their farm business. They're quite willing to answer questions about farm life. They have chickens and beef cattle. Neighbors have a dairy farm and horses and they welcome the Hagen's visitors. Children have the run of the farmyard with an old school ground merry-go-round and a hay mow to play in.

Tennessee

Smoky Mountains — Kodak

You'll want to spend months enjoying this beautiful area and the interesting attractions that are available. Kodak is near I-40, Exit 407, as you drive toward Pigeon Forge, Gatlinburg and Great Smoky Mountains National Park. Golfers will want to stay right here, in Kodak, and spend some time at the **River Islands Golf Club**. Several of the holes are on three islands in the middle of the river. If you head south on US 441 toward Pigeon Forge, you're sure to see the entrance to **Dixie Stampede** and **Dollywood**. Dollywood has many rides and attractions but it also has working crafts shops, musical entertainment and the Dolly Parton Museum. Dixie Stampede has an evening country-style meal served during a program of wild-west performances, music, and comedy. There's much more at Pigeon Forge. **Ogle's Water Park**, on US 441 at 115 N. Parkway, has waterslides, miniature golf, and a wave pool. **Rainbow Music Theater**, 1100 N. Parkway, has an evening variety show of comedy, country and bluegrass music.Continue on down US 441 to Gatlinburg and the entrance to **Great Smoky Mountains National Park**. The park contains some of the highest peaks in the U.S. and contains more than 100 species of trees and wildflowers that bloom in profusion from late April through July. Visitors can take short self-guided nature trails or they can rent a horse at the park stables. Visitor centers provide information and you'll be able to rent tapes for self-guided auto tours. **Cades Cove**, on Laurel Creek Rd., has an 11-mile loop of the cove. It contains restored buildings and a mill. From Kodak drive west on I-40 to SR 162, drive northwest to Oak Ridge. The **American Museum of Science and Energy**, is on S. Tulane Ave., between SR 62 and CR 95. The **Graphite Reactor**, on Bethel Valley Rd., is the world's oldest nuclear reactor and a national historic landmark. The **Children's Museum of Oak Ridge**, 461 W. Outer Dr., offers hands-on exhibits on Appalachia. The University of Tennessee Arboretum, on SR62, has trees, shrubs and flowers which can be viewed from nature trails.

● **Grandma's House Bed & Breakfast**
734 Pollard Rd., Kodak, TN 37764.
(615)933-3512.

$55-75. Discount for stay of 5 or more days.

Call 8 AM - 9 PM.
•V, MC.
•**Innkeepers: Charlie & Hilda Hickman.**
•*3 rms, 3 pb.*
•Full breakfast. A sample menu might include fruit, biscuits, jam or jelly, grits, Ham and Egg Puff, juice, and coffee.
•No pets, no smoking, no alcohol, no children under 6.
•2 miles from the Great Smoky Mountains National Park exit from I-40.

This old fashioned Colonial style farmhouse is on a quiet country road. It is decorated in a country decor with antiques, handmade quilts, crafts and paintings. Hilda paints, makes baskets, enjoys quilting and cross stitch. She also writes murder mysteries for special winter weekend entertainment packages.

For dining, Charlie and Hilda offer their own restaurant guide to guests with their own special rating system. Some places to try are Chinatown in Sevierville, Pop's Catfish Shack or Five Oaks Inn in Pigeon Forge the Peddler in Gatlinburg or Ye Old Steak House in Knoxville.

When you visit you'll love the big front porch with a swing or the upstairs balcony. Your B&B is on a tranquil country lane leading to the French Broad River. You'll love the Southern hospitality and the wonderful location with easy access to many things to see and do.

Texas

Abilene

You'll want to visit **Buffalo Gap Historical Village**, south on SR 89, to get a feel for 19th century Texas. It has a collection of 19th century buildings, including an old court house and jail. **Fort Phantom Hill**, northeast on FM 600, contains the ruins of a Texas frontier fort. The **Abilene Zoological Garden**, in Nelson Park, compares African animals with North American Plains animals living in similar habitats. See a classic movie at the **Paramount Theater**, restored to its 1930s best.

Take a short drive, northeast on SR 351 to Albany, then north on US 283, to see **Fort Griffin State Historical Park**. The park contains the ruins of a frontier town and fort of the 1860s. Drive west from Abilene on I-20 to Sweetwater. The **Pioneer City County Museum**, at 610 E. Third St., is in a 1906 house. Several rooms contain period furniture and decorations. Others contain pioneer artifacts and one room is dedicated to women pilots who ferried aircraft to the fronts in WWII. If you're here during the second weekend in March you may (or you may not) want to attend the **Rattlesnake Roundup**.

Continue west on I-20 to Big Spring. This city has a Rattlesnake Roundup in late March — if you just missed the one in Sweetwater. There's a **Rodeo** in June. **Big Spring State Park**, on FM 700 just south of the city, has a prairie dog town, a scenic mountain drive and nature trails. The **Heritage Museum**, 510 Scurry St., has displays chronicling the development of the area.

Finally, take a drive on a country road, away from the freeway and the city to see ranches, cattle and miles of range. In the spring see whole fields of Blue Bells — one of the most beautiful sights ever.

● **Bolin's Prairie House Bed & Breakfast**
508 Mulberry, Abilene, TX 79601.
(915)675-5855.
$40-50.

Call 10 AM - 5 PM.
•V, MC, D, AE, DC.
•Innkeepers: Sam & Ginny Bolin.
•*4 rms, 2 sb.*
•Full breakfast. Sample breakfasts might include fresh fruit, baked sausage, grits, eggs and sour dough biscuits; or oven baked Dutch Babies, apple syrup, fried ham and fresh fruit.
•No pets, no smoking, no alcohol, no children under 12.
•In the historic district, near downtown Abilene.

Built in 1902, the first thing you'll notice when you approach this large home is the large corner porch with swing. It is surrounded by pecan trees. Inside, it has hardwood floors, high ceilings and is furnished in period antiques. Ginny enjoys cooking, sewing, painting and gardening. Sam likes carpentry, fishing and golfing.

For dining, you'll want to sample the steaks at the Outpost or Perini Ranch. The Casa Herrera has great Mexican food.

When you visit you'll see birds galore — Blue Jays, Cardinals, Robins and several others. Relax in the swing on the front porch or take a walk through the historic neighborhood. If you want to read, you'll enjoy the library of magazines and books and if you feel like curling up in front of the TV, you'll enjoy the library of video tapes for the VCR.

Castroville

You'll want to take a walking tour of this historic village. One of the top attractions here is the **Landmark Inn**. On the grounds are a restored dam, gristmill and old bathhouse dating back to the 1850s. There are numerous antique shops for browsing or shopping. The town is beside the river, shaded with trees, a great place for quiet relaxation and peaceful walks.

Sea World of Texas is just 15 min. away, on Loop 1064 around San Antonio. This marine park covers 250 acres and is open daily, 10 AM - 10 PM. Since San Antonio is just a short drive away, it's well worth the drive to visit **The Alamo**, the famous mission turned fortress. It is downtown, near the river. Other attractions that should be seen are the Zoo and Witte Museum, in **Brackenridge Park**, 3903 N. St. Mary's St. The **San Antonio Zoological Gardens**, has about 3,000 animals. There is an aquarium, a petting zoo and a monkey island. Open daily 9:30 AM - 5 PM. **Witte Museum**, 3801 Broadway, displays various aspects of the natural history and science of Texas. There is a multimedia show, a dinosaur show, several 19th-century buildings, a sculpture garden and many exhibits. Also in Brackenridge Park is a sunken Oriental garden, an outdoor theater and a children's amusement park with several rides. The **San Antonio Botanical Gardens**, at 555 Funston Pl., have formal gardens, native plantings, a gazebo observatory, a series of greenhouse conservatories, a touch and smell garden for the blind and a children's vegetable garden.

While you're here, you'll probably want to visit the Natural Bridge Caverns and Natural Bridge Wildlife Ranch; Hemisfair Plaza with the Institute of Mexican Cultures and Institute of Texan Cultures. Perhaps you will want to visit San Antonio Missions National Historical Park, Fort Sam Houston, and the Spanish Governor's Palace. The San Antonio Museum of Art and Marion Koogler McNay Art Institute have exceptional art collections. Obviously this paragraph just touches on a few of the things to see and do in San Antonio. It has an enormous variety of sports and recreational activities, shops, restaurants and entertainment possibilities.

● Landmark Inn State Historical Park
402 Florence, Castroville, TX 78009. (512)538-2133.

$35/S; $40/D; $5/ex. prsn.

Call 8 AM to 5 PM.
- No cr. crds.
- Innkeeper: Park Superintendent.
- 8 rms, 4 pb, 2 sb.
- No breakfast is served, but we recommend nearby restaurants and the Alsatian Bakery.
- No pets; no smoking except in designated areas.
- In downtown Castroville, off of Hwy 90 W.

This 19th century restored plastered stone inn is uniquely furnished and decorated with antiques. In keeping with the traditional style of older inns, there are no televisions, telephones or air conditioning. The rooms have fans and panel heaters. The inn grounds cover over 4 acres and are landscaped with attractive flower beds. It was donated to the TX Parks and Wildlife Department by the owner in 1974.

For dining, enjoy one of several excellent restaurants in the area. Look through the Castroville visitor guide for suggestions. Choose from descriptions in the Castroville Visitor's Guide, or drive 15 min. to San Antonio for even more choices.

When you visit you'll feel as if you've stepped back in time. You'll want to stroll the scenic grounds, visiting the historic pecan tree, the river front, the grist mill and dam and the old bathhouse. There are a variety of interpretive presentations available. Or sit on the veranda and watch the evening fall while rocking in comfortable oak rocking chairs. A stay here has been described as, "like staying in the spare bedroom at Grandmother's house."

Utah

Park City

You'll want to come to Park City in the summer. Though this area is popular for wintertime skiing, it is also extremely expensive during the winter. In the summer, the mountains are beautiful, there are many things to see and do and it fits our category of "affordable" getaways. Once the scene of a silver rush, Park City has an interesting historic area. Pick up the map of a walking tour at the **Chamber of Commerce**, 509 Main St. Visit the Park City Ski Area, on Lowell Avenue, to find the **Alpine Slide**. Take a chairlift to the top and ride a specially designed sled, down a concrete slide, to the bottom. **Balloon Affaire**, 514 Main St., gives hot air balloon rides. The **Kimball Art Center**, at Main St and Park Ave., has galleries, art and craft shops displaying international art. You'll be able to hike or bike the surrounding mountains, fish, swim, golf, ride horseback, play tennis or shop.

Rockport Reservoir just north on I-80, has boat rentals, fishing, waterskiing, swimming, food service and picnic facilities. Just south of Park City, is the mountain town of Brighton, where the **Mount Milicent chairlift** operates throughout the summer and provides magnificent views of surrounding mountains. Just a little further south is **Alta**, known for many ski areas. In summer, a tramway runs to the summit of an 11,000 ft. peak, providing more thrills and views. Alta has tennis courts, a swimming pool, and many special events, ethnic festivals and concerts throughout the summer. On SR 92, east of American Fork, is **Timpanogos Cave National Monument**. Cave tours of the three large limestone caverns, with spectacular stalactites and stalagmites, helictites and crystals, are given daily mid-May to mid-Oct, 7-5. Tours fill up quickly so call ahead to make reservations. **Salt Lake City** is less than an hour away from Park City. There is much, much more to do in Utah's capital city. If you have time to visit, call or write the Salt Lake Valley Convention and Visitors Bureau, in the Salt Palace, (801)521-2868.

● **The Old Miners' Lodge, A Bed & Breakfast Inn**
615 Woodside Ave., P.O. Box 2639, Park City, UT 84060-2639. (801)645-8068/ (800)648-8068.

4/1-11/15, $45-85. Far exceeds our rate during winter months.

Call 8 AM - 10 PM.
•V, MC, D, AE.
•**Innkeepers: Hugh Daniels, Susan Wynne, Jeff Sadowsky**
•*10 rms, 10 pb. 4 rms fit our rates throughout the summer.*
•A fixed menu full breakfast is served in the dining room. Ten different menus are rotated and all sound delicious. Expect an evening beverage or other surprise.
•No pets, no smoking.
•In the National Historic District.

Established in 1893 for housing for local miners, the lodge has been restored to its original splendor. The rooms are named after historic Park City personalities. Each room has down pillows and comforters. Yours hosts enjoy sharing their knowledge of bicycling, education, travel, fine dining and community affairs.

For dining, there are many exceptional restaurants in the area. Highly recommended are Mileti's, Alex's, Wasatch Brew Pub, Ichiban, Cisero's and Adolph's.

When you visit you'll enjoy the outdoor hot tub after a busy day of sightseeing. If the weather is cool, there is likely to be a fire in the living room fireplace. This room is frequently a gathering place for guests in the evening. Here they find complimentary refreshments and one or more of your innkeepers are sure to be able to provide knowledgeable information about dining, entertainment or city history. The library is filled with interesting books for you to borrow.

St. George

You'll want to visit here in the cold winter. Known as "Utah's Dixie," semi-tropical temperatures prevail during the summer and the climate is warm in winter.

This is the site of the first **Mormon Temple** in Utah. The temple still stands, at Main and Tabernacle Sts. Guided tours are available to visitors. The **Brigham Young Winter Home**, 89 W. 200 North St., is the restored home of the Mormon leader. It contains 19th century furnishings. There are 8 golf courses in town, as well as numerous tennis courts. There are innumerable art shows, concerts, and theater.

Only 10 miles northwest of the city is **Snow Canyon State Park**. There you'll see lava formations from a volcanic eruption and pictographs on the red sandstone canyon walls.

Drive just a little farther, northeast on SR 9 to Hurricane and **Pah Tempe Springs**. There, in a canyon, is one of world's largest hot springs. Less than 1 hour northeast of St. George is **Zion National Park**. There you'll find the **Zion and Kolob Canyons**, with a spectacular gorge and huge and curious stone formations. The park has several footpaths and hiking trails. Inquire at the park office about accessibility and safety before starting a hike.

The **Dixie National Forest**, just north of St. George along I-15, encompasses almost two million acres, including canyons and parks. To take a free three-hour tour of the forest you'll need to drive farther to Ruby Inn, at the jct. of SRs 63 and 12. The tour leaves at 9 and 1, Tues.-Sat., Jun.-Sept. Several well stocked streams and lakes provide excellent fishing. You'll find boat rentals, hiking and nature trails and wonderful scenery in the forest.

Near Ruby Inn is the entrance to **Bryce Canyon National Park** where you'll find some of earth's most colorful rocks hiking trails, driving trails, horseback trail rides, as well as a van tour of the park (available Memorial Day through Labor Day).

● Greene Gate Village

76 W. Tabernacle, St. George, UT 84770. (801)628-6999 or toll-free for reservations (800)350-6999.

$45/D; $75/cottage. Travel agent discount.

Call early in the week.
- V, MC, AE.
- **Innkeepers: Barbara & Mark Greene.**
- *16 rms, 16 pb.*
- Full breakfast from a menu that includes homemade rolls, pecan waffles, whole wheat pancakes, muffins, croissants, omelets, bacon, sausage, juice, fruit and coffee. Breakfast is served buffet style on Sunday and family style Mon-Sat.
- No pets, no smoking, no alcohol.
- In St. George.

This two-story home, with thick adobe walls, was built by Orson Prat, a counselor in the historic Mormon Dixie Cotton Mission. Surrounding the house are a carriage house and other buildings. Dr. Mark Greene is an orthopedic hand surgeon and Greene Gate's handyman. Barbara Greene has a passion for restoration, writing and her grandchildren.

For dining, you'll find a number of recommended restaurants, including Bentley Supper House, Andelin's Gable House, the Holiday Inn, The Shed, the Pizza Factory, and Basila's Greek Cafe, in St. George; in Springdale, near Zion National Park, visit Pizza and Noodles, Driftwood or the Bit and Spur.

When you visit swim in the village pool, play tennis or take a historic tour. During the winter, sit by the fireplace in your room for an afternoon of reading a book from the library. Any afternoon, you are invited to Judd Store, the village's old-fashioned fountain and general store, for a soft drink and bread sticks.

● **Seven Wives Inn**
217 North 100 West, St. George, UT 84770. (801)628-3737.

$45/D; $100/Suites. Travel agent discount.

Call after 3 PM.
- V, MC, AE, DC, CB.
- **Innkeepers: Donna & Jay Curtis; Alison & Jon Bowcutt.**
- *12 rms, 12 pb.*
- Full breakfast of juice, fruit, entree such as granola with fruit, blueberry pancakes, sausage or meat, and beverage.
- No pets, no smoking.
- In the downtown historic district.

These two historical homes, built in 1873 and 1883, feature massive hand-grained moldings. They are furnished in antiques and both are St. George Landmark homes. Your hosts enjoy art and history.

For dining, you'll especially want to visit Andelin's Gable House or Basila's Greek Cafe, in St. George; the Bit and Spur, near Zion Park.

When you visit, after a busy day exploring St. George, you will want to relax at your comfortable B & B. Perhaps you'll take a refreshing swim in the private swimming pool. Then you can settle back and read a book, peruse an old photo album or play a game in the parlor with some of the other guests. If you like to play the piano or organ, be sure to try the pump organ in the parlor.

Bran-Ana Pancakes with Toasted Almonds

From Susan Maxwell, **Castle Inn**
Circleville, OH.

1/2 cup bran flakes or buds
1 cup all-purpose flour
2 tablespoons sugar
2 teaspoons baking powder
1 teaspoon cinnamon
1/2 teaspoon salt
2 tablespoons melted butter
2/3 cup milk
1 egg
1/2 cup sliced almonds
2 bananas

Put bran, flour, sugar, baking powder, cinnamon and salt in a bowl and mix. In another bowl mix the melted butter, milk and egg. Pour liquid into dry ingredients and stir. Add more milk if necessary to make batter to a pouring consistency. Pour about 1/4 cup batter onto a greased hot skillet. Sprinkle some sliced almonds over the uncooked side. Turn the pancake when it is bubbly and lightly browned on the cooked side. The nuts toast as the second side browns. Turn your oven to warm. As each pancake is baked, stack it on a plate in the warm oven and keep covered until all are ready. Arrange the pancakes on a platter or on individual plates and cover with sliced bananas. Serve with syrup Makes about 8 large pancakes.

This is one of the guests favorite entrees at this B&B.

Vermont

Bethel, Fairlee

You'll want to use these lovely towns as centers from which to explore the surrounding countryside. Two miles west of Bethel, on SR 107, is the White River National Fish Hatchery. The goal of the hatchery is restoring the Atlantic Salmon to the Connecticut River. There are displays on the hatchery and salmon.

Drive south from to US 4 and the Village of Woodstock to visit the **Billings Farm and Museum**, 1/2 mile north on SR 12. Here you'll get to see modern dairy operations contrasted with dairy operations in the 1890s. It's a living history museum, with guides reenacting daily activities. Also see the **Dana House**, 26 Elm St., built in 1807. It has exhibits and furnishings dating from the mid-1700s to 1900. Take a walking tour of the village historical area. Begin the tour from the Chamber of Commerce information booth on the green. There are also three covered bridges in the area, one in the center of town.

The Village of Strafford is between Fairlee and Bethel. The **Justin Smith Morrill Homestead**, on SR 132, is a Gothic-Revival house, built around 1850.

Go Southeast on SR 14 from Sharon to US 4, then go south on US 4 to Quechee. The Quechee Gorge, west of town is known as a "Little Grand Canyon." A bridge on US 4 spans the gorge above the Ottauquechee River and provides a superb view of the gorge. In the small town of Quechee is a complex of shops called The Mill. It includes a glass shop where visitors can observe glass blowing. Turn back north on US 4 to I-89, go east on 89 to then turn north on I-91 back toward Fairlee.

Make a stop at the Village of White River Junction. The **Catamount Brewing Company**, 58 S. Main St., offers tours, a history of the brewing industry in New England and a sample. The tours are offered at specific times on Fri-Sun and on some Mondays. Call for the times.

● **Greenhurst Inn**
River St., RD 2, Box 60, Bethel, VT 05032-9404. (802)234-974.

$50-95. Discounts for senior citizens, travel agent, length of stay.

Call anytime.
- V, MC, D.
- **Innkeepers: Lyle & Claire Wolf.**
- *13 rms, 7 pb, 2 1/2 sb.*
- Expanded continental breakfast of fresh fruit, cold cereal, hot muffins or quick bread, English muffins, toast, beverage, served buffet style.
- Restricted pets.
- One-half mile south of Bethel.

This Victorian mansion, overlooking the White River, was built in 1890. It became an inn in the 1930s. It is on the National Register; it has eight fireplaces; the rooms are decorated with antiques.

For dining, ask to see the Wolf's scrapbook of restaurant menus. They'll be happy to discuss options with you.

When you visit if you're a reader, you'll love the 3,000 volume library. There is a library of 50 movies for the VCR. You'll find a game cupboard in the North Parlor, a Victrola and piano in the South Parlor. When its cool, you'll love the electric blankets.

● Silver Maple Lodge and Cottages

RR 1, Box 8, Fairlee, VT 05045.
(802)333-4326 / (800)666-1946.

$46-64. Discounts for senior citizens and travel agent.

Call 8 AM - 10 PM.
- V, MC, D, AE.
- Innkeepers: Scott & Sharon Wright.
- *14 rms, 12 pb, 1 sb.*
- Continental breakfast with juice, homemade breakfast breads, beverage served buffet style.
- No pets, limited smoking.
- On US 5.

This antique farmhouse was built in the 1790s. You can still see the 200-year-old hand-hewn beams. It was expanded in the 1800s and converted to an inn in the 1920s. The knotty pine cottages were built in the 1940s from lumber cut on the property. The lodge is filled with many of the inns original antiques.

For dining, you'll like Leda's Restaurant next door. For an exceptional meal drive to Lyme, NH to D'Artagnans.

When you visit you'll love reading or sitting on the large wrap-around porch. Enjoy croquet, badminton or horseshoes on the side lawn. You're welcome to enjoy a picnic under the apple trees and Scott will allow you to help him weed his garden.

Mushroom Crust Quiche

From Myrtle Haldeman, **Conifer Ridge Farm**
Clearville, PA

5 tablespoons butter or margarine
1/2 pound mushrooms, coarsely chopped
1/2 cup finely crushed saltine crackers
3/4 cup chopped green onion or shallots
2 cups (about 8 ounces) shredded Swiss or mozzarella cheese
1 cup cottage cheese
3 eggs
1/4 teaspoon cayenne
1/4 teaspoon paprika
1 teaspoon chives, chopped

Melt 3 tablespoons butter in frying pan over medium heat, add mushrooms and cook until limp. Stir in crackers and turn mixture into 9 inch pie pan. With a wooden spoon, press mixture over sides and bottom of pan. Melt remaining butter, add onion and cook until limp. Spread onions in the crust, cover with cheese. In a blender mix eggs, cottage cheese and cayenne until smooth. Pour into crust. Sprinkle with paprika and chives.

Bake in 350F oven for 20-25 minutes or until set. Let stand for 10 - 15 minutes and cut. Makes 4 to 6 servings.

East Burke — Northeast Kingdom

You'll want to look forward to country living. You'll be able to enjoy jogging, walking or bicycling on country roads without having to dodge traffic. Streams for fishing are within a mile or two. Additional summertime fishing can be found at **Willoughby** or **Crystal Lakes**. They're only about an hour away. If you like to play golf, bring your clubs. There are four golf courses close by. If you prefer tennis, Lyndon State College has courts that you will enjoy using. Visit **Fallow Deer Farm** to see beautiful deer. They'll eat apples out of your hand. Visit a dairy farm and see the farm animals. Enjoy band concerts in the park. In the fall see the beautiful colored leaves as you drive, hike or bike the gravel roads.

Visit in the winter to enjoy downhill skiing at **Burke Mountain Ski Resort**. Cross country ski trails are easy to find and well groomed. Public ice skating is available at the **Fenton Chester Ice Arena**. Other popular seasonal activities include snowmobiling, snowshoeing, ice fishing and sledding. Spring starts with maple sugar season. You're sure to find a sugar house tour. Enjoy a horse-drawn sleigh ride through the melting snow. Whitewater canoeing is at its best during this season.

Drive south on US 5 from East Burke to St. Johnsbury. The **Fairbanks Museum and Planetarium**, on Main and Prospect Sts., has programs on history, science and the arts. Collections include 2,500 mounted birds and animals. The museum also has a planetarium, the Northern New England Weather Center and the Children's Nature Corner. It is open daily except on major holidays. The **Maple Grove Museum**, east on US 2, has exhibits, a film and demonstrations of the sugaring process. The **St. Johnsbury Athenaeum Art Gallery**, at 30 Main St. in the library, has a collection of paintings by 19th century artists and artists of the Hudson River School.

If you'd like to see more of the maple sugaring process, drive US 5 northeast from E. Burke to Barton. At SR 16 turn south to **The Sugarmill Farm**. Tours are given daily 8 AM - 8 PM. You'll see the orchards, the processing and packaging of maple syrup.

*If you'd like to see more of the maple sugaring process, drive US 5 northeast from E. Burke to Barton. At SR 16 turn south to **The Sugarmill Farm**. Tours are given daily 8 AM - 8 PM. You'll see the orchards, the processing and packaging of maple syrup.*

● **Laniers' Hilltop B&B**
P.O. Box 103, East Burke, VT 05832. (802)626-9637.

$35/S; $50/D. Family and length of stay discount.

Call 7 AM - 7 PM.
•V, MC.
•**Innkeepers: Lionel & Marilyn Lanier.**
•2 *rms*, 2 *sb*.
•Full breakfast of fruit, juice, entree, homemade breads or muffins. Entrees may be a special pancake recipe, with Vermont syrup, Eggs Supreme, bacon, sausage or ham.
•No pets, restricted smoking.
•Five miles from I-91.

This modern split-level home is on a hill, at the foot of Burke Mountain. It has a panoramic view of the countryside. Surrounded by four acres of woods, a bubbling brook runs past the gazebo. Patios surround the in-ground pool. Lionel and Marilyn own a golf shop in town. They enjoy golfing, bridge, fishing, traveling and their perennial gardens.

For dining, there are four wonderful restaurants in town. They are the Wildflower Inn, Riverside Cafe, Cutler Inn and The Pub Out Back.

When you visit you'll enjoy country living as you relax on the four wooded acres surrounding your B&B. Enjoy the gazebo next to your own stream. Go swimming in the pool. Jog, walk or bike on the country roads with little traffic. A deer farm is just a mile away. Children love to feed apples to the friendly deer. Sleigh rides and ice skating are available just two miles away. The B&B is at the foot of Burke Mountain with great climbing and cross-country ski trails.

Hyde Park, Stowe, Waterbury

You'll want to ski if you come here in the winter. The region is noted for its many downhill ski slopes as well as its cross-country skiing. In the summer, you can play golf on its lovely golf courses. Other summer activities that are available to you include tennis, horseback riding, mountain climbing, hiking, swimming, sailboarding and trout fishing. The **Hyde Park Opera House** provides entertaining theater throughout the summer. Shoppers will want to browse through the antique shops and attend a barn sale.

In nearby Morrisville, see the **Morristown Historical Museum**, on Main St. This brick mansion displays artifacts of early New England and a collection of miniature pitchers. Just east of Morrisville, on SR 15, is Wolcott. The last covered railroad bridge still used in Vermont is the **Fisher Bridge**. It was built in 1908.

*The **Stowe Alpine Slide** and the **Stowe Gondola**, north of Stowe on SR 108,* give rides to the top of Mount Mansfield, Vermont's highest mountain. The trip back down is more exciting on the slide.

*Waterbury is the home of the famous **Ben & Jerry's Ice Cream Factory**, north on SR 100.* A 30-minute guided tour through the factory includes a slide show and free samples.

*Southeast of Waterbury on I-89 is Montpelier, the capital of Vermont. It's especially interesting for the architecture of many of its buildings. At Burlington, the largest city in Vermont, you'll find the **Ethan Allen Homestead**.* Guided tours and a media show are given of the restored house and gardens.

*The **Spirit of Ethan Allen**, at Perkins Pier, is a Mississippi paddlewheeler.* Narrated cruises on Lake Champlain are given Memorial Day - Labor Day.

Fitch Hill Inn

RFD, Box 1879, Hyde Park, VT 05655. (802)888-5941.

Apr.-Dec. 15: $45; Dec. 16-Mar.: $55. Seasonal, travel agent and weekday business discounts.

Call anytime.
- V, MC.
- Innkeeper: Richard A. Publiese.
- 4 rms, 2 sb.
- Full breakfast is served in the large period dining room. A sample breakfast would include hot cereal, fresh squeezed juice, Ginger Pancakes with cream cheese and lemon sauce, fresh brewed Green Mountain Coffee.
- No pets, no smoking.
- 1/2 mile from center of Hyde Park, off Rts. 100 & 15.

This large colonial style house was built in 1797, by Darius Fitch. It is set in five acres of woodland, on a hillside, overlooking the Hamoille Valley and the two highest mountain ranges in Vermont. The inn is decorated with period antiques.

For dining, you may be able to arrange with your host to have a New England style dinner right here in the dining room. On other evenings or for lunch you might wish to visit the Isle de France, the Trapp Family Lodge, Ten Acres Lodge, the Green Mountain Inn or the Partridge Inn. There are many other fine restaurants available.

When you visit you'll enjoy tea or sherry in the outdoor garden. In the summer hike the five acres of woods and enjoy the mountain vistas on the property. In the winter you may use the ungroomed cross-country ski trails on the property. There is always abundant reading material and over 200 video movies in the library.

● Andersen Lodge - An Austrian Inn

3430 Mountain Rd., Stowe, VT 05672. (802)253-7336.

$50-65. Sr. citizen, family & travel agent discounts.

Call Noon to 5 PM.
- V, MC, AE.
- Innkeepers: Dietmar & Gertrude Heiss.
- *17 rms, 17 pb.*
- Full breakfast. A sample menu includes juice, fruit, hot or cold cereal, pancakes, French toast, eggs, bacon, sausage and ham.
- 3.6 miles from Stowe, 45 miles from Burlington.

This lovely lodge has a Austrian Tyrolean look and atmosphere. It is set in a scenic mountain setting. Your hosts give a special warmth and friendly atmosphere. The lodge is air conditioned. Tennis courts and a heated pool are available for guests. In the winter there is a heated mud room for skis, boots and equipment.

For dining, you will want to have some of your meals at the inn. Dietmar is a trained chef from Austria. You may also choose to visit the Trapp Family Lodge. There are many other fine restaurants in the area.

When you visit you'll be sure to relax in the mountain atmosphere. You'll enjoy using the tennis court and pool. In addition to the attractive dining room, the lodge has two living rooms with fireplaces. You'll find books there to read or other guests ready to talk. There is also a game room with ping pong, bumper pool and a piano. Trout fishing, horseback riding and mountain hiking trails are close by.

●Grunberg Haus Bed & Breakfast

RR 2, Box 1595, Rte 100 S., Waterbury, VT 05676. (802)244-7726/ (800)800-7760.

Apr.-Jul, Nov.-Dec. 20: $55. Dec. 21-Mar., Sep.-Oct.: $60-65. Sr. citizen, travel agent, military and length of stay discounts.

Call anytime.
- V, MC, AE, D, ER.
- Innkeepers: Christopher Sellers & Mark Frohman.
- *10 rms, 6 pb and sb.*
- Full breakfast, including muffins, fresh fruit and entrees. Expect to dine on house specialties like Pumpkin Apple Streusel Muffins, Maple Poached Pears and Ricotta Stuffed French Toast.
- No pets, no smoking. Pets may be boarded nearby.
- 3 mi. south of Waterbury.

This hand built Austrian mountain chalet is on 40 wooded acres with a sweeping view of the mountains. In typical chalet style, it is built of wood and has many balconies. Inside is a massive stone fireplace, whirlpool and sauna. Hiking trails and a tennis court are on the property. Each guest room opens onto the large second floor balcony that surrounds the chalet.

For dining, we think you'd enjoy Tanglewoods, Villa Tragara, Thatcher Brook Inn, Arvad's or Crust 'n' Cauldron.

When you visit hike or cross-country ski on the 40 acres of trails, use the tennis court, enjoy the greenhouse and library. Look out over the mountains from your balcony, sit by the fireplace that's used almost year-around. Use the grand piano or the antique pump organ, help feed the chickens and "Ike." Borrow your hosts' snowshoes in the winter, borrow their inner tubes in the summer. Walk through the gardens.

Morgan

You'll want to bike to the lake and hike on the country roads. You'll enjoy the sunny beaches, fishing and golfing in the summer and skiing in the winter.

Drive northwest on Route 5A to Newport where you may tour the **American Maple Products** candy factory, at Union and Bluffs Rds, Mon-Fri. Continue North on I-91 to the Canadian border. Just across the border is the Province of Quebec where French is the native language. Enjoy being in a "foreign country." At the Derby Line is the **Haskell Free Library and Opera House**. It sits on the international boundary between Canada and the U.S. The library is open on Tue., Thur.-Sat.

If you'd like spectacular mountain scenery and summer and winter sports, drive west from Newport on SR 100, then north on 101 and then west again on 242 to **Jay Peak Ski Area**. The tramway to the peak is open for sightseeing rides from late June thru mid-Oct. if the weather permits.

South of Newport on I-91, on the Derby-Brownington Village Road, is the **Old Stone House Museum**, in Brownington. It has displays of early American furniture, decorative arts and historical items. It is open daily, 11-5, Jul.-Aug. It is open Fri.-Tue., 5/15-6/30 and 9/1-10/15.

Continue south on I-91 to Barton, then take Exit 25 to SR 16. It's just 1/8 mile south to **The Sugarmill Farm**. Tours are given daily 8 AM - 8 PM. You'll see the orchards, the processing and packaging of maple syrup. A film and a maple museum are included in the tour. The most interesting time to visit, of course, is in early spring when you can see the sap gathering process.

● **Hunts' Hideaway**
RR 1, Box 570, West Charleston, VT 05872. (802)895-4432 (home) or 334-8322 (office).

$25/S; $35/D. Discount for family or stay of a week or more.

Call 7 AM to 11 PM.
•No cr. crds.
•**Innkeeper: Pat Hunt.**
•*3 rms, 2 sb.*
•Full breakfast. A sample breakfast might include orange juice, sausage, pancakes with Vermont maple syrup, and beverage.
•In the town of Morgan.

This is a modern split-level house on 100 acres of woods and fields, with a brook and pond. Jay Peak can be viewed from here. Your host has an income tax and financial planning service during the winter. She enjoys golf, bridge, gardening and swimming.

For dining, you'll find many outstanding restaurants in the area. Your host has menus available for you and she'll be happy to help you with choices that suit your taste.

When you visit you're welcome to swim in the pool, use the picnic table, play billiards, weed in the garden, enjoy the many indoor and outdoor games available. The 100 acres has many interesting areas for walking and exploring. There is a pond and brook on the property and lots of comfortable space for reading, tanning or chatting. Pat shares vegetables from her garden, her kitchen and gas grill with guests. There are nearby golf courses, ski areas, and lakes with beaches. The B&B is only two miles from a public beach.

Shrewsbury

You'll want to take a short trip to Killington, an all-year recreational community. There is a summer theater and during July both the **Killington Music Festival** and the **Killington Equestrian Festival** are held here. West on US 4 is **Killington Ski and Summer Resort**. A gondola tramway and chairlift carry sightseers to the observation deck at the summit of Killington Peak. Also on US 4 is the **Pico Alpine Slide**. You may ride a chairlift to the top and then take your choice of two slides down the mountain.

From Shrewsbury drive north to Plymouth, the birthplace of Calvin Coolidge, the 30th president of the U.S. **Plymouth Notch Historical District** off SR 100A, includes the birthplace, early home and burial place of President Coolidge. Rutland is northeast of Shrewsbury on SR 103 and US 7, where you can find the **Norman Rockwell Museum**, on US 4 east. There are more than 2,000 Rockwell pictures and other articles on display. Drive northwest on SR 3 to the Village of Proctor to learn about the quarrying industry. In Proctor the streets are marble and many of the public buildings are built from marble. The **Vermont Marble Exhibit** is on Main St. Visitors can view a film, watch a sculptor at work, see displays of the processing of marble and see marble from Proctor and from other parts of the world. On West Proctor Road, 3 1/2 miles south of downtown is **Wilson Castle**. This lavish mansion was built in 1867 on an 115-acre estate. The 32 rooms are extravagantly furnished with antiques, museum pieces and art. Tours are given daily, late May to mid-Oct.

From Proctor continue north on US 7 to Pittsford. The **New England Maple Museum**, on US 7, has displays, demonstrations and a slide show to describe the historic and modern maple sugaring process. Visitors can sample different grades of syrup. At the **Federal Fish Hatchery**, 4 miles northeast of US 7, the visitor can see Atlantic salmon in various stages of development. One of the entrances to the **Green Mountain National Forest** is northeast of Rutland on US 4. The combination of forest and mountains provide a wealth of scenic beauty.

● **Buckmaster Inn**
Lincoln Hill Rd., Shrewsbury, VT 05738. (802)492-3485.

$50-60/D. Family and length of stay discount.

Call 8:30 AM - 8:30 PM.
• No cr.crds.
• Innkeepers: Sam & Grace Husselman.
• *4 rms, 2 pb, 1 sb.*
• Full breakfast served in the dining room or on the porch. You'll have a choice of juice, muffins, homemade breads and jellies and beverage.
• No pets, no smoking, no alcohol, no children under 3.
• 8 mi. southeast of Rutland.

This historical **1801** building is built on a knoll overlooking a picturesque valley. The inn has wide pine floors, fireplaces, a wood-burning stove and a library.

For dining, you'll want to visit Hemmingway's Royal Hearthside, the Sirloin Saloon, or Brookside Furnace Market Place.

When you visit you're welcome to look at the antiques throughout the home. You'll rest by the fireplace, reading books from the library, or, during the summer, you'll enjoy the two large screened porches. You're welcome to visit the sugar house next door where maple syrup is made. Most of all you'll want to stroll the country roads enjoying the beautiful Vermont scenery.

Virginia

Cluster Springs

Danville, west of Cluster Springs on US 58/360, is one of the largest tobacco auction centers in the U.S. There are nine auction warehouses in the area and visitors are welcome during the auctions, mid-Aug. through mid-Nov.

Millionaires' Row Historic District has many fine Victorian and Edwardian residences. A walking tour map of Millionaires' Row and schedules of auction warehouses are available from the **Danville Chamber of Commerce**, 635 Main St.

East of Cluster Springs on US 58/360 is Clarksville. The **Prestwold Plantation**, north on US 15, was built in 1795. It has original furnishings. Costumed guides give tours of the house, outbuildings and gardens. The plantation is at the edge of Buggs Island Lake, where you can enjoy a swim, the beach or boating.

Drive north on US 501 to Brookneal. **Red Hill**, the last home of Patrick Henry is near Brookneal. It is 5 miles east on SR 600. The house has been reconstructed and contains furniture from the Henry family. Here you can see Patrick Henry's grave, his law office, other outbuildings and a garden. Drive south on US 501 to Durham, Raleigh and Chapel Hill, North Carolina. It's only an hour drive from Cluster Springs. You could spend days in these cities enjoying the sights, shopping and entertainment available. If you prefer not to get lost in city traffic, you might want to drive south on US 501 to Roxboro then west on US 158 to Reidsville, NC. Although it is a slightly longer drive, people who enjoy beautiful old mansions will think it is worthwhile to see **Chinqua-Penn Plantation House**. The 30-room mansion is 3 miles northwest off of US 29 bypass. It is filled with art and furnishings from throughout the world. On the grounds is a Chinese pagoda and 30 acres of landscaping.

Oak Grove Plantation Bed & Breakfast

P.O. Box 45, Hwy. 658, Cluster Springs, VA 24535. (804)575-7137.

$45/S; $50/D. OPEN MAY-SEP.

Call anytime.
- No cr. crds.
- **Innkeeper: Pickett Craddock.**
- *2 rms, 2 sb.*
- Full breakfast of juice, fruit salad, egg casserole, bread and coffee.
- No pets, no smoking in bedrooms. Children are welcome.
- Just off of US 501, 5 mile south of South Boston and 50 miles north of Durham, NC.

This antebellum house was built in 1820 and is still owned by a descendent of the builder. It has ornate woodwork, a 19th century furnished parlor and a sun porch. It is furnished in authentic antiques. The house sits on its own 400 acres of land. During the off-season Pickett is a preschool teacher and a caterer.

For dining, you'll want to talk to Pickett about dining right here at Oak Grove Plantation. Other popular spots are Oliver's, Ernie's, Clarksville Station, Steve's or Billy's Steak House.

When you visit arrange to bring your children. Pickett is a preschool teacher and she welcomes children. She has a midweek package that includes special activities and supervision for children. You'll also appreciate the play equipment on the grounds. You'll enjoy hiking and biking on the trails in the 400 acres surrounding your B&B. It's a great place for bird watching, too. If you prefer, you may read or relax on the porch.

Monterey

You'll want to enjoy the beauty of nature during your stay in the county that is called "Virginia's Switzerland." It is nestled in the foothills of the Allegheny Mountains and just a short drive from the Appalachians. The **Monagahela National Forest** with its green woods, hiking trails, and fishing streams is nearby (see Elkin, WV).

During your stay in this picturesque village you'll want to relax and to exercise outdoors. It's famous for its hunting and fishing. The mountain trails are superb for summertime hiking and wintertime skiing. In the spring the area is filled with sugar houses and sugar camps producing maple syrup. The **Maple Museum**, on US 220 S., has displays and artifacts used in sugar making historically and today. There is a nearby golf course, swimming, shopping areas and many antique stores. Just east on US 250 is McDowell where a sign and monument mark the site of the **McDowell Battlefield,** where one of the first battles in Stonewall Jackson's campaign took place.

From Monterey, drive west across the West Virginia border on US 250 and then south on SR 28/32 to Green Bank. The **National Radio Astronomy Observatory** does research in radio astronomy. Visitors see a slide show that provides information about six radio telescopes. Then a narrated bus ride is given to the site of the telescopes. After you leave the observatory, drive west to Cass. The **Cass Scenic Railroad State Park** starts right downtown where you can take a trip on a Shay steam locomotive that was once used for logging trains. During the summer you can take a 2-hour trip to Whittaker Station, a 4 1/2-hour trip to the top of Bald Knob or a Saturday Night Dinner Train ride. While you are in Cass, you may want to see the **Cass Country Store**, once the largest company store in the world. The **Wildlife Museum and Historical Museum** has displays relating to the history of the timber and mining industries in the area and a collection of wildlife exhibits. If you'd like to do more traveling and sightseeing, it's only about an hour drive east from Monterey on US 250 to Staunton and Swoope, Virginia (also listed in the book).

● Highland Inn
Main Street, P.O. Box 40, Monterey, VA 24465. (703)468-2143.

$45-64. Discounts to sr citizen, government, AAA, travel agent.

Call 8 AM to 9 PM.
- V, MC.
- **Innkeepers: Michael Strand & Cynthia Peel.**
- *17 rms, 17 pb.*
- Continental breakfast with fruit, fresh baked bread and beverage.
- No pets.
- On Main St. in Monterey.

This classic Victorian Inn, has two-tiered Eastlake style porches with gingerbread trim. Furnishings are period antiques. It is listed on the National Historic Register. Your hosts enjoy antiques, classical music, the local wildflowers and birds.

For dining, you'll want to enjoy the Highland Inn dining room. There are several other excellent restaurants within driving distance.

When you visit you'll want to relax in one of the rocking chairs on the porches. The parlor has reading material, games, and a piano for guests' use. You'll find shopping, antique stores, golf and swimming or skiing nearby.

Shenandoah Valley — Staunton, Swoope

You'll want to pay special attention to the exceptional old buildings in Staunton, because none were destroyed during the Civil War. Self-guided walking tours are available from the Chamber of Commerce, 30 N. New St. This is also the birthplace of **Woodrow Wilson**. The **Museum of Frontier Culture**, five miles west on US 250, shows how the background of European settlers from various cultures fused to become a part of the early American family farm.

Drive southwest on I-64/I-81 to Lexington, the home of four American Generals. The **Stonewall Jackson House**, 8 E. Washington St., has been restored and furnished with many of the family's original furnishings. **Washington and Lee University** is on S. Jefferson and Washington Sts. General Lee and his family are buried beneath the chapel. **Virginia Military Institute** is on US 11. The **George C. Marshall Museum and Library**, at the end of the VMI parade ground, houses papers and materials relating to the career of General Marshall.

New Market Battlefield Historical Park, is 1 mile north of I-81. This is the site where 247 cadets from Virginia Military Institute aided the confederate troops in winning a strategic battle.

East of Staunton on I-64 or US 250 is the home of Thomas Jefferson and James Monroe. **Monticello**, I-64 to SR 20, 1/2 mile south to SR 53, 1 1/2 miles east, was built by Thomas Jefferson from 1769 until 1809. **Ash Lawn-Highland**, 2 miles southeast of Monticello on CR 795, is a 535-acre estate owned by James Monroe. Visitors may receive guided tours of the main house, see the gardens, spinning and weaving demonstrations.

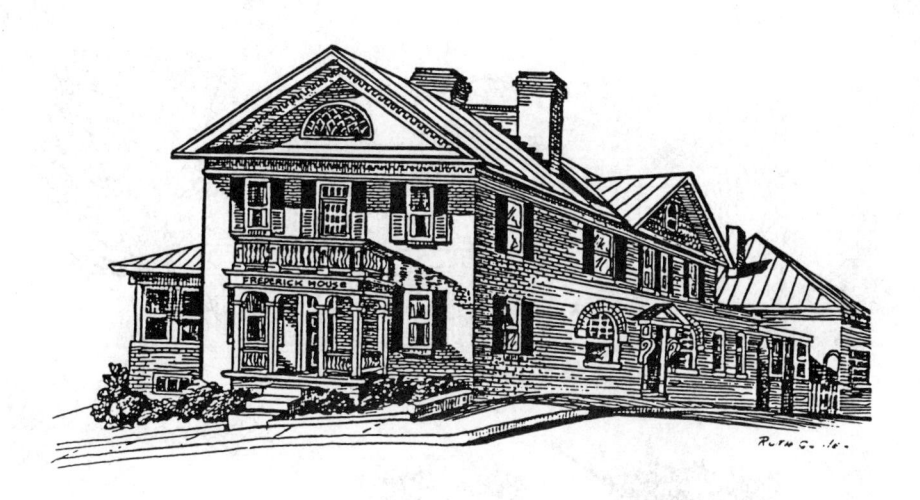

● Frederick House

Frederick and New Sts., Staunton, VA 24401. (703)885-4220 / (800)334-5575.

$50-95. Sr citizen discount.

Call 7 AM - 10 PM.
- V, MC, D, AE, DC.
- **Innkeepers: Joe & Evy Harman.**
- *14 rms, 14 pb.*
- Full breakfast is served in the tea room. The menu will include choices like Apple Raisin Quiche, strata, Ham & Cheese Pie, waffles, hot or cold cereal, fruit, homemade bread.
- No pets, no smoking.
- Across from Mary Baldwin College in the center of Staunton.

The inn is composed of five restored townhouses, built between 1810 and 1910. Each is furnished with period antiques. Each guest bedroom has terry robes, ceiling fans, cable TV, radio, air conditioning, telephone and a private entrance.

For dining, you'll enjoy McCormicks, the Concourse Cafe, the Ruggles Warehouse, the White Star Mill, 23 Beverley or the Depot Grill.

When you visit you'll enjoy the privacy and convenience offered by this B&B. It is convenient to all downtown Staunton attractions. You'll have the use of the adjacent athletic club with its exercise facilities and swimming pool. Guests enjoy strolling through the gardens and viewing the art collection in the inn.

●Thornrose House at Gypsy Hill

531 Thornrose Ave., Staunton, VA 24401. (703)885-7026.
$55-65.

Call anytime.
- No cr. crds.
- **Innkeepers: Suzanne & Otis Huston.**
- *5 rms, 5 pb.*
- Full breakfast. A typical breakfast would include juice, fruit, a whole grain entree such as waffles or pancakes, an egg entree such as omelet, frittata or strata and beverage.
- No pets, no smoking.
- Adjacent to a 300-acre park and six blocks from historic Staunton.

This Georgian Revival home has been recently redecorated and renovated. It has a wraparound veranda, a garden with Greek pergolas, interior columns and fireplaces. Your hosts enjoy travel, skiing, gourmet cooking and gardening.

For dining, you may choose to dine at 23 Beverley, the Buckhorn Inn, the Belle Grae Inn or in the Depot Grill or Concourse Cafe, in Staunton Station.

When you visit you'll want to enjoy afternoon tea, served on the veranda or in the fireplace parlor. You can stroll on the spacious grounds, or, if you're energetic you can play tennis in the park directly across the street. If you've forgotten your tennis racket, they'll supply one.

● **Lamsgate Bed & Breakfast**
Rte. 1, Box 63, Swoope, VA 24479.
(703)337-6929.
$35/S; $45/D. Discount to families and for stay of 5 nights or more.

Call anytime.
- No cr. crds.
- Innkeepers: Dan & Elizabeth Fannon.
- 3 rms, 1 sb.
- Full breakfast. A sample breakfast might include juice or fruit, bacon or ham, eggs, grits, homemade muffins and jellies. When you stay for a second night, you're likely to be served Gingerbread pancakes.
- No pets, no smoking.
- 6 miles east of Staunton.

This **1816 brick farmhouse** has been modernized and furnished in a casual country style with antiques, collectibles and needlework. You'll enjoy the working sheep farm that surrounds the house. Elizabeth is a quilter, gardener and retired librarian. Dan is a sheep farmer, Civil Air Patrol chaplain and a semi-retired clergyman.

For dining, you'll want to choose between the Belle Grae Inn, the Buckhorn Inn, the Depot Grille, McCormick's and Bowe's Family Restaurant.

When you visit you'll undoubtedly enjoy the sheep and lambs, and observing a working sheep farm. In early spring there are newborn lambs to watch. The veranda is a perfect spot to relax, visit or enjoy the scenery which includes the pastures and the Allegheny Mountains.

Woodstock

You'll be immersed in the breathtaking scenery of mountains and forests. The **Shenandoah River** runs nearby and provides excellent fishing and canoeing. Visit the **Woodstock Museum**, 137 W. Court St., and take a walking tour of this town that has buildings that predate the Revolutionary War.

Drive north from Woodstock on US 11 to Strasburg. The **Strasburg Museum**, on SR 55, is in an old railroad station. It contains a pottery collection, and other collections in Victorian and colonial settings. The **Vintage Village Americana/Transportation Museum**, south on US 11, displays old autos, aircraft and other Americana. Continue north on US 11 to Winchester. A historic community that was first settled in 1732, Winchester played a major part in the French and Indian and Civil Wars. Stop at the **Winchester-Frederick County Visitor Center**, 1360 S. Pleasant Valley Rd., to get a driving tour map of the area. The oldest house in the city is **Abram's Delight Museum**, at 1340 S. Pleasant Valley Rd. It was built in 1754 and has period furnishings. **George Washington's Office**, at S. Braddock and W. Cork Sts., is now a museum. This was where he began his surveying career and contains colonial items and antique surveying equipment. **Stone-wall Jackson's Headquarters**, 415 N. Braddock St., is an 1854 Gothic Revival House. On another day, drive east to US 340, then north to Front Royal. During the Civil War this town was a base for the famous Confederate spy, Belle Boyd. The **Ivy Lodge Museum** and **Belle Boyd Cottage** are at 101 Chester St. The **Warren Rifles Confederate Museum**, 95 Chester St., has items from Belle Boyd, and other Civil War artifacts. Take a drive south from Woodstock on US 11 to Edinburg. Drive west to SR 686, then 1 1/2 miles north to **Shenandoah Vineyards**. Take a self-guided tour of the vineyards and enjoy a taste of the wine produced here.

Continue south on US 11 or I-81 to **New Market** for another interesting day. **George Washington National Forest** and **Shenandoah National Park** are all within easy driving distance of Woodstock.

●Country Fare Bed & Breakfast

402 N. Main St., Woodstock, VA 22664. (703)459-4828.
$45-55. Discounts for extended stays.

Call 8 AM - 9 PM.
- No cr. crds.
- **Innkeeper: Bette Hallgren.**
- *3 rms, 1 pb, 1 1/2 sb.*
- Expanded continental breakfast of juice or fruit, home baked bread and beverage. Often there may be a surprise addition to the menu.
- No pets, restricted smoking.
- In Woodstock, right on US 11.

Built in the late 18th century, with an addition in 1840, this inn has been authentically restored. It was used as a field hospital from 1861-1864 during the Civil War. It is furnished with antiques, many from the host's grandmother. The inns sits on a half-acre of land, circled by magnolias, boxwood and Japanese cherry trees. Betty enjoys many crafts, especially stenciling. She shares her craft books with guests.

For dining, you'll want to visit the Spring House restaurant, the Hotel Strasburg (in Strasburg), McSylvia's or a nearby B&B that serves gourmet dinners. Bette will help you find a restaurant of your choice.

When you visit you'll find the upstairs porch and the living room are marvelous places to read or just relax. You're welcome to catch some sun on the patio or to stroll the grounds. You'll feel very comfortable at this B&B. In fact, Bette says she's happy to have you bring home a pizza and relax with a drink.

Washington

Edmonds, Seattle

The Puget Sound waterfront, at Edmond, has a public fishing pier, beaches and a wonderful view of the Olympic Mountains. **Edmonds Underwater Park** for scuba divers is at Brackett's Landing Beach. Ferries regularly cross the sound to Kingston. The **Edmonds Museum**, 118 N. 5th Ave., has historic displays on Edmond. The exhibits include a marine room and a model shingle mill.

Just south of Edmond is the city of Seattle. **Blake Island Marine State Park** is accessible only by boat. There are exhibits, trails, activities, including clamming, and **Tillicum Village**, a recreation of a Native American settlement. The island is reached by a 45-minute boat cruise. The admission fee, which includes the boat ride, ranges from $9 for small children to $40 for adults. The **Lake Washington Ship Canal and Chittenden Locks** are in the northwest section of the city, 4 miles west of I-5, Exit 169. The **Maritime Heritage Center**, S. Lake Union, is a 3-acre park. and includes the **Center for Wooden Boats** with replicas and original boats of many different cultures and eras. Boat rentals are available. The **Northwest Seaport**, 1002 Valley St., has tours of an 1897 sailing schooner. A restored shipyard, education center and various nautical tours are also a part of the Maritime Center. The **Seattle Center**, near Elliott Bay, encompasses 74 acres on the site of the 1962 World's Fair. Included is an amusement park and the space needle. The **Pacific Science Center** is a hands-on science museum for children including a science playground. The **Museum of Flight**, 9404 E. Marginal Way S., has exhbits on the history of aviation. The **Seattle Aquarium**, 1483 Alaskan Way, has a number of special exhibits including an underwater dome where visitors can view sea life in Puget Sound. The **Bill Speidel Underground Tour**, leaves from Doc Maynard's Public House, Pioneer Building, First Ave. and James St. This walking tour includes the old buildings around Pioneer Square and the sidewalks and stores that are below ground as the result of an 1889 fire.

● **Harrison House**
210 Sunset Ave., Edmonds, WA 98020. (206)776-4748.
$35-45/S; $45-55/D.

Call anytime.
- No cr. crds.
- **Innkeepers: Jody & Harve Harrison.**
- *2 rms, 2 pb.*
- Full breakfast with fruit, entree and beverage. A sample entree might be waffles with strawberries & cream, pancakes & sausage or ham & eggs.
- No pets, no smoking, no children.
- In downtown Edmonds.

This new waterfront home has a spectacular view of Puget Sound and the Olympic Mountains. You will have a large room with your own king size bed, television, wet bar, telephone and private deck. Your hosts enjoy travel, golf and skiing.

For dining, there are numerous waterfront restaurants with assorted specialties. Discuss your preferences with your hosts.

When you visit you'll have the privacy of a large room with your own deck. You may entertain on your own deck or just relax and view the boating activities on Puget Sound. Harrison House is just 15 min. from the University of Washington and you can walk to the boat harbor, fishing pier, beaches and shopping. Some of the northwest's finest restaurants are within walking distance.

- **Prince of Wales Bed and Breakfast**
133 Thirteenth Ave. E., Seattle, WA 98102. (206)325-9692.
$55-80. Discount for longer stay.

Call 10 AM - 7 PM.
- V, MC.
- **Naomi Reed & Bert Brun.**
- *4 rms, 2 pb, 1 sb.*
- Full breakfast of juice, fresh fruit cup, muffins, quiche and beverage.
- No pets, no smoking.
- About 1 1/2 miles from Pike Place Market.

This **turn-of-the-century Capitol Hill house** is well located and has excellent views. Three rooms view the Seattle skyline, Puget Sound and the Olympic Mountains. A fourth room has a panoramic view of downtown Seattle. Your hosts are interested in adult education, travel and current events.

For dining, we recommend Chinook's. For other recommendations, discuss your personal preferences with your hosts.

When you visit you'll enjoy the comfort of the fireplace on a cool, rainy afternoon. When the climate is better you'll want to enjoy the views from the deck. The location of this B&B makes it especially convenient.

Overnight Caramel French Toast

From Joy Hagen, **Lakeside Farm Bed and Breakfast**
Webster, SD

1 cup firmly packed brown sugar
1/2 cup butter of margarine
2 tablespoons light corn syrup
12 slices sandwich bread
6 eggs beaten
1 1/2 cups milk
1 teaspoon vanilla
1/4 teaspoon salt

Combine sugar, butter and corn syrup in a small saucepan. Cook over medium heat until thickened, stirring constantly. Pour syrup mixture into a lightly greased 13 x 9 x 2 baking pan. Place 6 slices of the bread on top of the syrup mixture. Top with the remaining 6 slices. Combine milk, eggs, vanilla and salt. Pour egg mixture evenly over the bread slices. Cover and chill 8 hours or overnight. In the morning, bake uncovered at 350F. for 40 to 45 minutes or until lightly browned and bubbly. Watch closely to adjust for differences in oven temperatures and baking pans.

Mrs. Hagen frequently substitutes her own homemade bread for the sandwich bread but sandwich bread is specified because it fits the pan so well.

Mt. Adams Country: Glenwood

You'll want to go hiking or cross-country skiing on Mt. Adams and in the nearby Gifford Pinchot National Forest; go downhill skiing on Mount Hood; take a sno-cat ride up to the Mt. Adams Wilderness; hike, bike or bird watch in the Conboy National Wildlife Refuge.

Mt. Adams is the second highest mountain in Washington State and Glenwood is the community closest to the mountain. Order a **Mt. Adams Country** brochure from the Mt. Adams Chamber of Commerce, P.O. Box 449, White Salmon, WA 98672. Then drive one or all four of the scenic driving tours. Fish in the Klickitat River, ride horseback near Glenwood or Trout Lake, ride a dogsled in the National Forest, bicycle paved backroads, pick huckleberries in the Indian Heaven country, windsurf or sail on the Columbia Gorge, raft or kayak the White Salmon River. In season, you can pick fruit in the cherry, apricot, peach, pear and apple orchards of Hood River and Mount Adams. Golf at Husum Hills. Bicycle the country backroads and enjoy blossoming orchards or autumn colors. West of White Salmon, on SR 14, is the **Broughton Log Flume**, which was one of the last operating log flumes in the U.S. See the **Spring Creek National Fish Hatchery**, 3 miles west of Hood River - White Salmon Bridge on SR 14. It has a visitor center, ponds and a fish ladder. Chinook salmon can be seen in varying stages of maturity, depending upon when you visit.

Southeast of Glenwood is Goldendale. In the **Goldendale Observatory State Park**, has a large reflecting telescope for public use. The **Klickitat County Historical Museum**, 127 W. Broadway, is in a 1902 mansion. It has exhibits of pioneer items and a large coffee mill collection. Maryhill is just south of Goldendale. The **Maryhill Museum of Art**, on SR 14, has a large collection of European and American art. There is a collection of Rodin originals and several outstanding collections. **Stonehenge**, is on a cliff overlooking the Columbia River. The concrete replica of the Stonehenge in England is a memorial to soldiers from Klickitat who were killed in World War I.

● **Flying L Ranch**
25 Flying L Lane, Glenwood, WA 98619. (509)364-3488.
$55-85. Family and seasonal discounts.

Call 9:30 AM - 9:30 PM.
- V, MC, AE, DC, CB.
- **Innkeepers: Darvel & Darryl Lloyd.**
- *13 rms, 9 pb, 1 sb. This includes 2 cabins.*
- Full breakfast. A sample menu might include juice, fresh fruit salad with yogurt sauce, Mt. Adams Huckleberry Pancakes, ham slice, beverage.
- No smoking, no pets except in cabins.
- 1 mi. NE of Glenwood. Paved all-weather highways lead to the ranch.

This quiet retreat has lodging facilities which include a 3000 sq. ft. lodge, a 2-story guest house and two cabins, on 160 acres of private meadows and woodland with protected wildlife and wildflowers. Your hosts are brothers. They are veteran mountaineers, hikers, cross-country skiers and active conservationists.

For dining, you'll enjoy Mio Amore Pensione and Serenity's Restaurant in Trout Lake. The Cookhouse Dining Room at the lodge is available for group dinners or for special occasions.

When you visit you'll be able to walk or cross-country ski over one or two miles of trails on the property, groomed, marked and mapped. Rental bikes are available. The pond in the front meadow is great for swimming, ice skating and wildlife observation. A large hot tub with room for 6-8 people is in a gazebo with a view of Mt. Adams. There are outdoor games (volleyball, badminton, horseshoes etc.) and indoor games for you to play. And, there's a library filled with books that you can read in front of the big fireplace or on the front porch.

San Juan Islands and surrounding area: Deer Harbor, Ferndale

You'll want to revel in the fresh sea air, enjoy the many recreational opportunities, watch the wildlife, gasp at the beautiful scenery. The San Juan Islands consist of 172 different islands. Orcas, Fidalgo, Lopez and San Juan are the largest and most populated. Deer Harbor is on Orcas. The **Washington State Ferries** leave Anacortes for Orcas Island on an established schedule. The **San Juan Airlines** fly regularly from Seattle and Bellingham. The **San Juan National Wildlife Refuge** contains 48 islands with only two open to the public. The islands are home to many bald eagles, tufted puffins, great horned owls, many other birds and a large assortment of mammals. The waters are filled with salmon, dolphins, seals and killer whales (orcas). **Orcas Island Historical Museum**, Eastsound, has Native American items and artifacts from six homestead cabins built in the 1800s. **Moran State Park**, on the east side of Orcas Island and 8 miles southeast of Eastsound, contains 4,934 acres. It has hiking trails, a 2,400-ft. mountain and mountain lakes. On San Juan Island is the **National Historical Park**. Parts of British and American forts are preserved. These were built during a quarrel over possession of the islands between Great Britain and the U.S. **Western Prince Cruises**, depart from Friday Harbor. They offer 4-hour narrated wildlife cruises of the islands. The **Whale Museum**, 62 First St. N., Friday Harbor, has exhibits on whales, their behavior, sounds, and history. The **Hovander Homestead**, south on Hovander Rd., in Ferndale, is a restored early Whatcom County farm. It includes a 1903 Victorian house, a large red barn, a children's farm zoo, gardens and an orchard. The **Tennant Lake Natural History Interpretive Center**, is 1 1/2 miles southwest of I-5, Exit 262. It contains a Fragrance Garden designed for the visually impaired, a boardwalk trail around a marsh, a lookout tower and displays on the seasons. **Pioneer Park**, First and Cherry Sts., contains 10 restored pioneer log buildings.

Bellingham overlooks Bellingham Bay and the San Juan Islands. Chuckanut Drive, SR 11, follows the shoreline offering wonderful views of Puget Sound and the islands. At the junction of SR 11 and Hawthorn Road, in Fairhaven Park, is a large rose garden. Sehome Hill Arboretum, off Bill McDonald Parkway, is 165-acres filled with native plants. There are two miles of trails and many scenic views of the surrounding countryside. The Whatcom Museum of History and Art, 121 Prospect St., has displays of antique furniture, Native American items and logging tools. Two floors have art exhibits and historical items. The Children's Museum Northwest, 227 Prospect St., has hands-on displays including a craft area, train and medical clinic.

● Palmer's Chart House

P.O. Box 51, Orcas Island, Deer Harbor, WA 98243. (206)376-4231.

$50/continental breakfast; $55/full breakfast. To receive these rates, mention this book.

Call before 8 PM.
• No cr. crds.
• Innkeepers: Majean & Donald Palmer.
• 2 rms, 2 pb.
• Expanded continental breakfast: Fruit, fruit juice, cold cereals, beverage. Full breakfast: Fruit, fruit juice, entree, breads, beverage. Entrees would include Canadian bacon and eggs, quiche, French toast and other recipes. Breakfasts are served on a variety of table settings collected by Majean in her travels about the world.
• No pets, no smoking, restricted alcohol, no children under 12.
• On Orcas Island.

This modern island home is exceptionally clean. Guests have their own private deck. Don is an educator; Majean is a businesswoman. They spend as much time as possible sailing their 33 ft. sloop, the *Amante*.

For dining, you'll want to try Rosario's, Bilboa's, La Famiclia, Christina's or the Bungalow. There are also some terrific delicatessens. The Palmers say you are welcome to take out food and enjoy it on the deck.

When you visit you'll enjoy the privacy of a room with your own private entrance, private bath and private deck. You're also welcome to use any of the outside areas surrounding the B&B. They will share travel information and slides with guests who ask. You may be able to charter a "sail tour" with the Palmers on their yacht, the *Amante*.

● **Hill Top Bed & Breakfast**
5832 Church Rd., Ferndale, WA 98248. (206)384-3619.
$39/S; $44-54/D. Sr. citizen, travel agent, length of stay discounts.

Call before 10 AM or after 4 PM.
• V, MC.
• **Innkeepers: Paul & Doris Matz.**
• *3 rms, 2 pb, 1 sb.*
• Expanded continental breakfast. A sample menu might include blueberry coffee cake, muffins, applesauce and beverage. Other menus might include Dutch Babies or Oatmeal.
• No pets, no smoking.
• 2 miles west of I-5, 12 miles south of Canada.

This modern brick home gives guests a panoramic mountain view in quiet surroundings. The large rooms and private entry make this B&B special. The rooms have fine quilts and wall hangings made by your hostess.

For dining, you'll enjoy the Douglas House, Tres Sombreros, Bob's Burger & Brew or the Kowloon Garden.

When you visit you'll need to get up early one morning and watch the glorious sunrise over Mt. Baker and the Cascade Mountains. You'll find croquet and badminton games to play, a backyard for sunbathing, upper and lower decks for lounging, books to read, a cable TV to watch and a player piano to play.

Yogurt Granola Parfait

From Julie Snider, **Two Sisters Inn**
Laurens, SC.

1 single serving tub of your
favorite fruit yogurt
1 cup granola cereal
Whipped topping

In 2 parfait glasses, place alternate layers of granola and yogurt until filled. Top with a dollop of whipped topping. Serve with an iced tea spoon. Makes 2 servings.

This dish is beautiful and delicious.

Sunnyside

You'll want to visit a winery and enjoy some of the great Northwest. The area around Sunnyside is wonderful for vineyards. There are at least 20 **wineries** in the area.

To visit the sister cities of Kennewick, Pasco and Richland, drive southwest on I-82 to I-182. Richland is a center for technology and atomic research. The **Hanford Science Center**, 825 Jadwin, is a U.S. Dept. of Energy information center. **Sacajawea State Park**, southeast on US 12 and 395, has an interpretive center with an Indian artifacts room. Exhibits tell the story of the Lewis and Clark expedition and the role played by their guide, Sacajawea. At Kennewick, you can find a cruise on the Columbia River. The **Spirit of Washington Dinner Train**, Canal Dr. and Dayton St., has a narrated 3hr. excursion to Prosser, every Friday. Gourmet dinners are served on board.

From Sunnyside, drive north on I-82 or SR 22 to Toppenish and Yakima. **Toppenish** is the headquarters of the Yakima Indian Nation. The **Yakima Nation Cultural Center**, north on US 97 has exhibits depicting the history of the Yakima Indians. It also displays a recreation of a historic winter lodge. The **Toppenish Historical Museum**, 1 S. Elm St., has a collection of Native American baskets and bead work. The **Toppenish National Wildlife Refuge**, is south 4 3/4 miles on US 97, then west 1/2 mile on Pump House Rd. It has a nature trail and interpretive center. At **Fort Simcoe State Park**, 27 miles west, is a partially restored fort built in the 1850s. In Yakima you can find several major shopping centers, Class A baseball and basketball and horse racing. Indian petroglyphs can be seen at a spot 5 miles west on US 12. The Yakima Canyon is a popular spot for hunting rocks. Take a ride on a 1906 **Yakima Trolley**. During the summer trolleys leave from 3rd Ave. and Pine St. Tour the **Boise Cascade Corp.**, 805 N. 7th St. Phone 5 days in advance for reservations. The **Yakima Valley Museum**, in Franklin Park, at 2105 Tietcn Dr., has a large collection of horsedrawn vehicles, recreated historic shops and Native American artifacts.

● **Sunnyside Inn Bed & Breakfast**
800 E. Edison Ave., Sunnyside, WA 98944. (509)839-5557 /(800)221-4195.

$40-75.

Call 9 AM 9 PM.
● V, MC, AE.
● **Innkeepers: Don & Karen Vleger, Jim & Geri Graves.**
● *10 rms, 10 pb.*
● Full breakfast served restaurant style. A sample menu would include orange juice, fresh baked muffins, pancakes, ham, fresh fruit and coffee.
● No pets, no smoking.
● In Sunnyside, off of I-82.

This lovely old house was built in 1919. Each room has a private bath, color TV, phone and daily maid service. 7 rooms have double occupancy whirlpool tubs. 4 rooms are suite sized. Jim & Geri are gourmet chefs and bakers. Jim was head chef at the Trump Plaza in New York City.

For dining, you'll enjoy Le' Ma' Cuisine at the Sunnyside Inn, the Greystone or the Blue Goose.

When you visit you'll enjoy relaxing to the classical music in the parlor, sunbathing on the patio or in your own personal room. The central location and the many things to do in surrounding areas make this B&B particularly attractive.

West Virginia

Elkins

You'll want to take time to see and enjoy the fabulous scenery in this area of West Virginia. It is surrounded by some of the state's highest mountains, spectacular scenery, and huge forests.

Just east of town on US 33 is the **Monongahela National Forest** on more than 900,000 acres in the Allegheny Mountains. It has picturesque drives, miles of hiking trails and multitudes of trees, plants, wildflowers, animals and birds. Several special recreation areas and wilderness areas are contained within the forest.

The **Dolly Sods Wilderness Area**, west of Hopeville, covers more than 10,000 acres. It is noted for its views and wetlands filled with unusual plants. At the eastern side of the forest is **Seneca Rocks**. Starting at the town of Seneca Rocks, you can see an imposing 900-foot eroded rock formation that is popular with rock climbers. **Smoke Hole**, north of Seneca Rocks, is a deep gorge of the Potomac, with exceptional rock formations. **Spruce Knob**, west of US 33, is the highest point in West Virginia. Although the road to the top requires good driving conditions and an experienced driver, the views are exceptional for those who drive it. **Spruce Knob Lake** is said to be a good trout lake.

Twenty-five miles east of Elkins (US 33 to SR 32 N) is Harman. The **Old Mill** was built in 1877 and used to grind white flour and to plane wood. It is powered by water turbines. Today it still operates grinding various whole grain flours. A craft shop on the second floor has daily demonstrations of local crafts.

A drive northeast on US 250 will take you to the town of **Philippi**. This is the site of the first land battle of the Civil War. A covered bridge spanning the Tygart River was used by both Union and Confederate forces during the war. A museum is across from the bridge.

● The Retreat at Buffalo Run

214 Harpertown Road, Elkins, WV 26241. (304)636-2960.

1993: $37/S; $48/D. 1994: $41/S; $52/D.

Call 8 AM 8 PM.
- No cr. crds.
- **Innkeepers: Bertha, Earl & Kathleen Rhoad.**
- *6 rms, 3 1/2 sb.*
- Full breakfast served family style in areas guests prefer. Menus include fruit salad, muffins, beverage and a variety of delicious homemade entrees.
- No pets, no smoking.
- Within walking distance of Elkins shops and 10 minutes from the commuter airport.

This Greek Victorian style house has porches that almost wrap around the entire home. The retreat and many of the trees are nearly 100 years old. The grounds are filled with tall shade trees, hemlock rhododendron, roses, fruit, vegetable and herb gardens. The house is furnished with family antiques, art and contemporary pieces.

For dining, choose among the Cheat River Inn, The Starr Cafe, the 1863 Tavern, Beander's, or the Red Fox Inn. Take a 45-minute drive through the mountains to the small Swiss village of Helvetia and have dinner at The Hutte.

When you visit your hosts will invite you to pick roses, raspberries, tomatoes or herbs from the gardens. Enjoy an afternoon nap in the lower yard hammock or front porch swing. You can watch the hummingbirds and other birds at the feeder. If Kathleen is free, she may be willing to drive a dirt road to the Cheat River where you can float, in an inner tube, for four miles to a beautiful swimming hole.

Summit Point

You'll want to hide from the rest of the world for a relaxing getaway or, as an alternative, use this lovely rural village as a center base for all sorts of busy sightseeing at nearby attractions.

Located in West Virginia's eastern panhandle, Summit Point is a lovely spot for hiking, walking or biking. It's not far from the Shenandoah and Potomac Rivers where visitors can fish, canoe or raft. It's just a short drive to the Appalachian Trail for great mountain hiking.

Just 20 minutes away, on the Potomac, is **Harpers Ferry Historical Park.** At this famous Civil War site, you'll find many restored buildings, a walking trail, guided tours and living history programs. It's a 10-minute drive to Charles Town. Horse racing at the racetrack is open Feb.-mid-Dec. Auto races take place at **Summit Point Raceway,** Apr.-Dec. The **Courthouse,** George and Washington Sts., and the room where John Brown was tried for the Harpers Ferry incident, is open to the public. The **Jefferson County Museum,** 200 E. Washington, has artifacts from the Civil War, John Brown and the Washington family.

From Summit Point it's a 30-minute drive to Sharpsburg, MD, and **Antietam National Battlefield.** It's also 30 minutes to Winchester, VA, steeped in Civil War and colonial history. Other short drives are to Sherpherdstown, the oldest town in West Virginia (20 min.), and Martinsburg Outlet Mall (30 min.).

● Countryside
P.O. Box 57, Summit Point, WV 25446. (304)725-2614.

$50-55. Lowest rates apply to two day stay, and are guaranteed if seen in this guide.

Call 8 AM-10 AM or 8 PM-10 PM.
- V, MC.
- **Innkeepers: Lisa & Daniel Hileman.**
- *2 rms, 2 pb.*
- A continental breakfast on a white tray or in a lovely wicker basket, is brought to your room. A typical breakfast includes huge muffins, juice and beverage.
- No pets, no children under 10.
- In Summit Point.

Tucked away on a quiet, treelined street in the village, Countryside is decorated with a mixture of old and new. It sits on the edge of a 500-acre apple orchard. Afternoon tea is served every day.

For dining, some of the best known restaurants include the Bavarian Inn and the Yellow Brick Bank, in Shepherdstown or the Charles Washington Inn, in Charles Town. There are many other excellent restaurants in the area.

When you visit you'll want to take walks through the apple orchard, where guests sometimes see deer and rabbits. In the patio, you may sit and watch the birds. Countryside has hundreds of books and magazines about country life and the civil war and other subjects. Daniel and Lisa enjoy telling their guests about all the out of the way places to visit near Summit Point.

Wisconsin

Menomonee Falls — Milwaukee Area

You'll want to enjoy the luxury of staying in the tranquil, lovely village of Menomonee Falls, just 20 minutes from the activities of Wisconsin's largest and most famous city, Milwaukee.

In Cedarburg, northeast of Menomonee Falls, you can explore the **Cedarburg Mill**, built in 1855. One of the last covered bridges in the state crosses Cedar Creek. The **Cedar Creek Settlement**, in an 1864 mill, has a cluster of shops, galleries, restaurants, a blacksmith, and a winery you can tour. Eleven miles north of Cedarburg, on Co. Rd. I, is **Ozaukee County Pioneer Village**, a village of restored log and half timber buildings from throughout the country. Crafts and skills are demonstrated on Sunday. The **Cedarburg Visitor Information Center**, in City Hall, has information on the historic district and a map for a self-guided walking tour. In Milwaukee, try visiting a brewery, since Milwaukee is famous for its beer. The **Pabst Brewery**, 915 Juneua Avenue, offers walking tours of the brewery and samples, Mon.-Fri., 10 AM-3 PM. The **Miller Brewing Co.**, 4251 W. State St., has a media presentation, guided tours and samples of beer and soda, Mon.-Sat., 10 AM-3:30 PM. The **Milwaukee County Zoo**, west on US 18, at 10001 W. Bluemound Rd., is one of the largest in the U.S. Animals are seen in natural habitats. Tours are available in zoomobiles and trains. The **Mitchell Park Horticultural Conservatory**, 524 S. Layton Blvd., has three huge glass domes, seven stories high, featuring seasonal exhibits in tropical, desert and themed habitats. The **Milwaukee Public Museum**, 800 N. Wells St., is a natural history museum. The visitor walks through exhibits with lifesize dinosaurs, a tropical rainforest, European Village etc. Sports fans can see the **Brewers** play baseball, the **Bucks** play basketball. There also are art museums, parks, theater, old homes, many other museums and things to do.

● **Dorshel's Bed & Breakfast Guest House**
W140 N 7616 Lilly Road, Menomonee Falls, WI 53051.(414)255-7866.

$35-50.

Call anytime 3 to 5 days ahead.
•No cr. crds.
•**Innkeepers: Dorothy and Sheldon Waggoner.**
•*3 rms, 1 pb, 1 sb.*
•Expanded continental breakfast with a different menu each day of your stay. Typical menu would include juice, cereal, fruit bowl or cheese and apple plate, warm rolls and beverage.
•No pets, no children under 10.
•In the village of Menomonee Falls.

A contemporary country manor filled with antiques on 1 1/2-acres of blue spruce, white willow and cedar. There are two screened porches. On the upper level are floor to ceiling windows for an unrestricted view of the surrounding countryside.

For dining, you'll find a variety of exceptional restaurants. Dorothy and Sheldon will be happy to help you choose something to fit your taste.

When you visit you'll enjoy watching the birds bathing in the bird bath or feasting at the feeders. Read a good book beside one of the fireplaces, have a game of pool in the Miller room or take a stroll on the 1 1/2 acres of property surrounding your B&B. You'll have access to a nearby developed quarry swimming area with excellent facilities.

Wyoming

Alta

You'll want to use this as a jumping off spot for your visit to the Grand Teton National Park, just 7 miles away.

Within the park are miles of trails for short walks, longer hikes and overnight trips. Take a drive to see the spectacular mountains, canyons, lakes, glaciers, forests of evergreens and ground covered with snow throughout the year. If you like to fish, the lakes and streams are inhabited by all manner of fish. Not only is this an ideal spot for mountain climbers, but authorized guide services are available. Rangers will help prospective climbers with information on routes and equipment. Horses are available for trail rides and there are also evening horse or wagon rides with dinner. Visitors can rent boats, go on float trips or take scenic boat cruises. In the winter, ice fishing, snowmobiling and crosscountry skiing are popular.

Jackson is southwest of Alta and at the southern entrance to Grand Teton National Park. In town you can find a number of float trips or whitewater river trips of varying difficulty and length. More unique are the wintertime dog sled trips offered by **Freebird Alaskan Adventures**. Call (307)733-7388 for more information. The **Jackson Hole Aerial Tram**, northwest on SR390, is at the base of the Jackson Hole Ski Area. Passengers ride to the top of Rendezvous Mountain where they can look out over the Teton Range and Jackson Hole Valley. **Snow King Chairlift and Alpine Slide**, is at 400 East Snow King Ave. The chairlift takes passengers to the top of Snow King Mountain. The slide descends from halfway up the mountain. The **National Elk Refuge**, east on Broadway to Elk Refuge Rd., is the winter home of one of the largest Elk herds in North America. They can be seen from November through April. The **National Fish Hatchery and Aquarium**, north on US 26/89/191, raises lake and cutthroat trout. **Wax Museum of Old Wyoming**, 55 S. Cache St., has life-size characters from the Old West. **Wildlife of the American West Art Museum**, displays the work of North American wildlife artists. Exhibits change throughout the year.

● **Inn of the Lost Horizon**
Rte. 1, Box 3590, Alta, WY 83422.
(307)353-8226.

$40/D.

Call after 5 PM.
- No cr. crds.
- **Innkeepers: Chuck & Shigeko Irwin.**
- *4 rms, 2 pb, 1 sb.*
- Continental breakfast including coffee, juice and a croissant or Belgian waffle.
- No pets, restricted smoking, no children under 14.
- 6 mi. from Driggs, ID (the most direct route to the inn).

This chalet is furnished with artifacts from around the world, to simulate the ShangriLa in the book, "Lost Horizon." It was built in 1976. Chuck is a retired air force officer. He met and married Shigeko in Japan. They searched the world for their own "ShangriLa" and finally decided on Alta, WY.

For dining, make reservations for a dinner at the Lost Horizon Dinner Club, here in the inn. The service of the 10 course dinner takes 3 hours so there is only one seating. The cuisine is a blend of Chinese and Japanese. Other fine places to dine include nearby Grand Targhee Ski and Summer Resort and the British Rail, in Driggs, ID.

When you visit you'll be amazed at the scenery, with the mountains and wilderness so near your doorstep. The Lost Horizon has its own private Lake Nola. It's stocked with fish and guests are welcome to fish it. The B&B also has its own stream which is fine for swimming in the summer. Hiking trails start right at the doorstep and lead into the Grand Tetons. There is an excellent golf course just a mile away and it's just 100 miles to Yellowstone National Park.

Casper

You'll want to spend days exploring this city of 50,000, where you will find a college, civic center, recreation center, symphony orchestra, parks and swimming pools and many museums.

Fort Casper Museum, 4001 Ft. Casper Rd., is a recreation of a fort built in the 1840s. Indian and pioneer artifacts are exhibited in an interpretive center. The **Werner Wildlife Museum**, 405 E. Fifteenth St., has a collection of mounted wildlife specimens. The **Nicolaysen Art Museum**, 400 E. Collins St., has changing exhibits of art by regional and national artists. It also has a children's center with hands-on displays. **Casper Mountain Park** has numerous picnic sites and trails for hiking, crosscountry skiing and snowmobiling. The **Casper Planetarium**, 904 N. Poplar, has daily shows of celestial movements every evening June-August.

West of Casper on US 20/26, 5 miles west of Powder River, is **Hell's Half Acre**. Covering 320 acres, it is a depression filled with strangely colored and shaped rock figures and shapes.

Take a trip east from Casper on US 20/26 to Glenrock. East of the town is a spot where ruts made by pioneer's wagon wheels can still be seen. In downtown Glenrock are several buildings that date from the late 1800s.

Continue east on 20/26 to Douglas. On the state fairgrounds is the **Wyoming Pioneer's Memorial Museum**. It has clothing and a large collection of artifacts and photos from early Wyoming. There is also a changing art exhibit and a research library on Wyoming history. The **Ayres Natural Bridge** is 12 miles west on I-25 then 5 miles south on Natural Bridge Rd. Water from Prele Creek has worn a path through a huge rock, leaving a huge natural bridge.

At **Fort Fetterman State Historic Site**, 11 miles northwest on SR 93, is a partially restored 1867 fort. A museum has displays on the history of the military.

●Bessemer Bend Bed & Breakfast

5120 Alcova Rt., Box 40, Casper, WY 82604. (307)265-6819.

$35/S; $45/D; $10/ex. prsn.

Call after 4 PM.
- V, MC.
- Innkeeper: Opal and Stanley McInroy.
- 3 rms, 2 sb.
- Full breakfast. A sample breakfast may include fresh fruit or juice, sourdough pancakes, maple syrup, sausage, eggs if desired, beverage.
- No pets, no smoking.
- 10 mi. southwest of Casper on Hwy 220.

This charming home is located on the North Platte River, on the Oregon Trail crossing and the Pony Express route. Opal is a retired teacher with a great knowledge of western history and a background in ranching. Stan is a petroleum engineer who enjoys fishing, hunting and hiking.

For dining, the Goose Egg Inn is recommended.

When you visit you will appreciate the peace, quiet and beauty the area has to offer. This home faces the North Platte River and as you dine a variety of wildlife may pass by. Muledeer may cross on either side of the house on their way to water. Meadowlarks sing from the fence posts. Bald Eagles fish in the early spring and Canadian Geese nest on the islands. Pelicans arrive early in the spring and stay until fall. Sunrises and sunsets are spectacular. Bring your camera. You'll find lots of reading material and enjoyable games: horseshoes, croquet, and ping pong.

● Durbin Street Inn
843 South Durbin, Casper, WY 82601. (307)577-5774.

$48-53. Extra charge for fireplace. Sr citizen and travel agent discounts.

Call 10 AM 9 PM.
- V, MC, D, AE, DC, CB.
- **Innkeepers: Don & Sherry Frigon.**
- 4 rms, 2 sb.
- Full breakfast. A sample menu might include fruit or juice, scrambled eggs, bacon, sausage, hash browns, homemade danish, blueberry pancakes or biscuits and gravy.
- No pets, restricted smoking, limited alcohol, no children under 15.
- 7 blocks from downtown.

This historic inn was built in 1917. It is decorated in period style with soft color throughout to create a warm, comfortable, relaxing atmosphere. It is in a quiet, residential neighborhood. Your hosts' hobbies include photography, cooking, decorating, real estate, old homes and furniture refinishing.

For dining, you might want to eat right at the Durbin Street Inn. Other superb places to dine include Bosco's Italian Restaurant, the Goose Egg Inn or Armor's Restaurant.

When you visit you'll find a relaxing, comfortable "home away from home." You're welcome to play the old piano. In the summer you can enjoy fresh fruit and vegetables from the garden, sit on the side porch to enjoy warm evening breezes and try to count the stars. If you want, your hosts will volunteer to take you to their secret place where you can find a lovely hidden waterfall and hand-feed wild deer.

Chipmunk Pie

From Bette Hallgren, **The Country Fare B&B**
Woodstock, VA

3/4 cup sifted cake flour
1 cup firmly packed brown sugar
1 1/2 teaspoon baking powder
1/2 teaspoon salt
dash mace
dash cinnamon
2 eggs
1 1/2 teaspoon vanilla
1 1/2 chopped tart apples
3/4 cup walnuts

Mix and sift the first 6 ingredients. Stir in unbeaten eggs and vanilla. Fold in apples and walnuts. Turn into a well greased 9 inch pie pan. Bake at 350F. for 25 to 30 minutes. Serve plain and warm or cool with whipped cream.

Bette once ate a similar pie and asked for the recipe. The cook refused to divulge her secret so Bette experimented until she developed her own version.

Cheyenne

You'll find a town filled with colorful history. Cheyenne was the home of the first U.S. woman governor, the first woman justice of the peace and is the capitol of the first state to grant women the right to vote. There are hundreds of stories about the early days, when it was on the frontier of the "wild west." And, most of the stories are true!

Visit during the last week in July to attend **Cheyenne Frontier Days** and the world's largest rodeo. The **Cheyenne Frontier Days Old West Museum**, on N. Carey Ave., has artifacts dating from 1897. The **State Capitol**, between 24th and 25th on Capitol Ave., has murals and displays of native wildlife within the neoclassic sandstone building. Also see the **State Museum**, in the Barrett Building, at 24th St. and Central Ave and the **Historic Governors' Mansion State Historic Site**, 300 E. 21st St. Visit the **Wyoming Hereford Ranch**, to see a working cattle ranch. In Lions Park there is a small **zoo**, where buffalo and elk can be seen. The **National First Day Cover Museum**, 702 Randall Ave., has original artists drawings used for first day covers, and the covers for postage stamps issued throughout the world. The **Wildlife Visitor Center**, of the Wyoming Game & Fish Dept., 5400 Bishop Ave., has photographs of the animals that can be found in the state. It also has a grassland display.

Take a scenic drive west on I-80 toward Laramie. Although Laramie is filled with entertaining things to see and do, we'll suggest just a few. **Wyoming Territorial Park**, 975 Snowy Range Rd., is a re-created wildwest town with restored buildings. A barn has a dinner theater and craftspeople demonstrating their skills. Open 5/25-10/14. **Laramie Plains Museum**, 603 Ivinson Ave., is a restored mansion filled with period furnishings. The **University of Wyoming**, at 9th St. and Ivinson has **planetarium** shows when school is in session. It also has an **Art Museum** with art from many artists of many periods. It also has historic, geological and anthropological museums.

Drummond's Ranch Bed & Breakfast

399 Happy Jack Rd., Cheyenne, WY 82007. (307) 634-6042.

$55-60.

Call anytime.
- No cr. crds.
- **Innkeepers: Kent & Taydee Drummond.**
- *3 rms, 1 pb, 1 sb.*
- Full breakfast. A sample menu might include fresh fruit, homemade English or blueberry muffins, eggs, cereal, orange juice and beverage. Sourdough waffles are served every Sunday.
- No smoking.
- 20 minutes from Cheyenne and 1/4 mile off of SR 210.

This large modern home is centrally located between Cheyenne and Laramie. It's quiet and secluded and you'll have fresh flowers in your room. There'll be snacks, fruit or beverage available throughout the day. Terrycloth robes are provided for your comfort. Your hosts' hobbies include backpacking, mountain biking, cross-country skiing, reading, playing soccer and horseback riding.

For dining, you may make special arrangements to have lunch and/or dinner at the ranch. Other excellent places to eat include Lexes Cafe, Poor Richards and Carriage Court.

When you visit you'll be adjacent to a state park where boating and fishing are popular. It's just five miles to Medicine Bow National Forest. The library has a large supply of reading materials. There are a number of table games to play. You can use the outdoor hot tub or raid the refrigerator whenever you are hungry.

CANADA

ALL PRICES ARE IN CANADIAN DOLLARS UNLESS OTHERWISE NOTED.

Alberta

Calgary

This large Canadian city has a plethora of things to see and do. **Heritage Park Historical Village**, west on Hwy 2, and south on Heritage Dr., is a recreation of a village built before 1915. More than 100 buildings are clustered on 60 acres. Many of the buildings are actual restored buildings. The **Calgary Tower**, 101 Ninth Ave., is 627 ft. high. There is a revolving observation terrace and restaurant at the top. **Calaway Park**, west on Hwy. 1 at Springbank Rd. exit, is a children's amusement park. Shows, with live music, are presented daily. The **Calgary Zoo, Botanical Garden and Prehistoric Park**, 1300 Zoo Rd. N.E., includes a large zoo, a children's zoo, a large conservatory and a park containing life-size replicas of dinosaurs. The zoo has approximately 1,400 animals including endangered species.

Glenbow Museum, 9th Ave. and 1st St. S.E., has a museum, art gallery and library. Items displayed in the museum include Native American and pioneer objects, European armor and weapons, geological samples, and art from a range of periods. **Alberta Science Center and Centennial Planetarium**, 7th Ave. S.W. and 11th St., has interactive exhibits and star shows. **Devonian Gardens**, between 2nd and 3rd Sts., at 8th Ave., has 2 1/2-acres of glass covered gardens and a pool/ice-skating rink. The **Canadian Olympic Park**, Hwy. 1 and Bowfort Rd., was the site of the 1988 Winter Olympics. It is now used as a training center and winter ski area. Bus tours are available. The **Alberta Historical Resources Foundation**, 102 8th Ave. S.E., has brochures for a self-guided walking tour of downtown and a driving tour of interesting residential areas. Calgary also has many fine shopping areas, recreation facilities, golf courses, biking and cross-country skiing, and horse racing. It has several major sports teams.

Harrison's B & B Home
6016 Thornburn Dr. N.W., Calgary, AB T2K 3P7.
(403)274-7281.

$50-55.

Call 7 AM - 8 AM or 4 PM - 7 PM.
- No cr. cds.
- **Innkeeper: Susan Harrison.**
- *2 rms, 1 sb.*
- Full breakfast. A sample menu might include fresh baked scones or toast from homemade bread, baked beans or potato cakes, cereal, eggs or bacon, ham or sausage, juice or fresh fruit, beverage.
- No pets, no children under 10, restricted smoking.
- In Calgary, 2 min. from Deerfoot Trail and 64th Ave. N.E.

This cozy bungalow is in a quiet, residential area with many trees. Birds and squirrels visit all year. Your host enjoys gardening to attract birds, walking, hiking and cross-country skiing, art exhibitions and hunting for treasures in second-hand shops.

For dining, you'll find many choices of restaurants ethnic and traditional western food. For help in choosing spots that you'll enjoy ask Susan for help.

When you visit you'll be able to watch birds and squirrels during breakfast because the dining room looks out on the front garden and bird bath. When you lounge on the quiet, secluded patio you'll be able to watch birds attracted by the two large pines, sunflowers and the neighbors feeders. The B&B is on the morning side of Nose Hill, a prairie-covered hill in its natural state. There are marvelous walks available within a short distance of Harrison's.

● **Turgeon's B & B**
4903 Viceroy Dr. N.W., Calgary, AB T3A 0V2.
(403)288-0494.

$30/S; $45/D.

Call after 5 P.M. or leave a message on the answering machine and calls will be returned collect.
● No cr. cds.
● **Innkeepers: Eileen & Denis Turgeon.**
● *2 rms, 2 sb.*
● Full breakfast served in the dining room or on the patio. A sample menu might include cereal, pancakes, sausage or bacon, fresh farm eggs, fresh muffins and scones, homemade preserves, beverage.
● No pets, no children, restricted smoking.
● 1/3 mi. from Hwy 1A & 1/2 mi. from Trans Canada Hwy 1.

This comfortable bungalow is in a residential area, next to a quiet park at the end of the street. It is air conditioned and close to two major shopping centers. Denis speaks French and loves gardening. Eileen enjoys crafts, gardening, cooking and sewing. They both enjoy singing.

For dining, you will find many diverse restaurants within walking distance. Eileen and Denis will be happy to help you choose. With 24-hour notice, dinner is available at the B & B.

When you visit relax on the patio, enjoy the friendly Cocker Spaniel or Siamese cat; play cribbage with Denis. A TV, stereo, VCR and darts are all available for guests. In cool weather, enjoy the gas burning fireplace in the family room.

Mount Adams Huckleberry Hot Cakes

From Darvel T. Lloyd, **Flying L Ranch**
Glenwood, WA

Dry Mix:
8 cups unbleached all-purpose flour
2 cups old fashioned oats
2 cups 100% bran cereal
1/4 cup baking powder
2 tablespoons baking soda
1 tablespoon salt

Added ingredients:
1 dozen eggs
3/4 cup vegetable oil
3 quarts lowfat buttermilk
6 cups huckleberries (preferably from the Mount Adams area)

In a large bowl, combine flour, oats, cereal, baking powder, baking soda and salt. This mixture can be stored in an air-tight container for future use. For every 1 cup of dry mix add 1 egg, 1 tablespoon oil, 1 cup buttermilk and 1/2 cup berries. Beat the eggs, then add the buttermilk and oil, mixing well. Stir the egg mixture into the flour mixture until just mixed. If it seems too thick, add more liquid. Heat a large non-stick griddle to 400F, and oil lightly. Just before frying, gently fold in the huckleberries. For each pancake, pour 1/4 cup batter onto hot griddle and cook until bubbly. Flip and cook other side until golden brown. The entire recipe makes about 4 dozen hotcakes.

At the Flying L Ranch, these hotcakes are often served with thawed freezer jam made with fresh local peaches. Darvel says the recipe was actually developed by his mother, Ilse Lloyd. They've been serving guests at the ranch since 1960.

Claresholm

In Claresholm, visit the **Claresholm Museum**, 5126 First St with its displays of the late 1800s and pioneer life. There is a one-room schoolhouse, an early motorized school van, and many other early artifacts. There is an antique shop and live theatre Jul.-Aug. Drive south on Hwy. 2 to Fort Macleod. You'll want to visit **Head-Smashed-In Buffalo Jump**, W. on Hwy. 785, off Hwy. 2. An interpretive center has exhibits on one of North America's best preserved Plains Indian buffalo hunting areas. The center has displays interpreting the excavations and the history of the property. There are short trails leading to the main sections. The **Fort Macleod Museum**, 25th St. and 3rd Ave., is built to represent the original fort. There are exhibits on the history of the fort and the mounted police. Musical Mounted Patrol rides are presented daily Jul.-Aug.

West from Ft. Macleod, on Hwy. 3, is Lethbridge. If you are interested in gardens, visit the **Nikka Yuko Japanese Garden**, on Mayor Magrath Dr. in Henderson Pk. Hostesses in kimonos conduct tours. **Indian Battle Park**, on Scenic Dr., west of 3rd Ave. S, is the site of the last Native American battle in North America. Fort Whoop-up was a trading post and the incentive for the formation of the North West Mounted Police. Visitors can ride a train through the park, visit replicas of shops and houses and visit an interpretive center. South of Ft. Macleod and Claresholm, on Hwy. 2, is Cardston, home of a large Mormon settlement. Visitors may visit the site of the temple but cannot enter it. The **C. Ora Card Home**, 337 Main St., is a log cabin that once was the home of this Mormon leader, a son-in-law of Brigham Young. The **Alberta Carriage Centre**, 339 Main St., has antique horse-drawn vehicles. West of Cardston, on Hwy. 5, is **Waterton Lakes National Park**. This park joins Glacier National Park, in the U.S. to form the Waterton-Glacier International Peace Park. The scenery here is breathtaking with mountains towering above lakes. The park is home to many native prairie and mountain wildflowers and to a wide range of wildlife. There are hiking, driving, and horseback riding trails in the park. Horses may be rented at riding stables north of the town of Waterton Park.

● **Anola's Bed & Breakfast**
Box 340, Claresholm, AB T0L 0T0.
(403)625-4389.

$50. Cottage: $95.

Call before 10 AM or after 4 PM.
•No cr. cds.
•Innkeepers: Anola & Gordon Laina.
•*2 rms, 1 sb. 1 cottage with private bath.*
•A full hearty farm style breakfast, served in the solarium or in the country kitchen. A sample breakfast might include juice, homemade granola, creamy scrambled eggs with bacon, cornbread, homemade breads and jams, beverage.
•No pets, no smoking.
•9 mi. E of Claresholm and 1 mi. N.

This 3,800-acre farm in South Alberta has a home decorated with antiques. The guest cottage has been restored and decorated with antiques and a wood burning stove. Your hosts are both private pilots. Anola enjoys quilting and collecting antiques.

For dining, visit the Casa Roma Restaurant, in Claresholm.

When you visit you'll find a lot to do without ever leaving the farm. Grandad's Museum has a collection of old cars, tractors and Western Canadian antiques. A neighboring Hutterite Colony will welcome your visit. You're free to tour the farm and learn the story of how wheat becomes bread and pasta. You'll be able to soak in the hot tub or curl up in front of a glowing fire with a best-seller.

British Columbia

Kelowna

You'll want to visit Lake Okanagan, 90 miles long, to watch for its legendary Loch Ness-type monster, the Ogopogo. To get a better viewpoint, you may want to take a summer-time cruise on the **M.V. Fintry Queen**. The lake is also used for water sports and fishing. The area surrounding the lake is noted for its vineyards, fruit and vegetable crops. There are many wineries in the area offering tours. The **Hiram Walker & Son** distillery, is east of Hwy 97 N. on Beaver Lake Rd., then S. on Jim Bailey Rd. It produces 50 brands of brandy, gin, rum, vodka and whiskey. Tours and tastings are given Mon-Fri, May-Labor Day. **Sun-Rype Products**, 1165 Ethel St., gives tours of its fruit processing plant. The **Okanagan Orchard Tours Ltd.**, 2755 K.L. O. Rd., has a narrated tram tour of an orchard. The **B.C. Orchard Industry Museum**, 1304 Ellis St., is devoted to the history and current production of fruit in the area.

Children will be interested in **Wild Waters Waterslide Park**, N. on Hwy. 97 at McCurdy Rd. It has waterslides, miniature golf, a video arcade, hot pools and picnic facilities. Next door is **Flintstones Bedrock City**, at 990 McCurdy Rd. Featured in this recreation of the cartoon village are figures of the Flintstone characters, a train ride, boat ride, carrousel, miniature golf and Flintstone movies. The **Kelowna Sunshine Theatre** is considered an excellent Canadian summer theatre group. the area. The **Okanagan Game Farm**, S. on Hwy. 97, has native wildlife and animals from all over the world sharing the property. The **Canada Dept. of Agriculture Research Station**, N. on Hwy. 97, has 741 acres of ornamental gardens and picnic facilities. In Vernon you'll find yet another waterslide, **Atlantis Waterslides and Recreations**, N. on Hwy 97A at Pleasant Valley Rd. Don't worry there's more to see and do. The **O'Keefe Historic Ranch**, N. on Hwy. 97, was a pioneer cattle ranch. The original buildings, including mansion, church and general store have period furnishings. The **Okanagan Bobslide**, N. on Hwy. 97A, offers a 1,900 ft. ride. There is a picnic area, gold panning and go-carts.

● The Cat's Meow

5299 Chute Lake Rd., Kelowna, BC V1Y 7R3.
(604)764-7407.

$35-45/S; $40-55/D; $25/ex. prsn.

Call in the morning.
- No cr cds.
- Innkeepers: John Moelaert.
- *3 rms, 2 sb.*
- Your choice of breakfast from a menu. A sample breakfast might include orange juice, an egg, toast and beverage or grapefruit, cereal, biscuits or toast, beverage.
- No pets, no smoking, no children under 10.
- 8 miles from downtown Kelowna.

This architect-designed cedar home is on a one acre lot. The surrounding Ponderosa pines provide a home for many birds, squirrels and chipmunks. Your host is a writer and author/photographer who has traveled to many different places.

For dining, you'll find many restaurants in Kelowna. Some favorites are the Vintage Room of the Capri Hotel, the Shalimar or The Carvery.

When you visit you will want to relax on the sundeck, browse through the private library. It's close to a fine beach and a winery. It's in a tremendous area for nature walks. Just a short walk will take you to a ridge overlooking Okanagan Lake, the floating bridge and the city.

● The Gables Country Inn
2405 Bering Rd., Box 1153, Kelowna, BC V1Y 7P8.
(604)768-4468.

$50-60/D. Seasonal discounts for stays of 3 days or more.

Call 7 AM - 11 PM.
- No cr. cds.
- **Innkeeper: Patricia Graham.**
- *4 rms, 1 1/2 sb.*
- Expanded continental breakfast of juice, fresh fruit compote, hot biscuits, homemade jams, beverage.
- No pets, no smoking, no children under 12.
- One block off highway, 10 min. from downtown Kelowna.

A Heritage Award-winning home, this inn has spacious upstairs bedrooms, furnished with antiques. Guests will enjoy views of orchards, vineyards and Okanagon Lake. Patricia enjoys travel and is also interested in antiques, dolls, art and crafts. She enjoys meeting people.

For dining, you'll have superb dining at Lake Okanagan Resort, the Capri Hotel, Case Marguerites, Finer Choice, Jean's Bistro, or Cattle Country.

When you visit you'll be able to swim in the pool in the secluded sunken garden, enjoy relaxing on the old-fashioned covered porch. Breakfast is frequently served on the glass-windowed porch, where guests can view the lake, pool and surrounding countryside. On cold days, guests may prefer sitting by the huge brick fireplace. If you feel like cooking, you can use the barbecue. You're welcome to help pick fruit from the B&B's trees. There are peaches, cherries, apricot, plum, walnut and apple.

Cottage Cheese - Yogurt Pancakes

From Joyce Johnson, **Joha House**
Quathiaski Cove, British Columbia

4 eggs, separated
1 cup (1/2 pint) plain yogurt
1 cup (1/2 pint) small curd cottage cheese
3/4 cup flour
3/4 teaspoon soda
1/2 teaspoon salt
1 tablespoon sugar
1/2 teaspoon cream of tartar

Add cream of tartar to egg whites and beat until they stand in peaks but are not dry. Beat egg yolks until light colored. Add yogurt and cottage cheese, blend thoroughly.

Stir or sift together flour, soda, salt and sugar and add to egg yolk mixture. Drain any liquid from egg whites and gently fold into the mixture.

Lightly grease or spray griddle that is heated to 325F. Make pancakes that are about 4 inches in diameter and cook slowly until the top begins to dry. Turn and brown on the other side.

Serve immediately with warm applesauce or fruit syrups. Serves four.

Vancouver and Vancouver Island: North Vancouver, Quathiaski Cove, Ucluelet, Victoria

Vancouver is on the mainland and just across the Strait of Georgia from Vancouver Island. **Stanley Park**, downtown peninsula, is an outstanding natural park that has an aquarium, zoo, children's zoo, miniature train, rose garden, and biking and jogging trails. **Vandusen Botanical Gardens**, 521 Oak St., has 39 sections with walks that wind past sculptures, streams, lakes and waterfalls. **Dr. Sun Yat-Sen Classical Garden**, 578 Carrall St., in Chinatown, is designed like classical gardens developed during the Ming Dynasty. **Science World**, 1455 Quebec St., has interactive exhibits and shows on a variety of scientific subjects. The **Maritime Museum**, 1100 Chestnut St., has exhibits associated with boats and the sea. It also has the St. Roch, an Arctic supply and patrol schooner, which was the first vessel to circumnavigate North America. The **Burnaby Village Museum**, 6501 Deer Lake Ave., recreates the sights and sounds of a late 19th century B.C. village. Quathiaski Cove is on Quadra Island, near Campbell River on the northeastern side of Vancouver Island. The water surrounding the island is said to be the second clearest in the world. The **Kivagiulth Museum** at Cape Mudge has an exceptional collection of Potlatch artifacts. The area is noted for its marvelous fishing. **Ucluelet** is on the west coast of Vancouver Island. This is a fabulous spot for walkers, with trails for nature walks, wharves and beaches to investigate. Rent a bike or charter a boat for fishing, scuba diving, whale watching or sight-seeing. During the summer the **M.V. Lady Rose** sails between Ucluelet and Port Alberni on Mon., Wed., and Fri. In Victoria see the world famous **Butchart Gardens**, Brentwood Bay, off Hwy. 17. At **Sealand**, Beach Dr., you can view ocean creatures through windows. Seals and a whale perform daily. **Undersea Gardens**, 490 Belleville St., allows visitors to observe marine life through large windows. Also: Take a ferry trip to Vancouver, a harbour tour, or a horse-drawn carriage ride.

● Poole's Bed & Breakfast
421 W. St. James Rd., North Vancouver BC V7N 2P6
(604) 987-4594.

$45-50. Family, repeat customer and weekly discounts.

Call 9 AM - 9 PM.
- No cr. cds.
- **Innkeepers: Arthur & Doreen Poole.**
- 3 rms, 2 sb.
- Full breakfast served in the dining room. A sample breakfast might include juice, hot or cold cereal, fruit, bacon & mushroom stuffed crepes or waffles with blueberry sauce or yogurt sauce, beverage.
- No pets, no smoking.
- Across Burrard Inlet from Vancouver. It's a 20 min. drive to downtown or a 15 min. ride by SeaBus.

This comfortable home is tastefully decorated with some valuable antiques mixed with contemporary. Your hosts are retired and both consider entertaining B&B guests to be a hobby. Arthur is a retired banker who enjoys giving information and directions to the guests. Doreen enjoys cross-country skiing and gardening. Both enjoy travel.

For dining, you'll find a variety of fine restaurants. Our suggestions are the Salmon House, with a lovely view of the city and excellent sea food, in West Vancouver; the Prow Restaurant, on the waterfront at Canada Place; Seven Seas Restaurant, a floating ship with excellent seafood, in North Vancouver; and the Teahouse Restaurant, overlooking the water in Stanley Park. There are many excellent Chinese, Thai and Japanese restaurants in the area.

When you visit you'll find books in every room and a library upstairs. Guests are welcome to sit on the porch, under the umbrella, when they relax or when they have breakfast or a snack. They also like to sit on the patio, under the shade of the old apple tree. Some guests like to help pick raspberries when they're in season.

Joha House
Box 668, Quathiaski Cove, BC V0P 1N0. (604) 285-2247.

$55-65/D. Garden Suite: $70.

Call at your convenience. Leave a message on the machine if no one answers.
- No cr. cds.
- **Innkeepers: Harold & Joyce Johnson.**
- *3 rms, 1 pb, 1 sb.*
- Full breakfast served in the dining room. A sample breakfast might include scrambled eggs with smoked salmon, scones, melon wedges, homemade jams, fresh fruit cup and beverage.
- No pets, no smoking inside. Inquire about children.
- 15 min. ferry ride from Campbell River.

Wood and glass are the focus in this contemporary home. The living areas and the deck overlook the inside passage to Alaska. The house is furnished in an eclectic blend of antiques and contemporary furniture.

For dining, visit Tsa-Kwa-Luten Lodge, a new resort with an excellent dining room. Two excellent grocery stores on the island have great produce, bakery items and deli sections for picnic menus. It's only a short ferry ride to Campbell River and many more dining choices.

When you visit, you'll want to sit on the 55 ft. deck and view the water in its many changing moods. You can use binoculars to observe the many birds, such as eagles, herons, hummingbirds and kingfishers. Take a walk to the private dock to view nature from another level. From here you'll see purple starfish and sea anemone on the pilings. Ask Joyce and Harold to show you their suggested "Quadra Island Adventures," an entire week's itinerary, to give you ideas of things to see and do on the island. Use the spacious guest living room to relax in privacy, if you'd like. Books and games are available to while away an occasional rainy day and your hosts might join you for bridge or pinochle.

● **Burley's Lodge**
1078 Helen Road, Box 550, Ucluelet, BC V0R 3A0.
(604)726-4444.

$40-50/D.

Call anytime, although best time is evening.
- V, MC.
- **Innkeeper: Micheline Riley.**
- *6 rms, 4 sb.*
- Expanded continental breakfast served buffet style. A sample menu would include juice, a selection of cereals, a variety of breads for toast, bran muffins and a selection of spreads.
- No pets, no smoking, no children under 12.
- On the waterfront, 3 blocks from Main Street in Ucluelet.

This **waterfront home** is on a small island at the mouth of the harbor. You'll look out on the waterfront. At the back of the house is lawn, garden and forest. There is a view from every window.

For dining, the Wickinninish Restaurant, Whales Tale and the Pot Belly Restaurant have excellent food.

When you visit, you'll want to spend some time just looking at the world around your B&B. Sunbathe on the deck while you watch the fishing boats go by. Walk on the beaches or into the woods. Watch the birds. Play horseshoes on the lawn, or billiards in the recreation room. Borrow a book or magazine from the large library to read on the deck or next to the fireplace in the large living room. Borrow the canoe for a trip around the harbor.

● Our Home on the Hill B&B

546 Delora Dr. Victoria, BC V9C 3R8.
(604)474-4507.

$55. Family discount.

Call anytime. Calls left on answering machine will be returned promptly.
- No cr. cds.
- **Innkeepers: Grace & Arnie Holman.**
- *3 rms, 1 pb, 1 sb.*
- Full breakfast served in the formal dining room. A sample menu might include fresh kiwi and orange juice, cheddar cheese - sour cream oven omelette, carrot muffins, homemade blackberry jam, choice of cereal, beverage.
- No pets, no smoking.
- Close to Trans-Canada Hwys. 1 and 14, about 20 min from downtown Victoria.

This **modern home** is built in a quiet, wooded residential area on the side of Triangle Mountain. Your hosts collection of antique furnishings and collectibles give an appearance of old-fashioned charm and comfort.

For dining, you'll find many of the world's finest restaurants in Victoria. Perhaps you'd like to order curry in the Empress' Bengal Room, or have afternoon tea at the James Bay Tea Room. Louie, Louie has a fifties theme and is a teen favorite. Spinnakers is a pub style restaurant where they brew their own beer and offer live entertainment.

When you visit enjoy the sheltered spa after a busy day of sightseeing or relax in the privacy of the special TV room. Grace and Arnie take pride in offering guests a tranquil and peaceful place to stay, welcoming them as personal friends.

Oatmeal and Coconut Cookies

From Jeanette Rowland, **Jeanette Rowland's B&B**
Hudson Heights, Quebec

1 cup butter
1/2 cup white sugar
1 cup all-purpose flour
1 cup medium shredded coconut
2 cups rolled oats
1 teaspoon vanilla

Cream butter and sugar together. Then add flour, oats and coconut. Roll out to approximately 1/8 - 1/4 inch thick. Cut in rounds. Bake at 325F for 15 to 20 minutes or until pale brown.

Jeanette adapted this recipe from the cookies her mother made in Ireland. She says she has baked thousands of them, frequently serving them to guests who arrive in time for tea or giving them as gifts.

New Brunswick

Fredericton

You'll want to wander the tree-lined streets, admiring beautiful old buildings, and stroll through "The Green," a lovely park-like walk along the St. John River. Fredericton is one of North America's oldest settlements and the capitol of New Brunswick.

Spend a day at **Kings Landing Historical Settlement**, west on Hwy. 2, a living history village of restored 19th-century buildings. It has shops, homes and farms. The costumed staff conducts tours and gives wagon rides around the village. Take a stroll down Queen St. and vicinity for another day of sightseeing. The **Guard House**, 4 Carleton St. at Queen, is reconstructed to look like it did in 1829. The **Fredericton National Exhibition Centre**, 503 Queen St., is in a renovated 1880s building. It has exhibits on history, science, technology and art. The **York-Sunbury Historical Society Museum**, Officers' Square and Queen St., has historical exhibits on the area. The **Beaverbrook Art Gallery**, St. John and Queen Sts., has art by British artists from the 18th through the 20th century. Across the street from the gallery is the Provincial Legislative Building. Tours are available daily. The library has a complete set of Audubon's bird paintings and a copy of the Doomsday Book of England. At Church St. turn right to **Christ Church Cathedral**,, between King and Brunswick Sts. Built in 1853, it is a replica of St. Mary's Church in Snettisham, Norfolk, England.

You can visit **Woolastook Wildlife Park**, west on Hwy. 2. You can buy feed for some of the animals, follow nature trails or have a picnic on the grounds. **O'dell Park and Arboretum** covers more than 430 acres (175 Hectares) at Smythe St and Wagoners Lane.

Some of the oldest buildings in New Brunswick are on the campus of the **University of New Brunswick**, on the hill east of the city. If you like history, or discovering interesting old cemeteries, see the **Loyalist Cemetery**, near St. John River off Waterloo Row, and the **Old Burial Ground**, on Brunswick between York and Regent Sts.

● **Appelot Bed & Breakfast**
RR 4, Fredericton, NB E3B 4X5.
(506)472-6115.

$45-50/D. Open May 1 to Oct. 31.

Call mornings and early evening.
- No cr. cds.
- **Innkeeper: Elsie Myshrall.**
- *3 rms, 1 pb, 1 sb.*
- Full breakfast served on the sunporch overlooking the St. John River. A sample menu would include beverage, juice or fresh fruit, homemade muffins with homemade jams or jellies, cereal, choice of eggs, meat, pancakes or French Toast.
- No pets, no smoking, no alcohol.
- 14 km. from Fredericton.

This 1905 refurbished farmhouse overlooks the St. John River. It has an orchard and woodlands, with lots of space for walking. Elsie grows flowers, enjoys crafts and travel.

For dining, you'll find superb food at La Vie en Rose, Dimitri's or the Lobster Hut.

When you visit walk through the orchards and tree lots, or laze around in the lawn swing. Read a book and enjoy the view. Use the gas barbecue and picnic table. There are books, magazines, board games, a TV and VCR available for guests.

● **Happy Apple Acres**
RR 4, Fredericton, NB E3B 4X5.
(506)472-1819.

$45-51 US. Lowest rates 11/30-3/30.

Call 9 AM - Noon or 4 - 8 PM, and weekends.
•V, MC.
•Innkeepers: Angus & Margaret Hamilton.
•*3 rms, 3 pb.*
•Full gourmet breakfast, beautifully presented, served at the big old-fashioned table.
•On Hwy 105, 7 miles from downtown, 1 mile from city limits.

A renovated 1840's farm house is one of two houses available. There are three units in two sites overlooking the beautiful St. John River. A clean stream gurgles through a ravine at one side of the property. Your hosts enjoy the Anglican church, cross-country skiing, traveling, art, music and books. Margaret is a home economist; Angus is a retired professor, part-time lecturer and apple grower.

For dining, visit Benoit's for fine French food, Kingsclear Lodge for salmon, Canadian food and a lovely view, Puzzles, a bistro specializing in crepes, or Panos for tasty souvlakia and donair.

When you visit swim in the funny pool, have a sauna—your hosts will encourage a roll in the snow in season, climb Currie Mountain, ride on the Happy Apple Express, watch a movie from the video library of over 100 titles, play with the friendly dog or read a book from the large library.

● **Carriage House Bed & Breakfast**
230 University Ave., Fredericton, NB E3B 4H7.
(506) 452-9924.

$50. Extended stay discount.

Call 10 AM - 7 PM.
● V, MC.
● Innkeepers: Joan & Frank Gorham.
● *10 rms, 2 pb, 4 sb.*
● Full breakfast served on an antique table in the solarium. A sample breakfast will include beverage, juice, muffins, pancakes, maple syrup made by your hosts, eggs, cereal and bacon.
●
● Downtown, next to St. John River.

This 32-room, 3-story, Victorian mansion, was built in 1875. It is furnished in antiques. A veranda extends across the front of the building. The large ballroom is now a guest lounge. Your hosts enjoy their pets, motorcycling, cross stitch, reading and music.

For dining, you'll like the very special food at Benoit's, Puzzles and Dimitri's.

When you visit you'll love having the St. John River just 2 minutes away. Walking and biking trails are easily accessed. When you're at home at the B&B, you'll be able to sit on the first or second floor verandas, set up the badminton net for a game, enjoy the library, piano, TV and VCR for guests. The pets are sure to welcome your attention.

Nova Scotia

Annapolis Royal

Fort Anne National Historic Site and Museum, is on 27 acres (11 hectares) just north of the junction of Hwys. 8 and 1. This is the original location of the fort built by the French in the 1630s. When the British took control in 1710 the name was changed to Annapolis Royal. There are several remaining structures. The Fort Anne Museum is in the restoration of the old officers' quarters. There are displays on the history of the region, artifacts, ships, guides and brochures. **Annapolis Royal Historic Gardens**, just a block south of the junctions of Hwys. 8 and 1, has paths that wind among several theme gardens, ponds and fountains. An Acadian section demonstrates the lifestyle of early settlers. **Lower Saint George St.** is the oldest section of Annapolis Royal. Many of the restored buildings offer tours, collections and museums. **Upper Clements Park**, west on Hwy. 1, is a theme park that offers train rides, craft demonstrations, miniature golf, a petting farm, water rides, roller coaster, carrousel, live music and dancing. Visit the **Annapolis Tidal Generating Station**, E. on Hwy. 1. It has a model, audiovisual presentations, and observation decks.

Across the river from Annapolis Royal is the small village of Granville Ferry. It has many houses that were built in the 18th century. If you enjoy old homes, you'll want to walk or drive through this settlement. Note the iron door hinges shaped like H's or L's. Called Holy Lord hinges they were thought to ward off witches. The **North Hills Museum**, off Hwy. 1, is a restored 18th-century residence filled with Georgian furniture, glass, silver and ceramics.

Port Royal National Historic Site, south of Granville Ferry, is the oldest European settlement in Canada. Founded in 1604 by French colonists, it was captured by the English in 1613. The Habitation has been rebuilt to original measurents, including fastening without spikes or nails. Open mid-May to mid-October.

● The Poplars Bed & Breakfast
124 Victoria St., Box 277, Annapolis Royal, NS B0S 1A0.
(902)532-7936.

$35-50. Length of stay discount.

Call anytime.
•V.
•Innkeepers: Syd & Iris Williams.
•*9 rms, 6 pb, 1 1/2 sb.*
•Expanded continental breakfast served in the dining room. A sample breakfast includes juice, cold cereal, toast, beverage.
•No pets, no smoking.
•18 miles from the ferry at Digby.

This gracious Victorian home is a Registered Heritage Property. It has wide verandas and is surrounded with large trees and is centrally located within walking distance of major attractions. Your hosts enjoy knitting, sewing, making quilts and upholstery.

For dining, you'll enjoy Newman's Restaurant. If you'd like additional suggestions, your hosts will be happy to offer suggestions.

When you visit you'll like the lawn furniture that allows you to relax around the property under the trees, the wide verandas and the convenient location.

Ontario

Cardinal

You'll want to spend a day at **Upper Canada Village**, in Morrisburg, a reconstructed 19th century community. A day in the life of this loyalist village will be recreated through the living history presentation. You'll attend quilting sessions, see a grist mill in operation, go on wagon rides, smell bread baking and, when you're hungry, you'll order your 19th-century meal at the hotel.

When visiting **Prehistoric World**, E. on Upper Canada Rd., also in Morrisburg, you'll be able to touch and see life-sized reproductions of animals from the past, including giant dinosaurs. Morrisburg is north of Cardinal on Hwy. 401.

South of Morrisburg is Cornwall. The **Moses-Saunders Power Dam**, 2nd St. W., has an information center with audio-visual presentations and scale models on the construction of the St. Lawrence Seaway and the generation of electricity at the station. While you're in Cornwall, watch the manufacture of artistic free-form glass at **Rossi Artistic Glass**, 470 Seventh St. W.

The **North American Indian Travel College**, on Cornwall Island, is a recreated village representing traditional buildings and lifestyles of the Cree, Ojibway and Iroquois tribes.

Prescott is south of Cardinal on Hwy. 401. **Fort Wellington National Historic Park**, on Hwy. 2, is a restored fort. Staff in period costumes make you feel you're back in the 1800s, when the British Troops were garrisoned here.

● **Roduner Farm**
RR 1, Cardinal, ON K0E 1E0.
(613) 657-4830.

$20-25/S; $25-35/D. Discount to sr. citizens and families.

Call 7:30 AM to 9 PM.
• No cr. cds.
• **Innkeepers: Margareta & Walter Roduner.**
• *2 rms, 1 pb, 1 sb.*
• Full breakfast of juice, pancakes with maple syrup or eggs and bacon, homemade bread and muffins, cereal, Margaret's granola and beverage.
• 3 mi. from Cardinal; 1 1/2 mi. from Trans Canada Hwy. 401.

This comfortable B & B is on an active dairy farm. Children (of all ages) love to see the working farm. In addition to farming, your hosts are interested in gardening, fruit trees and crafts.

For dining, you can make advance reservations to eat at the farm, except in the busy months of July and August. During those months ask your hosts to help you find area restaurants. Guests are welcome to use the barbecue and your hosts will provide dishes.

When you visit you'll relax on the spacious lawn, shaded by maple trees, in the swing and comfortable chairs. The library contains many books. Adults and children love to collect eggs from the 100 hens. You may even help with farm chores. Two bicycles are available to explore the country roads.

London

You'll want to compare this city with the capital of Great Britain. This busy city is also located on the Thames River, and it shares many of the same street names such as Picadilly and Oxford. It also has double-decker buses offering tours of the city. However, it is distinctively Canadian.

The **Ska-Nah-Doht Indian Village**, in the Longwoods Road Conservation Area, Hwy. 402 to Hwy. 2 W., is a re-creation of an ancient Iroquois settlement. The **Museum of Indian Archaeology and Lawson Prehistoric Indian Village**, 1600 Attawandaron Rd., has an excavation site and a museum. The **Fanshawe Pioneer Village**, is in the Fanshawe Conservation Area, Hwy. 401 to Hwy. 100, N. to Oxford St., W. to Clarke Sideroad, turn N. This 19th-century village has many original buildings with costumed guides demonstrating crafts.

Children will enjoy **Storybook Gardens and Springbank Park**, in West London on Springbank Dr. A boat, the **London Princess**, offers a 45-minute cruise from Storybook Landing to the fork of the Thames River downtown, during the summer. The **London Regional Children's Museum**, 21 Wharncliffe Rd., has participatory exhibits on geology, archeology, history, communication and science.

Look for the **Royal Canadian Regiment Museum**, on the Canadian Forces Base, at Oxford and Elizabeth Sts., and the Guy Lombardo Museum, at 205 Wonderland Rd. S. The **London Regional Art and Historical Museum**, 421 Rideout St. N., has a large art gallery with a fine collection of paintings. Visit the **Eldon House**, 481 Rideout St. N., built in 1834. The oldest residence in the city, it has 19th century furnishings and a large garden.

- **Annigan's Bed & Breakfast**
194 Elmwood Ave. E., London, ON N6C 1K2.
(519)439-9196.

$40/S; $55/D. Weekly and monthly rates.

Call after 6 PM. Answering machine at all times.
- MC.
- Innkeeper: Anne Humberstone.
- 3 *rms, 2 sb.*
- Full or expanded continental breakfast. Menus vary according to season. A sample menu might include fresh fruit, muffins, homemade preserves and beverage or quiche, muffins, preserves and beverage.
- No pets.
- In an old established neighborhood called "Old South." 5 min. from downtown.

This Edwardian home has many special architectural details such as a turret, an egg-dart fireplace, beamed ceiling and curved window glass. It is a heritage designate. It has stained glass windows and antique furnishings. Anne is a graduate interior designer and writes a decorating column.

For dining, look for Auberge du Petit Prince, with superb novelle cuisine; Cafe Bruges is a contemporary bistro with a creative menu; La Cucina has exceptional Italian cuisine; Maestro has excellent Dutch and Indonesian dishes; Waldecks specializes in quail, venison and pheasant.

When you visit you'll have a wonderful place to relax in the TV lounge, the library or the English garden. You'll enjoy meeting other travelers, including many international visitors. You'll be perfectly situated for walking tours of historic "Old South" London and perhaps Anne will give you a conducted tour of the restored Palace Theatre.

Niagara-on-the-Lake

You'll want to explore this picturesque town on Lake Ontario, "one of the loveliest in Ontario," with its distinctive "19th-century aura." Every summer this city has a **Shaw Festival** that begins in late April and lasts until mid-November. Plays by George Bernard Shaw and other writers are held at the Festival Courthouse and Royal George Theatre. It is one of the most famous theatre happenings in Canada. The **Fort George National Historic Site**, just south of the city, was originally built in the 1790s. The **Laura Secord Homestead**, Niagara Pkwy. S. to Queenstone, was the home of heroine Laura Secord. The two-story cottage has been restored to its 1812 appearance. Drive along the **Niagara Parkway** for a scenic drive through the Niagara Parks system. Wineries offer tours and tastings. Two possibilities: **Chateau Des Charmes** on Four Mile Creek Rd. and **Inniskillin Wine Inc.** on Line 3 of Service Rd. 66.

Just west of Niagara-on-the-Lake is St. Catharines. The **Old Town** area is a wonderful area for walking tours. St. Catharine's Centennial Library, 54 Church St., or St. Catharine's Historical Museum, 343 Merritt St., have maps and brochures. The **St. Catharine's Museum at Lock 3**, is right on Canal Rd. from the Glendale Ave. exit off Queen Elizabeth Way. The museum has a model of the lock, a 1912 Reo auto, a gallery, a library and changing exhibitions. South is famous Niagara Falls. Favorite attractions include: the **Maid of the Mist** boats which take passengers directly in front of the falls. On the Canadian side they depart from the dock at River Rd. and Clifton Hill St. The **Niagara Spanish Aero Car**, Niagara Pkwy, carries passengers over the Niagara Gorge and back in a cable car. **Queen Victoria Park**, Niagara Pkwy. at the falls offers exceptional views of the falls and beautiful flower gardens. From **Table Rock House**, you may take an elevator to the level of Horseshoe Falls and the river. Tunnels leading from the elevator provide wonderful observation points. **Great Gorge Adventure**, north of Whirlpool Rapids Bridge on Niagara Pkwy, provides elevator service to the river where visitors walk along the boardwalk besides the rapids.

● **Janzen Guest House**
991 East & West Line, Niagara-on-the-Lake, ON L0S 1J0.
(416)468-3569.

$55/D.

Call anytime.
• No cr. cds.
• **Innkeepers: Nick & Mary Janzen.**
• *3 rms, 2 sb.*
• Expanded continental breakfast served in the sunroom. A sample menu might include juice, homebaked raisin bread, whole wheat bread and muffins, homemade jams, fresh fruit, 2 kinds of cheese, cereals, beverage.
• No pets, no smoking, alcohol in moderation.
• 2 1/2 miles from town, 1/4 mile from Hwy 55.

This bungalow is situated among the beautiful fruit orchards of the Niagara Peninsula. The backyard is spacious with a swimming pool, picnic tables, chairs and barbecue. Mary makes her own quilts and comforters. She enjoys playing the piano and organ.

For dining, you'll find wonderful food at Lawrenceville Restaurant, The Oban Inn, Prince of Wales Hotel, Pillar and Post Country Inn or Queens.

When you visit after enjoying one of the prettiest towns in Canada, enjoy a swim in your host's pool.

Ottawa

You'll want to visit the **Rideau Canal**. In the winter, it is the world's longest ice-skating rink; in warmer weather, joggers, walkers and bikers use the pathways bordering the canal and canoes traverse the water.

You'll also want to view the **Parliament Buildings**, on Parliament Hill, in Canada's capital city. Free tours are given daily. A popular ceremony is the **Changing of the Guard**, on the lawn of Parliament Hill daily at 10 AM, Jun. 26 - Aug. 30. The **Royal Canadian Mint**, 320 Sussex Dr., has tours of the coin production plant, a film on the process and a display of coins and medals from all over the world. The **Royal Canadian Mounted Police Stables**, at the N. end of St. Laurent Blvd., has tours, Mon-Fri. Occasionally, you may be able to watch the training of riders and horses for the musical ride. **Rideau Hall**, 1 Sussex Dr., is the official residence of the governor-general of Canada. 87 acres (35.2 hectares) of property surround the residence and can be toured daily, except during official functions. The **National Gallery of Canada**, 380 Sussex Dr., has works by Canadian artists from the early 19th century.

The **National Museum of Science and Technology**, 1867 St. Laurent Blvd., has displays of antique steam locomotives, horse-drawn vehicles, bicycles, motorcycles, and autos. **Central Experimental Farm**, Maple Dr., is a 1,200 acre (500 hectare) farm in the suburbs. The research branch of the Canada Dept. of Agriculture, it has an agricultural museum, gardens, arboretum, fields, herds of cattle, sheep, pigs and horses. The **Log Farm**, in Nepean, is a working farm functioning as it would have in the late 1800s. Visitors may watch or help with the activities. Guides, in costume, demonstrate activities.

Boat tours are offered during the summer at the Hull Municipal Wharf, the Rideau Step Locks and the Ottawa Locks. The National Arts Center has excellent performances and plays.

Australis Guest House
35 Marlborough Ave., Ottawa, ON K1N 8E6.
(613)235-8461.

$45-55. Sr. citizen discount.

Call after 4 PM or leave a message on answering machine.
- No cr. cds.
- **Innkeepers: Carol, Brian, Olivia Waters.**
- *3 rms, 1 pb, 1 sb.*
- Full breakfast served family style at dining table. A sample breakfast might include juice, fruit salad, homemade breads, muffins and pastries, eggs and sausage or bacon, beverage.
- No pets, no alcohol, no children under 6.
- 1 mile from downtown Ottawa and 1 mile from Hwy. 417.

This older home sits on a quiet, tree-lined street one block from the Rideau River. It has two 8 ft.-high stained glass windows, fireplaces, oak floors and antique English furniture. Your hosts enjoy making braided rugs, papier mache and recycled crafts.

For dining, there are many exceptional restaurants in the city. Ask your hosts for their suggestions.

When you visit you'll find many magazines in the library for relaxed reading. The convenient location makes it easily accessible to the many attractions in Ottawa.

Rossport

Rossport is on the north shore of the world's largest fresh water lake, Lake Superior. Founded as a stop on the Canadian Pacific Railroad, it's now a quiet fishing village. You may charter a boat for your own fishing or for scuba diving. Lake Superior is far too cold, even in midsummer, for any but the most hardy to swim.

Walk westward along the railroad tracks to look for agates. The **North Superior Hiking Trail** extends between Rossport and Terrace Bay. The distance is approximately 16 miles (or 25 kilometers) but it can be rough walking. If you don't want to go the entire distance, hike a short way, have a picnic and return. Along the way there are Indian pictographs and the remains of an old mining camp.

Just a short 4 mile drive east from Rossport is **Rainbow Falls Provincial Park**. The scenic portion of the park includes the hills around Whitesand Lake and the Whitesand River which cascades over Rainbow Falls. There are hiking and nature trails through the park. If you stand on the wooden bridge over the Whitesand on a bright sunny day you're likely to see a rainbow in the mist over the falls.

West from Rossport is Nipigon. The **Nipigon Historical Museum** exhibits a large number of items. Open Jun.-Sep. North of Nipigon is **Lake Nipigon Provincial Park**. The beaches in this park are of black sand. A short historic trail goes past an ancient Hudson's Bay Company post and an Indian village. Just west of Nipigon is **Ouimet Canyon Provincial Park**. The spectacular Ouimet Canyon is two miles long and 350 ft. tall. Because the canyon is so deep and dark the plants that grow at the bottom are usually found only in the arctic tundra.

● **Rossport Inn**
6 Bowman St., Rossport, ON P0T 2R0
(807)824-3213.

$50. U.S. OPEN 5/15 - 10/15.

Call 1 week in advance.
•V, MC.
•**Innkeepers: Ned & Shelagh Basher.**
•*7 rms, 1 pb, 2 sb.*
•The rate quoted above does not include breakfast. Full or continental breakfast may also be ordered from the inn's menu. You may eat in the dining room or take your food to the balcony overlooking the harbor.
•Only well-behaved pets are accepted.
•1 km. off the Trans-Canada Highway in Rossport.

This historic inn was built in 1884 as a railroad inn. It is charmingly decorated with many period antiques. Your hosts enjoy kayaking, canoeing, hiking and trout fishing.

For dining, you'll enjoy every meal at the Rossport Inn. The dining room has been listed for five years in "Where to Eat in Canada." They specialize in fresh fish, seafood, homemade soups and desserts.

When you visit you'll marvel at the wonderful location of this inn. The view of the jewel-like harbor from the second floor balcony is spectacular. The food is marvelous and your hosts are gracious and friendly. You'll enjoy using the Finnish-style log sauna. The inn has an extensive library and each room has books. Guests like to read in the lobby or while sitting on the balcony. Rental kayaks and canoes are available for your use. Ask Ned to tell you the story of the wreck of the ship Gunilda and to show you its mast.

Toronto

You'll want to come back again and again to this metropolitan city. Spend a day downtown, beginning with the **Art Gallery of Ontario and the Grange**, 317 Dundas St. W., in Grange Park. The art gallery has thousands of art works by Canadian and international artists, from old masters through contemporary. The Grange is one of the oldest houses in Toronto and is restored as an 1830s house. Go east on Adelaide to the city's **First Post Office**, at 260 Adelaide St. E. It is still in operation with workers in period costumes. You may also buy stationery, a quill pen and sealing wax to write a letter in 1830s style. Go back west and south to the **CN Tower**, 301 Front St. W. It is the tallest free-standing structure in the world. The tower has a revolving restaurant, a nightclub and three observation decks. At the foot of the CN Tower is **Tour of the Universe**, 301 Front St. W. Visitors can participate on a simulated flight into space. Be certain to visit the **Royal Ontario Museum**, 100 Queen's Park Crescent W., the **George R. Gardiner Museum of Ceramic Art**, 111 Queen's Park; and The **McLaughlin Planetarium**, just south of the museums. Continue north on Spadina Rd. to **Casa Loma**, 1 Austin Terrace, at Spadina and Davenport Rds. This medieval looking castle has 98 rooms and was built between 1911 and 1914. Self-guided audio tours are provided and include an underground tunnel, secret passageways and the stables. **Ontario Place**, 955 Lakeshore Blvd. W., is considered a showplace for the nation and includes canals, lakes, park and groups of buildings. There is a Children's Village and theatre, a WW II destroyer, a waterslide, and a wilderness adventure ride. At Lakeshore Blvd. W. and Strachan Ave., is the **Marine Museum of Upper Canada**. Displays are on shipping on the Great Lakes and the St. Lawrence Riverway. Continuing east, you'll next stop at **Fort York**, off Fleet St., between Bathurst St. and Strachan Ave. Established in 1793, eight original buildings have been restored to look as they did early in the 19th century. Guards in uniform give daily demonstrations. Take a **Gray Line Boat Tour** of the harbor and the islands. During summer tours leave from the foot of Yonge St and from Harbourfront at York St and Queen's Quary.

*Visit the suburb of North York to see **Gibson House**, at 5172 Yonge St., with costumed guides cooking and demonstrating rural life in the 1850s. **Black Creek Pioneer Village**, at Jane St. and Steeles Ave. W, has costumed workers carrying out daily work in a restored Canadian farm settlement of the late 18th century. The **Toronto Zoo**, north of Hwy. 401 on Meadowvale Rd, is a huge zoo that has animals representing six geographic regions. A zoomobile or monorail will give you a ride through the attraction.*

● **Beaches Bed & Breakfast**
174 Waverley Rd., Toronto, ON M4L 3T3.
(416)699-0818.

$48-68. Discounts for Sr. citizen, family, travel agent. Seasonal discount Nov.-Apr.

Call before 11 AM. Answering machine is always on.
•No cr. cds.
•**Innkeeper: Enid Evans.**
•*4 rms, 2 pb., 1 sb.*
•Expanded continental breakfast is served at the dining table. A sample menu might include fresh in-season fruit, hot and cold cereals, fresh baked bread, butter, Scottish marmalade, Niagara jelly, and coffee.
•No smoking.
•East of downtown, 2 blocks north of the lake.

This delightful home is noted for its warm and friendly atmosphere and is located in a distinctive section of the city known for its famous boardwalk beside the lake, called "Beaches." Enid's favorite things include antique hunting, yard sales and car trips to the country. She enjoys having children stay at her B&B.

For dining, you'll enjoy Clemantine's, Il Fornello, The Owl's Nest and Beaches Tea Room.

When you visit you'll find a host who enjoys her guests. Three minutes from the house is one of the most popular walks in Toronto: the Beaches Boardwalk. It provides a beautiful view of Lake Ontario and wildlife. On Summer Sundays there are free band concerts, craft shows and a free Olympic swimming pool in the adjacent park. After a day of sightseeing, you'll truly appreciate this comfortable home, relaxing in the "Secret Garden," possibly with afternoon tea. Feed and enjoy the birds, squirrels and raccoons who visit the back yard and you may wish to join the group on the front porch.

Quebec

Gaspe Peninsula: New Carlisle West

You'll want to stay forever when you first glimpse the unbelievable beauty of the rugged coastline surrounded by mountains and forests.

The villages are still frequently thought of as Acadian, Loyalist, Basque or Micmac Indian. New Carlyle is a Loyalist community. West on Hwy. 132, which circles the peninsula, is Bonaventure, an Acadian community. To understand the depth of feeling and the history surrounding the area visit some of the local museums. The **United Empire Loyalist Museum** will provide some insight. A trip to Bonaventure to see the **Acadian Historical Museum of Quebec**, at 95 av. Port Royal, will give you a more complete understanding.

Take long hikes to enjoy the beauty of the countryside. This is a popular area for skiing in the winter. In the Spring, sugar camps spring up for the tapping of the maple trees and the processing of the sap into syrup and candy. Maybe you can even enjoy a "sugaring off" party. If you arrive during the second week in August, attend the Bayview Folk Festival.

Take a drive past Bonaventure, on Hwy. 132, to Carlton. **St.-Joseph-de-Carleton Church** on rue Principale, has silver, paintings and vestments from the early 1800s. Drive to the summit of mont St. Joseph, one of the high peaks in the Chic-Choc Mountains. **Oratoire Notre-Dame du mont Saint-Joseph** is a chapel on the summit. Back in Carlton, the **Moluque Theatre** offers plays Tue.-Sun., from mid-Jul.-Aug. The "Festival of Carleton" is held the first two weekends in August with windsurfing competitions.

Take drives down Hwy. 132; go down to the sea and relax; thrill to the beauty of the Gaspe Peninsula.

● **Bay View Farm B&B**
337 Main Hwy. Rt. 132, Box 21, New Carlisle West, PQ G0C 1Z0.
(418)752-2725 / (418)752-6718.

$25/S; $35/D. Length of stay discount.

Call 7-8 AM or 7-8 PM.
•No cr. cds.
•Innkeepers: Helen and Garnett Sawyer.
•5 rms, 2 sb.
•Full breakfast served in the dining room, country kitchen or on the veranda. A sample breakfast might include juice or fresh fruit, cereal, eggs, bacon, sausage, ham, hashbrown potatoes, homemade jams, homemade scones and muffins, toast, beverage.
•No pets.
•On the main highway, 132, in New Carlisle West.

This large farm home has a large wrap-around veranda. It's comfortable and homey. Helen teaches pre-school children. Garnett is a carpenter and farmer. The family has helped to organize the Bay View Folk Festival each August.

For dining, you may ask your hosts to prepare light meals for you at an additional charge. The Au Petit Cafe and Le Chateau Hotel Dining Room in Bonaventure also have fine food.

When you visit you may want to walk through the fields or along the beaches on the property. Sometimes you may be able to join a folk music jam session or a quilting and craft workshop. Enjoy fresh produce from the B&Bs gardens and orchards. In the evening view sunsets and moon over the water of the bay and relax on the large wrap-around veranda.

Hudson

You'll want to come to this lovely, quiet village, on the banks of the Ottawa River, to combine the advantages of staying in a small, peaceful area with easy access to the nearby sophisticated large city of Montreal. Hudson has fine restaurants, excellent shopping, antique and craft shops, flea-markets, wonderful bicycle routes, cross country and downhill skiing, golf and tennis. You'll find historical sites, provincial parks with swimming and boating, sailing competition and equestrian events. There are rugged mountains close by, and a wildlife refuge for bird and animal watching. It's only about a 40 min. drive to Montreal.

You must see **Old Montreal** and **Underground Montreal**. Old Montreal grew in this area from the original settlement in 1642 until the 1800s. It now has one of the largest concentrations of 17th, 18th and 19th century buildings in North America. You'll want to take a walking tour of the area. The **Underground City** developed when the city planners made provision for the Metro. It's possible to spend an entire day shopping without ever having to go outside. Montreal is a sophisticated city and the second largest French speaking city in the world.

You'll love dining and shopping here but there is much more too. There are many parks and gardens. Among them are **Angrignon Park**, with a children's zoo and winter activities; the **Aquarium de Montreal**; and **Jardin Botanique de Montreal**, third largest botanical garden in the world. Art lovers will be interested in **Musee des beau-arts de Montreal** (fine arts), **Musee des arts decoratifs** (decorative arts), **Palais de la Civilisation,** summer museum for major exhibitions. The gigantic **Olympique Stadium**, the site of the 1976 Olympic Games, is exciting and monumental.

Take a tour of the city by bus or by horse-drawn carriage. Enjoy a boat cruise of the St. Lawrence. Go to the theatre. This fascinating city could hold your attention for years.

Jeanette Rowland's Bed & Breakfast

76 Oakland Ave., Hudson Heights, PQ J0P 1J0.
(514) 458-5893.

$45/S; $55/D. OPEN APR. - OCT.

Call evenings.
- No cr. cds.
- Innkeeper: Jeanette Rowland.
- *2 rms, 1 pb, 1 sb.*
- Full breakfast served on the sunny porch. A sample menu might include juice, cereal, eggs, bacon, homemade scones, muffins, jams, marmalade and beverage.
- No pets, no smoking, no alcohol.
- 5 min. from village, 35 min. to Montreal.

In a quiet residential area, this B&B looks like a lovely roomy cottage set within a pretty English garden. It is within easy commuting distance of attractions. Your host loves gardening, skiing, walking, reading, playing bridge and the interesting people who visit her B&B.

For dining, you must search out Rube's Restaurant, Pierre de Rigance, mon Village, Willow Inn or Grandma Smythe's Irish Tea Room.

When you visit relax in Jeanette's garden, read by her fireside or on the veranda, and enjoy tea with her. Take long walks in the area around the B&B. Jeanette always has a lot of reading material for her guests.

Quebec City

You'll want to tour Old Quebec: Lower Town and Upper Town. Today much of the older section has been rebuilt to look as it did in the 17th and 18th centuries. A good place to start is at the interpretation center for the **Fortifications of Quebec National Historic Park**, at 100 rue St. Louis. There is an exhibit on the defense system and guided tours explaining the walls and the gates.

One of the highlights of your visit to the old city will be **The Citadel**, 1, cote de la Citadelle, the official residence of the governor general. You can watch the official changing of the guard at 10 AM, Mid-June to Labour Day. French and English guided tours are offered. **Artillary Park National Historic Site**, at Porte St. Jean, just within the walls, is a section of the city used for various military purposes. An interpretation centre for adults explains the evolution of the area and a children's interpretation centre uses games and other materials to compare life today with the past. Take the funiculaire (elevator) between the upper and lower town. There are many, many things to see in Old Quebec.

Outside the walls, you'll want to see the **Parliament Buildings**, on Grande Allee. Guided tours are available. **Place Royale**, at the center of Lower Town, is where French colonization began in North America. The settlement has been restored to its 18th century appearance. **National Battlefields Park**, has entrances on Grande Allee between rue Bougainville and the St. Louis Gate. The park includes the area where Gen James Wolfe and the Marquis de Mountcalm fought in 1759. There are tablets to explain the battle, an interpretation center and towers containing historical displays. The **Quebec Zoological Gardens**, 8191 avenue du Zoo, has more than 1,000 animals. There is a children's farm animal section and a natural wolf habitat. The Aquarium, 1675 avenue du Prc, has 250 species of fresh and salt-water fish, amphibians, and marine animals. Visit **Isle D'Orleans**, in the St. Lawrence River, reached by a bridge from Hwy. 138. Several of the buildings were built in the 18th century. Take a boat tour or a walking tour.

● **Battlefields Bed & Breakfast**
820 Eymard St., Quebec City, PQ G1S 4A1.
(418)681-6804.

$35/S; $50/D.

Call evenings.
•No cr. cds.
•**Innkeeper: Dolores Dumais.**
•*3 rms, 2 sb.*
•Full breakfast. A sample menu might consist of juice or fresh fruit, cereals, toast, eggs, ham, crepes, muffins, croissants, honey, marmalade, and beverage.
•No pets.
•Between the university campus and the walled city.

This charming house, in a quiet residential area of the city, is close to public transportation and just a few minutes from the walled city and the Battlefields. Your host is very interested in antiques and has furnished the house with beautiful furniture.

For dining, enjoy the delicious food at Serge Brnyere, Le Marie Clarice, Le Cavour, or Le Graffiti.

When you visit you will relax in the peaceful surroundings of this comfortable B&B, near the many historic and cultural attractions of this wonderful city. Your hostess is always delighted to help her guests practice the French language. You'll enjoy meeting and sharing experiences with other guests.

Reservation Services

If you're planning to visit a specific location that is not listed in our book, you may want to try one of these Reservation Service Organizations. RSOs list a variety of Bed & Breakfasts in their areas and try to match you with a host.

Alaska

● **Accommodations Alaska Style-Stay With A Friend**
3605 Arctic Blvd., #173, Anchorage, Alaska 99503 (907) 278-8800/ Fax: (907) 272-8800. $45+/S; $55+/ D. Call 9 AM - 5 PM Alaska time. •V, MC,D,AE. •**Contact Jean Parsons.** •50-60 homes. •Covers State of Alaska. •No smoking most homes. •Matches guest with host. •No charge for service. $2/ directory.

● **Alaska Private Lodgings**
P.O. Box 200047, Anchorage, Alaska 99502. (907) 258-1717/ Fax: 258-6613 $40-100/S; $50-100/D. Call 9 AM - 6 PM. •V,MC,AE. •**Contact Mercy Dennis.** •50 homes. •Covers South Central Alaska. •Restrictions vary with location. •Matches guest with host. •No charge. Free brochure. $3/ descriptive booklet.

Arizona

● **Bed & Breakfast in Arizona**
P.O. Box 8628 Scottsdale, Arizona 85252. (602)995-2831/ (800)266-7829. $30-120/S; $40-120/D. Call 10 AM - 5 PM, Mon.-Fri. 24- hr answering service. •V,MC, D, AE. • 70 homes. •Covers Arizona and New Mexico. •No pets, no children under 12, no smoking. •Matches guest with host. •No charge for service or brochure.

● **Old Pueblo Homestays**
P.O. Box 13603 Tucson, Arizona 85732. (800) 333-9RSO. $30-85/S; $45-105/D. Call 9:30 AM - 9:30 PM. •No credit cards. •Contact Bill Janssen. •30 homes. •Covers Southeast Arizona (Tucson, Bistre, Tombstone). •No children under 12. •Matches guest with host. •No charge.

Arkansas

● **Arkansas Ozarks Bed & Breakfast Res. Service**
HC 61, Box 72 Calico Rock, Arkansas 72519. (501) 297-8211/ (501)297-8764.$30-45/S; $35-55/D. Call 9 AM - 5 PM. •V,MC. •**Contact Carolyn S. Eck.** •15-20 homes. •Covers Ozarks, Northern Arkansas. •No smoking. •No charge. SASE/brochure.

California

● **Eye Openers Bed & Breakfast Reservations**
P.O. Box 694, Altadena, California 91003 (213) 684-4428/ (818) 797-2055/ Fax: (818) 798-3640. $35-150/S; $40-175/D. Call 9 AM - 6 PM. •V,MC. •**Contact Ruth Judkins or Betty Cox.** •100 homes. •Covers all of California. •No pets, no smoking. •Matches guest with host. •No charge. $1 and SASE for brochure.

● **Bed & Breakfast of Southern California**
1943 Sunny Crest Dr., Suite 304, Fullerton, California 92635. (714) 738-8361/ Fax: (714) 525-0702. $35-85/S; $40-100/D. Call 9 AM - 4 PM. •No credit cards. •**Contact Theresa Garrison.** •40 homes. •Covers entire State

of California & Baja Mexico. •Restrictions vary with home. •Matches guest with host. •No charge for service or brochure.

● Bed & Breakfast Intl.
P.O. Box 282910, San Francisco, California 94128-2910. (415)696-1690/ Fax: (415) 696-1699.$50-85/S; $50-125/D. Call 8:30 AM - 5 PM, Mon.-Fri., PST. 9 AM - Noon Sat., Apr.-Oct. •No credit cards. •450-500 homes. •Covers all of California and Nevada. •Restrictions vary with home. •Matches guest with host. •No charge for service or brochure.

● Bed & Breakfast San Francisco
P.O. Box 420009, San Francisco, California 94142. (415)479-1913/ Fax: (415)921-BBSF.$45+/S; $55-125/D. Call 9:30 AM - 5 PM, Mon.-Fri. •V,MC,AE. •Contact Susan or Richard Kreibich. •100 homes. •San Francisco, the Wine Country, Yosemite and Carmel/ Monterey. •Matches guest with host. •No charge for service or brochure (Please ask for free reservations).

● Bed & Breakfast of Los Angeles
730 Catalina Ave., Seal Beach, California 90740. (310)498-0582/ (800)383-3513 Out of CA. $45-65/ S; $55-95/D. Call 8 AM - 8 PM. •V,MC, AE. •Contact Robin Nahin. •200+ homes. •Covers entire State of CA with emphasis on Los Angeles. •Matches guest with host. •No charge for service or brochure.

● Kids Welcome
730 Catalina Ave., Seal Beach, California 90740. (310)498-0552/ (800) 383-3513 Out of CA. $45-60/ S; $50-95/D. Call 8 AM - 8 PM. •V,MC,AE. •Contact Robin Nahin. •160+ homes. •Covers entire State of California. •Matches guest with host. •No charge. $10/list of hosts.

Connecticut

● Bed & Breakfast, Ltd.
P.O. Box 216, New Haven, Connecticut 06513. (203)469-3260. $45-55/S; $50-75/D. Call after 5 PM, Wkdys, Jul.-Aug., anytime. •No credit cards. •Contact Jack Argenio. •125+ homes. •Covers Connecticut and Providence RI. •No pets, no smoking, no children under 12. •Matches guest with host. •No charge.

● Nutmeg Bed & Breakfast Agency
P.O. Box 1117, West Hartford, Connecticut 06127-1117. (203)236-6698/ (800) 727-7592. $45-120/S; $50-150/D. Call 9:30 AM - 5 PM, Mon.-Fri. •V,MC, AE. •Contact Michelle Souza. •200 homes. •Covers all of Connecticut and part of RI, MA and NY bordering CT. •Matches guest with host. •No charge. $5/directory.

Delaware

● Bed & Breakfast of Delaware
Box 177, 3650 Silverside Rd., Wilmington, Delaware 19810. (302) 479-9500. $45/S; $55-110/D. Call 9 AM - 5 PM, Mon.-Fri. Answering machine after 5 PM. •No cr. cds. •Contact Millie Alford. •35 homes. •Covers all of Delaware, SE PA, Chesapeake Bay area of MD & VA. •Matches guest with host. •No charge.

Florida

● Bed & Breakfast Co. - Tropical Florida
P.O. Box 262 South Miami, Florida

33243. (305)661-3270. $35-100/S; $38-150/D. Call 9 AM - 5 PM, Mon.-Fri., or answering machine. •V,MC,AE. •Contact Marcella Schaible. •100+ homes. •Covers all of Florida. •Restrictions vary with home. •Matches guest with host. •$3.50 serv. charge. $4/directory. $5/directory outside US. Free brochure.

● A&A Bed & Breakfast of Florida, Inc.
P.O. Box 1316 Winter Park, Florida 32790. (407)628-3233. $45/S; $55/D. Call 9:30 AM - 6 PM. •No cr. cds. •Contact Brunhilde Fehner. •40 homes. •Covers Central Florida. •No pets, no children under 4, restricted smoking. •Matches guest with host. •No charge.

Georgia

● Quail Country Bed & Breakfast, Ltd.
1104 Old Monticello Road Thomasville, Georgia 31792. (912) 226-7218/ (912)226-6882. $30-55/S; $40-65/D. Call 9 AM - 9 PM. •No cr. cds. •Contact Mrs. Mercer Watt or Kathy Lanigan. •8 homes. •Covers Thomasville Georgia. •No pets. •Matches guest with host. •No charge for service or brochure.

Hawaii

● Bed & Breakfast Honolulu (Statewide)
3242 Kaohinani Drive Honolulu, Oahu, Hawaii 96817. (800)288-4666/ (808)595-7533/ Fax: 595-2030.$35-100/S; $40-110/D. Call 8 AM - 5 PM, Mon.-Fri.; 8 AM - Noon, Sat. HI time. •V,MC. •Contact Gene Bridges or Mary Lee. •350 homes. •Covers all Hawaiian Islands. •No pets. Restrictions vary with home. •Matches guest with host. •$10 service charge. Free brochure.

● All Islands Bed & Breakfast
823 Kainui Drive Kailua, Oahu, Hawaii 96734. (808) 263-2342/ (800) 542-0344. $50-80/D. Most homes have 3 night minimum. Call anytime. •M,V,AE (with surcharge) to hold res. •Contact Ann Carlin. •350+ homes. •Covers all of Hawaii. •Restrictions vary with home. •Matches guest with host. •No charge for service.

● Pacific-Hawaii Bed & Breakfast
19 Kai Nani Place, Kailua, Oahu, Hawaii 96734. (808)262-6026/ (808) 263-4848/ (800)999-6026/ Fax: (808) 261-6573. $35-65/S; $45-100/D. Call 7 AM - 10 PM. •V,MC. •Contact Doris Epp or Ruth Winson. •350 homes. •Covers all islands of Hawaii. •Restrictions vary with home. •Matches guest with host. •$10 service charge. Free brochure.

Louisiana

● Bed & Breakfast Guesthouse & Reservation Service
1021 Moss St., Box 52257, New Orleans, Louisiana 70152-2257. (504)488-4640/ (800)729-4640. $36-51/S; $41-51/D. Call 10 AM - 5 PM, Mon.-Fri., or answering machine. •No cr. cds. •Contact Hazell Boyce. •25 homes. •Covers New Orleans. •Matches guest with host. •No charge for service or brochure.

● New Orleans Bed & Breakfast and Accommodations
P.O. Box 8163, New Orleans, Louisiana 70182 (504)838-0071. $40/S; $45/D. Call 8 AM - 5 PM. •V, M C, D,AE. •Contact Sarah Margaret Brown.

•*90 homes.* •*Covers New Orleans.* •*No children under 6.* •*Matches guest with host.* •*No charge.*

Massachusetts
● **Bed & Breakfast Folks**
48 Springs Rd., Bedford, Massachusetts 01730. (617) 275-9025. $40/S; $50/ D.Call 8 AM - 10 PM. •No cr. cds. •**Contact Phyllis Z. Phillips.** •*20 homes.* •*Covers North & West of Boston.* •*No pets, no smoking, no alcohol.* •*Matches guest with host.* •*No additional service charge.*

● **Greater Boston Hospitality**
P.O. Box 1142 Brookline, Massachusetts 02146. (617) 277-5430. $40-85/S; $47-90/D. Call 8:30 AM - 6 PM, Mon.-Fri., 8:30 AM - 1 P M Sat. •No cr. cds. •**Contact Kelly Simpson.** •*100 homes.* •*Covers greater Boston area.* •*No children under 5.* •*Matches guest with host.* •*No charge for service or brochure.*

Mississippi
● **Lincoln, Ltd, Mississippi B&B Reservation Service**
2303 23rd Ave., P.O. Box 3479, Meridian, Mississippi 39303 (601) 482-5483/ (800)633-MISS *for reservations.* $55-165/S or D. Call 9 AM - 5 PM, Mon.-Fri., Central time. •V,MC,AE. •**Contact Barbara Lincoln Hall.** •*60+ homes.* •*Covers all of Mississippi.* •*No pets, no children, no smoking.* •*Matches guest with host.* •*No charge for service. $3.50/directory. Free brochure.*

Massachusetts
● **Be Our Guest Bed & Breakfast, Ltd.**
P.O. Box 1333, Plymouth, Massachusetts 02362. (617)837-9867. $40-75/S; $50-125 /D. Call 10 AM - 7 PM. •V, M C, AE. •**Contact Mary Gill.** •*20 homes.* •*Covers Massachusetts, including Cape Cod.* •*Restrictions vary with home.* •*Matches guest with host.* •*No charge for service. $1/brochure.*

Missouri
● **Ozark Mountain Country Bed & Breakfast Service**
P.O. Box 295 Branson, Missouri 65616. (417) 334-4720/ (800) 695-1546. $35-145/S or D. Call 10 AM - 6 PM. •V,MC,V. •**Contact Kay Cameron.** •*90 homes.* •*Covers SW Missouri and NW Arkansas.* •*Restrictions vary with home.* •*Matches guest with host.* •*No charge for service. SASE/brochure.*

● **Bed & Breakfast K.C.**
P.O. Box 14781 Lenexa, KS Missouri 66285 (913)888-3636. $40-130/S; $50-135/D. Call 8 AM - 10 PM or answering machine. •No cr. cds. most homes. •**Contact Edwina Monroe.** •*40 homes.* •*Covers Kansas City Missouri area & St. Louis.* •*No pets, no alcohol. Most request no children under 12, no smoking.* •*Matches guest with host.* •*No charge for service.*

Princeton
● **Bed and Breakfast of Princeton**
Box 571, Princeton, New Jersey 08542. (609) 924-3189. $40-50+/S; $50 - 60+D. Call anytime. Answering machine also. •No cr. crds. •**Contact John Hurley.** •*15 homes.* •*Covers Princeton, NJ.* •*No pets, no smoking in some homes.* •*No charge for service. SASE/ brochure.*

New York

● **Rainbow Hospitality, Inc., B&B Reservation Service**
466 Amherst St., Buffalo, New York 14207. (716) 874-8797/ (800)373-8797 for reservations. $40-$150/S or D. Call 10 AM - 5 PM, Mon.-Fri. •V,MC. •Contact Karen Ruckinger. •60+ homes. •Covers W. NY. •Matches guest with host. •$5/admin fee. $3/ descriptive brochure.

● **American Country Collection of Bed & Breakfasts**
4 Greenwood Ln., Delmar, New York 12054-1606 (518)439-7001 / Fax: (518) 439-4301. $25-90/S; $35-130/D. Call 10 AM - 5 PM, Mon.-Fri. •V, MC, AE. •Contact Arthur Cope-land. •125 homes. •Covers E. NY, W. MA, VT, N. NH, St. Thomas, USVI. •$10/2 months. SASE/free brochure. $6/directory.

● **Elaine's Bed & Breakfast and Inn Reservation Service**
4987 Kingston Rd., Elbridge, New York 13060 (315)689-2082. $40/S; $60/D. Call 10 AM - 8 PM. •No cr. crds. •Contact Elaine Samuels. •60+ homes. •Covers Cen. NY and the Finger Lakes Reg. •Restrictions vary with location. •Matches guest with host. •No charge to guests for reservations. SASE/brochure.

● **Adventures Bed & Breakfast Reservation Service.**
Box 551, Lima, New York 14485. (716)582-1040/ (800)724-1932. $50 - $150/S or D. Call 9 AM - 9 PM. •V, MC,D, DC,CB. •Contact Millie Fonda. •50+ homes. •Covers area surrounding Rochester, NY. •Restrictions vary with home. •Matches guest with host. •No charge.

Ohio

● **Private Lodgings, Inc.**
P.O. Box 18590, Cleveland, Ohio 44118. (216)249-0400. $43-500. Call 9 AM - noon or 3 - 5 PM, Mon.-Tue., Th. - Fri. •No cr. cds. •Contact Elaine or Roberta. •40 rms, apts, and homes. •Cleveland and suburbs. •Matches guest with host. •No charge for service. SASE/brochure.

Oregon

● **Northwest Bed & Breakfast Reservation Service**
610 SW Broadway, Suite 606, Portland, Oregon 97205. (503) 243-7616. $30+/S; $40+/D. Call anytime. •No cr. crds. •Contact LaVonne Miller. •400 homes. •Covers British Columbia, Washington, Oregon, California. •No charge for service. $7.95/directory.

Pennsylvania

● **Bed & Breakfast Connections**
Box 21, Devon, Pennsylvania 19333. (215) 687-3565/ (800) 448-3619. $30-175. Call 9 AM - 9 PM, Mon.-Sat; answering machine Sunday. •V, MC, AE. •Contact Peggy Gregg or Lucy Scribner. •Over 60 homes. •Covers Philadelphia and suburbs, Lancaster County, Brandywine Valley, York, Reading and Poconos. •Restrictions vary w/location. •Matches guest with host. •Charge of $2-5.

● **Bed & Breakfast of Valley Forge**
Box 562, Valley Forge, Pennsylvania 19481-0562. (215)7 83-7838/ (800) 344-0123. $15-85/S; $40-125/D. Call 9 AM - 9 PM, daily. •V, MC, AE, DC. •Contact Carolyn J. Williams. •120 homes and inns. •Covers SE Pennsylvania. •Matches guest with host.

*No charge for reservation service. $3/directory & recipes.

● **Hershey Bed & Breakfast Reservation Service**
P.O. Box 208, Hershey, Pennsylvania 17033-0208. (717) 533-2928. $50-70/S; $50-95/D. Call 10 AM - 4 PM, Mon-Fri. •V, MC, AE. •Contact Renee Deutel. •*25 homes.* •*Covers South-Central Pennsylvania.* •*No pets, no smoking. Some restrict children.* •*Matches guest with host.* •*No charge for service or brochure.*

● **Charleston East B & B League**
1031 Tall Pine Rd., Mount Pleasant, South Carolina 29464. (803)884-8208 $35-80. Call 10 AM - 6 PM. •No cr. crds. •Contact Bobbie N. Auld, Coordinator. •*18 homes. 1 has wheelchair access.* •*Covers coastal South Carolina and Charleston area.* •*No pets, no children under 12. Restricted smoking.* •*No charge to guests for reservation. $1/brochure.*

South Dakota

● **Old West & Badlands Bed & Breakfast Association**
HCR 02, Box 100A, Philip, South Dakota 57567. (605) 859-2120. $25/S; $40- 50/D.Call early AM or late PM. •No cr. cds. •Contact Phillis Thorson or Marjorie Swift. •*10 homes.* •*Covers Western South Dakota.* •*No children under 4, no smoking, no alcohol.* •*Matches guest with host.* •*No charge for service. SASE/brochure.*

Tennessee

● **Bed & Breakfast -- Tennessee**
P.O. Box 110227, Nashville, Tennessee 37222. (612) 331-5244/ Fax: (615) 833-7701/ (800)458-2421 reserv. only. $45-75/S; $50-125/D. Call 10 AM - 5 PM, CST. •V,MC,D,AE. • •*100 homes.* •*Covers Tennessee.* •*Matches guest with host.* •*$5 charge for service. $5/pictoral guide.*

Virginia

● **The Travel Tree B & B Reservation Service**
P.O. Box 838, Williamsburg, Virginia 23187. (804) 253-1571/ (800)989-1571. $40-100/S; $50-120/D. Call 6 PM - 9 PM, Mon.- Fri. •No cr. cds. •Contact Sheila R. Zubkoff or Joann Proper. •*Covers Williamsburg, Virginia.* •*No pets. Other restrictions vary with home.* •*Matches guest with host.* •*No charge for service. SASE/brochure.*

Washington

● **Pacific Bed & Breakfast Agency**
701 NW 60th St., Seattle, Washington 98107. (206)784-0539. $45-100. Call 9 AM - 5 PM, Mon.-Fri. •V, MC, AE. •Contact Irmgard Castleberry. •*200 homes.* •*Covers the State of Washington, Victoria and Vancouver, British Columbia.* •*No pets, no smoking.* •*$5 booking fee, $5/directory.*

Canada RSOs

All prices are in Canadian dollars.

British Columbia

● **Town & Country Bed & Breakfast in B.C.**
Box 74542, 2803 W 4th Ave., Vancouver, British Columbia V6K 1K2. (604) 731-5942. $45-65/S; $65-130/D. Call 9 AM - 4:30 PM, Mon.-Fri. •No cr. cds. •Contact Helen Burich. •30+ homes. •Vancouver & lower mainland, Victoria & Vancouver Island. •Restrictions vary with home. •Matches guest with host. •$5/booking fee for reserv outside of Vancouver. Free brochure.

● **AA - Accommodations West Bed & Breakfast Reservations**
660 Jones Terrace, Victoria, British Columbia V8Z 2L7. (604)479-1986/ (604) 479-9999. $35/S; $45/D. Call 7 AM - 11 PM. •V, MC, AE, DC. •Contact Doreen Wensley. •80 homes. •Covers Victoria, Vancouver Island. •No smoking. •Matches guest with host. •No charge for service or brochure.

Ontario

● **Ottawa Bed & Breakfast**
488 Cooper St., Ottawa, Ontario K1R 5H9. (613)563-0161. $40/S; $50/D. Call 10 AM to 9 PM. •No cr. cds. •Contact Robert Rivoire. •10 homes. •Covers Ottawa. •Restrictions vary with home. •Matches guest with host. •No charge for service or brochure.

Province of Quebec

● **A Bed & Breakfast, A Downtown Network**
3458 Laval Ave., Montreal, Quebec-H2X 3C8. (514) 289-9749/ Fax: (514) 287-7386. $25-40/S; $35-55/D. Call 8 AM - 9 PM, Summer; 8 AM - 6 PM, Winter. •V, MC, AE. •Contact Bob or Mariko Finkelstein. •110 homes. •Covers Montreal. •Restrictions vary with home. •Matches guest with host. •No charge for service or brochure.

● **Bed & Breakfast a' Montreal, a B&B Network**
Box 575, Snowdon Station, Montreal, Quebec H3X 3T8. (514)738-9410. $45-55/S; $60-85/D. Call mornings or 4 - 8 PM. •V, MC, AE. •Contact Marian Kahn. •50+ homes. •Covers Montreal, Quebec City. •No pets, no smoking. •Matches guest with host. •No charge for service or brochure.

● **Bed and Breakfast Bonjour Quebec**
3765, Boul. Monaco, Quebec, G1P 3J3. (418) 527-1465. $35-60/S; $45-95/D. Call 9 AM to 5 PM. •No cr. cds. •Contact Denise Blanchet. •11 rooms. •Covers Quebec City. •No pets. •No charge for reservation or brochure.